System and Succession

System and Succession

The Social Bases of Political Elite Recruitment

By John D. Nagle

University of Texas Press, Austin & London

Library of Congress Cataloging in Publication Data
Nagle, John David
    System and succession.
    1. Elite (Social sciences). 2. Representative
government and representation. 3. Comparative
government. I. Title.
JF1057.N33   301.5'92   77-3936
ISBN 0-292-77537-7

Contents

Tables

Preface

For their considerable help in the critique and review of various parts of this four-nation study of political elites, special thanks go to John Hodgson, Ron McDonald, David Conradt, Ken Baker, Robert Miller, and Mark Ruhl. Dr. Adalbert Hess and Dr. Hermann Schunck were particularly helpful with their advice on the gathering of the German data, and Peter Smith has been most generous in sharing his data on the Mexican political elite. I am also indebted to Heribert Adelt, Kathy de Tulio, and Mike Smith for their painstaking work in the coding of the American, Soviet, and German data. My own data collection includes information on 1,000 members of the U.S. Congress from 1790 through 1960 (plus three update samples for the years 1964, 1968, and 1972); 6,005 parliamentary deputies in the German Reichstag and Bundestag assemblies from 1871 through 1972; and 1,114 members, both full and candidate, of the Central Committee of the Communist party of the Soviet Union (Bolsheviks). Peter Smith's data set contains information on 6,299 individuals at various levels of the Mexican political elite for the period from about 1900 to 1970. All figures presented in the tables are derived from these four data sets unless otherwise indicated in the tables themselves.

Collection and coding of data were made possible by grants from the American Philosophical Society and the Conference Group on German Politics and by a 1974 Fulbright-Hays Senior Research Fellowship at the University of Cologne and the Library of the Bundestag. My appreciation goes also to the personnel of the Academic Computing Center at Syracuse University for their aid in the archiving and statistical analysis of the data.

Responsibility for the judgments and evaluations which follow must rest, despite the above credits, with me.

Part 1. Introduction

CHAPTER I

Theoretical and Methodological Problems of Elite Background Analysis

Representation and Elite Composition: Theoretical Positions

Every beginning is hard. In a study which presumes to say something valuable about political elites, a first-order question of theoretical importance is: why is the study of political elites at all important? Fortunately, there are several fairly decent responses to this question, which is not always the case in the social sciences.

To begin, political elites are an important object of study because, if we have correctly defined our "elites," they are the most powerful or influential members of society in terms of government. In politics, they have (Lasswell, Lerner, and Rothwell 1952) more of what there is to get than the overwhelming majority of citizens. For the study of politics generally, and for any theory of politics, some cognizance of the political elite as an important element is vital.

On a very practical level, the *present* (but not immutable) understanding of politics, political systems, and political development is in fact inextricably bound up with the concept/issue of "Who governs?" (cf. Dahl 1961; Sartori 1962)—the concept of a political elite. Political history and events have been, for the most part, described in terms of the "men at the top," of leaders and their actions. Political systems are commonly designated and differentiated by the nature of political elite recruitment (e.g., military junta, parliamentary democracy, monarchy, one-party dictatorship); and it is widely presumed and perceived, whether correctly or not, that important system developments, including coups, revolutions, even policy reforms, are connected with changes in the political elite, with elite turnover or elite displacement.

So far so good. However, there are as many ways of approaching the study of political elites as there are of approaching the political behavior of people generally. This study concentrates on the social basis of political elite recruitment, on the social composition of political elites, studied comparatively and covering several generations for each polity. It is not directly concerned with specific behavior of the political elite, such as the decision-making process or a particular policy case study. No description or analysis is given for any single political leader, for his/her ideas or deeds. No attempt at developing an elite psychology is made here.

Without denying the contributions, both good and bad, of individual great leaders to modern civilization, this study is interested in the group profile of national political elites and analyzes the relationships between a political system and the social basis from which its political leadership is drawn.

Representation: Burke and Rousseau

In this sense a second theoretical question is raised: what is important in the (social) background of political elites? Unlike the first theoretical question, this second query finds no consensus among either scholars or average citizens. Rather, it raises some very different responses and conflicting opinions, which are rooted in varying views on the question of *representation* in government or in a political system. This question of representation (of needs, interests, ideas, values) in politics is an age-old point of dispute among adherents of various ideologies. Since the French Revolution, opinion on representation of interests through political leaders has been divided along two basic themes. First, there is the degree of latitude which the political leader should have in the representation of his/her constituents' interests. The Burkean view, the conservative orientation, is that the representative is more capable than his/her constituents and should use his/her own best judgment, not constituent opinion, in deciding how to represent them. The Rousseauean view, the radical position, holds that the political leader is the incorporation of her/his constituents' views and should represent these views as accurately as possible, even if she/he personally disagrees with them. Naturally, these are simplified polar positions which do no justice to the refined political theories of Burke and Rousseau, yet the tendencies, or rather the divergencies, of the two positions are nevertheless valid and critical for an understanding of the debate over the nature of political representation.

Representation: Pluralists and Marxists

A second theme which arises from this first issue over representation is precisely the question of how to achieve equitable representativeness in a political elite. Here the social composition of the political leadership may be seen as crucial or unimportant, depending in large measure on the answer to the previous question, the nature of representation. Here there are, in contemporary political science, two basic positions. The first position, dominant in Western social science generally since World War II, is the pluralist or revisionist democratic school of thought. Developed in the years of postwar reconstruction of parliamentary democracy in France, Italy, Japan, and West Germany by such scholars as Schumpeter, Aron, and Sartori, this school of thought holds that the political elite should not simply represent mass opinion, that the political elite is more capable of representing the masses if it is not directly bound to mass opinion, and that, as long as the masses have a choice every four or six years between or among competing elite groupings (parties), adequate representation of the electorate interests is provided. In this case the political elite cannot be expected to be representative of the population in its social composition, since the elite is made up of the presumably most capable and qualified in the society, not of people of average means, occupations, educations, or talents. For pluralists, the representativeness of a political elite in terms of social composition is meaningless with respect to the representation of the interests of the people or of different groups of citizens.

Competing with the pluralist school is the Marxist interpretation of representativeness, a minority position in Western scholarship, though perhaps a majority position in the social sciences worldwide. Developed originally by Marx and Engels and contemporarily by scholars like Miliband, Jaeggi, and Bottomore, this view holds that a political elite drawn only from the upper social stratum will not and cannot adequately represent the interests of the lower classes, the great majority of the population. Even if this upper-class political elite is divided into competing parties or groupings, these parties or groupings limit their competition so as not to disadvantage their own class interests. Resting on the empirically well established principle that social class is generally the *single* best indicator of political behavior, attitudes, and interests, Marxists view the exclusion or token representation of such groups as workers, blacks, and women in various political elites as signs of inadequate representation of the interests of these groups in the political system. For Marxists, the representativeness of a political elite in terms of social composition is meaningful with respect to equitable interest representation. In the long run, of course, the Marxist perspective foresees the gradual elimination of all elites and the withering away of the state as a governing body of leaders separate from the general citizenry.[1]

Again, the above positions represent only the outlines of the debate between pluralists and Marxists on the importance of social representativeness in a political elite. Most pluralists would admit that a political system which totally excludes a social group from the process of leadership recruitment, either by statute or in actual practice, is highly suspect in terms of fair representation of that group, even if members of that group have the formal right to vote (cf. Matthews 1954 for thoughtful commentary). Yet pluralists oppose any attempt to "mathematize" the relationship between elite composition and equitability of representation (cf. Rasmussen 1969: 165) or to establish "quotas" of representation.

Most Marxists also realize that the presence of workers, blacks, women, or other members of other social groupings in leadership positions does not necessarily insure fair representation of these group interests. It is clear, for example, that in the czarist Dumas there were peasant deputies from the most reactionary parties who were absolutely controlled by the local nobility in their districts (cf. Levin 1973: chap. 10) or that in many Western parliaments there are white-collar employees who are lobbyists for special industries or branches of commerce, but in no sense for their own occupational group. This also means that Marxists accept the notion that the ruling-class interests are not always literally represented "in person" in the governing elite, since members of the ruling class can "buy"

1. There is a third position, held by radical democrats, which tends to side with the Marxist position on the long-run abolition of political elites and with the notion of direct popular participation in government and economy, but nevertheless sides with the pluralists on the question of social representativeness in political elites as an indicator of interest representation. This position, neglected here, is considered in the concluding chapter as a contemporary competitor to the pluralist and Marxist perspectives.

or "control" members of intermediate or lower social strata. But the lower classes cannot do the reverse (otherwise it is doubtful that they could justly be termed "lower classes").

The position taken in this study is clearly the Marxist orientation. Analysis of changes in the social composition of political elites from a pluralist perspective, while perhaps interesting in other respects to pluralist theory, could not be the foundation of a study which attempts to connect systems and system changes with the social basis of elite recruitment. It is not possible to carry out a "value-free" analysis of this sort (cf. Connolly 1974), and the reader should bear in mind the theoretical underpinnings of this study, just as he or she should examine the ultimately political judgments which form the theoretical basis for pluralist-school research. In the following chapters, the emphasis will be on social composition of political elites as an important and fundamental indicator of the nature of interest representation in a political system and thus as an important indicator of the nature of the system itself. The closing chapter will deal in depth with the relationship of ideology to political-science research in the area of elite background analysis and will offer a postanalysis defense of the Marxist position.

Problems of Cross-Sectional Elite Analysis

Several years ago, William Quandt summarized the contribution of elite studies to the comparative analysis of political development:

> The study of political leadership will no doubt continue to occupy a central position in the analysis of political change. Among the numerous methods for analyzing political elites, the social background approach has been frequently employed, but thus far with mediocre results. The non-comparable focus of most of these studies is largely responsible for the absence of theoretically interesting and empirically testable hypotheses linking the socialization experience of elites to their political behavior and to the overall functioning of the political system. (1970: 197)

Quandt called for an attempt to make elite analysis more comparative through the inclusion of information on a large number (i.e., statistically significant) of elites taken at a single point in time, or on the study of trends in elite bodies over a considerable period of time, but again for a large number of polities. He himself was able to utilize data covering elite bodies in sixty-one countries at some points in time and was able to perform trend analysis of elite composition for about twenty nations taken as a group. This pioneering work, highly suggestive and rich in hypothesis generation for future testing, develops the basic motivating factors which should underlie comparative elite studies. This type of cross-sectional approach to elite analysis, also represented by the works of Banks and Textor (1963) and Russett (1964), among others (but cf. Searing and Edinger 1967; Searing 1969), presents certain problems. While accepting the basic call of Quandt for theoretical utility in elite analysis, this section presents some of the problems associated with the cross-sectional approach, illustrated through some examples from my recent research, and I shall propose an alternative "seminal-case" approach to the comparative study of political elites.

First of all, the cross-sectional approach to elite data analysis, covering as many national elites as possible, represents what Grew and Thrupp (1968) have termed "horizontal history." That is, the correlation and regression results of cross-sectional analysis don't represent the real world history of any polity but, rather, a composite pieced together from different polities, each of which presumably represents a stage or phase in some uniform relationship of political development. I doubt that correlations resulting from such data can in general validly be used in the testing of elite developmental hypotheses. Only by making the false assumption of a monolithic or universal pattern of development can one assume that each nation-state represents some point along a single continuum of development. The alternative is longitudinal analysis resting on complete time-series data for each political elite, so that our data analysis "remembers" the actual pattern of change for each system. This remembering process is vital, since stages of elite development not present in significant numbers in cross-sectional analysis at the sampling point in time among our collection of national elites are forgotten in the resulting analyses. Almost all the elite data utilized by Quandt and others in cross-sectional analyses date from the post-WWII period. There is a relative absence of data from the Western industrial nations during the interwar period of Depression and fascism, as well as an almost complete absence of data on political elites in feudal, traditional, or monarchical regimes.

To take one "seminal" example, that of Germany during Weimar and the Third Reich, when levels of urbanization, industrialization, education, and most other socioeconomic indexes are quite similar to Germany in the postwar period (at least up to the early 1960s), we can find examples of parliaments (Reichstag/Bundestag) in which the occupational composition of the political elite is quite similar under very different (centrifugal democracy, fascism, centripetal democracy) political systems. On the other hand, lack of complete longitudinal data may also mask the transformations of elite recruitment which may occur within a relatively short (10-year) timespan. For example, there is (see table 1) an almost complete change in occupational composition of Bundestag deputies from 1949 to 1961, as early high recruitment from workers and white-collar employees is rapidly replaced by recruitment from managerial and professional levels. Thus, even within stable political systems quite important developments in elite composition may occur which are overlooked or missed without systematic over-time data.

Additionally, the stages of feudal or traditional elite formations may never have existed in the actual histories of several "new" or "derivative" societies. Thus, for example, it has been asserted that the infusion of lawyers into the parliamentary elite is strongly related to the development of mass higher education ($r = .56$ in Quandt 1970: 194–195). However, the United States, which underwent a thorough bourgeois revolution far in advance of urbanization, industrialization, and the development of mass higher education, shows just the reverse trend in its actual history. While the representation of lawyers is still high in the U.S. House (55% of representatives, 1910–1960), it was even higher in the days of predominantly rural, nonindustrial America (64%, 1790–1860), when higher education was limited to a small minority. Complete longitudinal data have the potential advantage of keeping the records straight as to the real world process of elite development in actual, not composite, nations.

Second, the data which cross-sectional elite analysis has utilized are composed entirely of aggregate figures which do not allow for individual-level correlation of changes or for cross tabulation of elite composition by two or more variables. These aggregate measures are statistics of central tendency, whereas for many purposes measures of dispersion, distribution, and polarization are more important.

This inability to get at the less than aggregate-level relationships (without severe risk of ecological error) can show in several ways. We might, for example, assume that two elites with similar aggregate occupational recruitment patterns are more or less equally homogeneous. However, if we are able to correlate occupational cleavages with party affiliation for individual deputies or officehold-

TABLE 1. Occupational Composition of Selected
Bundestags, with Correlation by Party Affiliation

Occupation	1949 BT %	1961 BT %	1972 BT %
Worker	49	13	15
Owner	14	19	8
Manager	14	35	34
Professional	18	28	38
Other	5	5	5
Pearson's C	.41	.39	.36

Note: Figures in the tables have been rounded off to the nearest
percent. Because of normal rounding errors of individual entries,
some columns may not total 100%. In general, zero indicates any
amount more than absolute zero but less than .5%.

ers, we may find that one party system is much more integrative
than another. So, when we correlate, for example, elite composition
by occupation and party affiliation for the 1928 Reichstag, we get a
Pearson's Contingency Coefficient of .73, but for the 1957 Bundestag, with quite similar occupational distribution overall, the Contingency Coefficient is only .39. Conversely, despite the great shifts
in occupational recruitment patterns in the Bundestag in the
postwar era, the German Bundestag has retained a quite steady correlation level between elite occupation and party affiliation. (Contingency Coefficient is .41 in 1949, .39 in 1961, .36 in 1972.) The
difference of course lies in the greater homogeneity of elite recruitment patterns *across* party lines in the Bonn republic as opposed to
the Weimar party system.

Or, with regard to something as simple as average age of an elite
grouping, we might note that the average age of members of both the
1971 Soviet Central Committee and the 1969 U.S. Senate was quite
similar (58 and 56, respectively), yet the generational composition in
terms of pre-WWI, interwar, and post-WWII generations (i.e., those
who came to maturity before WWI, between the Great Wars, and
after WWII) is strikingly different. The Senate contains a greater
proportion of both older (28%) and younger (13%) generations,
while the Central Committee remains dominated by the same middle generation (77%) which was swept into power during the Great
Purges of the 1930s. Quandt (1970) concluded from his cross-
sectional analysis of elites that the average age of elites in "ideologi-

cal" systems is 42 (N = 9), with 51 (N = 11) being the average age in "non-ideological" systems. But the Soviet Central Committee, to continue our example from above, has had an average membership age ranging from 33 in 1917 to 63 in 1975. This may tell us that the Soviet leadership has gone from being hyperideological to hyper-pragmatic (some have argued this—cf. Tatu 1970), if we treat age only as a life-cycle variable, but a closer analysis tells us that the same generation (born 1900–1919) which, in very ideological fashion, was responsible for the construction of Soviet society along Stalinist economic and political lines in the 1930s is still in power today and still holds the same ideological outlook, which now, however, has become a conservative tradition rather than a ground-breaking radicalism. In my opinion, the question of ideological/ nonideological regimes measured in terms of an average age of elites is off the mark to begin with. The American political system is quite as ideological as the Soviet, and the ideology of American elites is quite as pronounced as the ideology of the Soviet leaders. The more relevant question would seem to be what substantive policy positions a particular elite grouping, whether defined in generational, occupational (class), or other terms, is oriented toward. This of course requires a greater in-depth knowledge of each polity and the development of its political leadership.

Third, it is not at all clear whether each of the political elites for which aggregate data have been collected in cross-sectional analysis is the result of internal political recruitment processes or is, on the other hand, "contaminated" through overt or covert influence of external nations or organizations. To take some obvious examples, it is not evident what relationships between system-type or level of economic development and elite composition exist at certain points in the history of communist Poland, Hungary, and Czechoslovakia or in South Vietnam, Cambodia, Lebanon, Guatemala, and Chile, given the extensive and often overriding, if not continuous, intervention of foreign powers in the recruitment process of the political leadership of these nations. Only for those nations where we can with some assurance assume that elite recruitment is the result of basic internal political and social processes can valid relationships to elite recruitment be drawn. It is of course of considerable interest to investigate the effects of foreign intervention on the process of elite recruitment, but this is another theoretical focus.

Fourth, it is clear that the taxonomies employed (perhaps unavoidably) in past cross-sectional analyses are at such levels of aggregation as to mask important differences, both between nations and within single polities. For example, under economic professions (including business owners and farmers), some distinction must be made between industrialists, bankers, and large landowners, on the one hand, and owners of small businesses, independent artisans, and smallholders, on the other. Otherwise it would appear, for example, that the Social Democratic party (SPD) deputy faction in the 1890 Reichstag, with 41% of its members from "economic professions," was almost tied with the middle-class National Liberal (NL) party (46%) or the aristocratic Conservative (K) party (43%) in recruitment from the propertied classes. In fact, however, all the Social Democratic self-employed deputies were either artisans or small businessowners (especially small restaurateurs), while the National Liberal deputies were predominantly large landowners (without titles) and the Conservative deputies were almost all titled estate owners. Similarly, it could be said that, during the 1920s and 1930s in Germany, the Nazi party recruited deputies to the Reichstag from wageworkers (30%) about as often as did the leftist parties (Social Democrats, Independent Socialists, and Communists). Only on closer (disaggregated) examination does it appear that the majority of Nazi wageworker deputies were white-collar employees (mainly sales personnel and bank employees), while nearly all leftist wageworker members of parliament came from the stratum of blue-collar production workers.

A Longitudinal Seminal-Case Alternative

Obviously, any quantitative analysis of aggregate data with a large number of polities as data base will contain some deviant cases in which general relationships will not hold, and there will be cases where aggregate categories are less than adequate in reflecting validly the concept intended. However, the deviant cases illustrated here represent major polities which are themselves examples of important political cultures and seminal political systems. The point is that distortions of the type demonstrated above are endemic to the aggregate type of cross-sectional elite analysis, as are the basic limitations of that approach to comparative elite analysis.

These basic considerations have led me to take a different course, to select a small (N = 4) number of nations which represent the internal workings of four distinct political cultures and significant system-types. The basic approach in my choice of the United States, Germany, the Soviet Union, and Mexico as the polities for which individual-level longitudinal elite data would be gathered can be summarized in terms of maximizing the differences in culture and system-type, while assuring that elite recruitment is operating under conditions of relative autonomy (see table 2). For each nation, two basic levels of the national political elite were included in the data base: one which corresponds to the top political executive (cabinets/politburos; an officeholding definition of each elite) and one which corresponds to a somewhat larger elite grouping (legislatures/central committees) which does not necessarily correspond to the effective political legislature but, rather, represents in each system an officially recognized body of effective national leaders.

I shall argue that this schema overcomes to a considerable extent the objections to cross-sectional analysis raised above. The data have been collected consecutively for all bodies in each polity, over a timespan covering several generations in each case. My longitudinal data can thus represent (remember) elite formation as it actually occurs in these four major systems. Additionally, it is possible for the researcher to be more than superficially familiar with four as opposed to sixty-one political cultures and systems, so that refined judgments or corrections in definitional schemes can help make cross-national comparisons more reliable (see esp. Mill 1888).

Since the data gathered for these four political elites are individual data, we can develop measures of distribution or polarization as well as multivariate correlation without fear of ecological error. For each polity, over 1,000 individuals have been coded along a variety of background and career variables (for Germany 6,005, for the U.S. 1,000, for Mexico 6,299, and for the Soviet Union 1,114 cases have been coded). This should allow for a variety of subgroup analyses with several control variables to test hypotheses relating to individual parties, occupational, educational, or other attribute groupings.

The fact that such analyses are based on examination of a small number of polities does not mean that findings must remain descriptive. Indeed, individual case studies of elites need not be atheoretical, if the researcher is careful to establish in advance the theoretical framework and hypotheses for which the case in point is to be a test case. The small "n" of national systems does mean that we shall not be able to make the extensive use of Pearsonian correlation and regression analysis (although see chap. 5) commonly

TABLE 2. Culture, System-Type, and Elite Levels of Four Seminal Cases

Country	Political culture	System-type	Elite levels
Germany	European	Multiparty parliamentary (except 1933–1945)	Cabinet Reichstag/Bundestag
United States	Anglo-American	Two-party presidential	Cabinet Congress
Mexico	Latin American	One-party dominant	Cabinet Congress
Soviet Union	Slavic	One-party communist	Politburo Central Committee

utilized with cross-sectional data, but this loss of some statistical possibilities should not diminish the theoretical relevance of our hypothesis testing.

Other types of statistical analysis, relating to association of nominal (Contingency Coefficient) or ordinal (gamma, Somer's D) scale variables, fractionalization (Rae's F_e) of representation, and time-series factor analysis (R-technique, see Michael Smith 1974: chap. 6), are available for analysis of each elite. For cross-national comparisons, less elegant but still valid methods, such as difference of means or analysis of variance tests, will be possible for hypothesis testing relating elite characteristics to system-type. The utility of seminal-case comparative elite analysis depends, in any case, not on the potency of the statistical methods used or usable but on the care with which the (seminal) cases relating to the theoretical focus of the research are chosen.

The longitudinal seminal-case method represents an attempt to develop a middle position between the static single-polity case study and the aggregate-level cross-sectional correlation analysis of political elites. We do not dispute the utility of either approach for particular cases or for certain research goals. We are in part returning to the method of comparison (method of agreement, method of difference) outlined by John Stuart Mill in the middle of the last century (1888: 278, 279–283, 610–612), in that we shall use agreement along system attributes—for example, the Mexican Party of Revolutionary Institutions (PRI) and the Communist party of the Soviet

Union (CPSU) cases as single-party systems—as a basis for evaluating similarities (and highlighting differences) in elite composition. Likewise, we shall use system differences (e.g., Germany as a political culture moving from imperial monarchy to unstable democracy to fascist dictatorship to stable democracy) in association with variation (and constancy) in elite recruitment. We are returning to Mill's method in part only, however, because we are not concerned principally with discovering laws of causation through logical induction, which Mill notes is strictly not achievable in the social sciences; rather, we are concerned with developing certain (noncausal) theses and associations between system and elite recruitment values (laws of phenomena, of which laws of causation are one subset).

Problems of Measurement

Despite the advantages of the longitudinal seminal-case alternative to cross-sectional analysis presented above, there remain some thorny problems which cannot be fully solved in this sort of research. Most of these problems, or problem areas, revolve around the questions of elite definitions, the boundary point between elite and nonelite for the purposes of this study, and the questions of variable measurement, accuracy, bias, and validity over time of background variables.

With any definition of an elite grouping, in this case the national political elite, there must be some method of selection which produces a data base of people considered to be members of this elite grouping. An institutional definition is used throughout this study, which has the advantage of providing a neat cutoff point between membership and nonmembership for each national elite sample. It is eminently suitable for over-time or historical research. The major methodological alternative—the selection of an elite sample by reputational criteria (cf. Merritt 1970; Bill and Hardgrave 1973)—is simply not a live possibility for such comparative research reaching back several generations and involving thousands of cases. On the other hand, the limitations of the institutional approach should be freely admitted. First of all, it is apparent that in every polity certain very influential political leaders do not hold an office, or at least not a government office, or not a government office at the national level. In the United States there are leaders like Mayor Daley who would not be included in our institutional definition; in Mexico a Cincinnatus figure like expresident Cárdenas, although still very powerful politically, would not be included after leaving office; and in Germany Adolf Hitler, who became a Reichstag member only in 1933, would not be included in the national political elite for the important years of 1928 to 1932. Second, the reverse situation, namely the inclusion of people in the elite sample who are not very influential, is also a possibility with an institutional definition. Thus, within the membership of Congress (Chamber of Deputies, Reichstag/Bundestag, or even Central Committee), there is a hierarchy of power or influence which strongly differentiates a one-term representative from a ten-term representative who heads an important House committee. This is unavoidable if there is to be any clear cutoff point; as long as we can assert that, for an elite political body in general, each member meets some minimal criterion of importance. This is a sticky problem, since over time each institution, be it Congress, Reichstag, Central Committee, or whatever, has experienced highs and lows of importance in the political system. The question is whether, as a body, an institutional grouping has ever fallen to a point where one can no longer generalize that, to be a member of that grouping, a person must have at least a minimum of political influence. Certainly this point has been *approached* in some cases here. During the late Porfirian dictatorship, for example, the Mexican lower house or Chamber of Deputies may have been populated by such lower-order figures in the Díaz machine that membership might not be counted as elite status. Yet because this is not clearly the case, and because in the Mexican system the national legislature has never been an effective legislature in Western parliamentary understanding, no exception was made for the late Porfirian period. In the German political development, the Reichstag/Bundestag has indeed experienced several highs and lows. Never an effective parliament under the kaiser, it was nonetheless *the* locus of national party competition, and its members were the top leaders of the national parties. More problematic, of course, is the Reichstag under the Third Reich, reduced to window dressing for the Nazi regime, meeting only once a year for purely symbolic and perfunctory activities. Here additional research has been necessary to show that the membership of the Nazi Reichstag (1933–1945) consisted of the *top* Nazi leadership, that, although the Reichstag itself was no longer a functional parliament or even a preparliament, its members were drawn from the top ranks of the National Socialist German Workers party (NSDAP) regime. The Soviet data base, resting on the membership of the top party institutions, the Politburo and the Central Committee, never presupposes any functional equivalence for the larger (Central Committee) elite grouping with Western legislatures. Even at the height of the Stalinist purges in the 1930s, when, according to Khrushchev's later revelations, neither the Politburo nor the Central Committee met as effective political forums, the members of these two bodies are widely regarded as the top national leadership under Stalin.

The problems of measurement for individual variables remain an area where often only approximate solutions are possible. Without going into detail as to the specifics of each variable for each national elite sample and the problems therein, we may divide these problems into two types: missing data and biased data. The problem of missing data appears in the Mexican sample with respect to the earlier (Porfirian and revolutionary) periods under study and with respect to lower political offices in the Mexican system. In general, the earlier the time period and the lower the office, the greater the probability of missing data for a member of the Mexican elite sample. A milder form of this problem appears in the Soviet data set for the 17th and 18th Party Congress Central Committees, when the biographical sketches of so many party leaders, victims of the Great Purge, were never included in the Great Soviet Encyclopedia. A still milder form of missing data appears with the Reichstag deputies from the Communist party of Germany (KPD) in the last years of the Weimar republic, when several KPD deputies refused to give occupation, education, or even date of birth information for the parliamentary handbook. Missing data become a problem when it is likely that the cases for which data are lacking represent a different distribution of values for some variable than the cases for which data are available. One suspects, for example, that for the earlier Mexican periods it is the deputy from humbler circumstances for whom data are lacking, while, for a deputy of higher social origins, data on date of birth, education, and occupation have been recorded. Thus a profile of education and occupation of members of the Mexican Chamber of Deputies for the late Porfirian and revolutionary years may well overestimate the educational level and understate the representation of lower-class occupation among deputies (cf. Peter Smith 1974). Decisions on the seriousness of potential bias have been made throughout this study on a case-by-case basis; in each situation where missing data may lead to biased results, conclusions have been tempered to include this possibility.

The problem of biased (nonmissing) data is a potential hindrance with respect to several variables. This arises when the data on social background from parliamentary handbook nonofficial "who's who" sources have been written out by the elite member. This rarely presents a bias problem with such variables as education, religion, date of birth, or birthplace. However, it does present a potential problem with respect to the most important variable involved in this study, namely, occupation. Occupation, when self-described, may be misleading due to diverse understandings of the term. One person may give his/her main career occupation even though not presently practiced, another may write "retired" or "pensioner," still another may give his/her political office whether or not this is a main source of income. In all four data sets, we have attempted to tap the main career occupation of each member according to the information at hand, although for several data sets we have also coded information on earlier, or secondary, occupations. It is clear, however, that the information at hand does not always give an accurate picture of main occupation. Two examples will suffice here. It is widely suspected that Soviet political leaders are prone to overstate their proletarian origins and perhaps the extent of their occupational career as either worker or simple employee (cf. Lewytzkyj 1970; Brzezinski and Huntington 1963: 133 ff.). An ongoing attempt by Western scholars has been made to correct this bias when possible, and the data used here reflect this work. Earlier experience with these data indicates that this problem may have been more acute during the Stalinist era than under Lenin or since the reconstruction of the collective leadership during the 1950s. With respect to the German data, there is a tendency for Bundestag deputies to describe their occupations in terms that do not provoke class-conflict images of interest representation (cf. von Beyme 1971: 52–54). Thus a Christian Democratic Union (CDU) deputy may describe himself/herself as a lawyer or an engineer when his/her main occupation, in terms of income and activity, is that of an entrepreneur or an industrialist. Not wanting to appear as the direct incorporation of business interests, a conservative deputy prefers to be seen as a free professional. Likewise, an SPD deputy, who is in fact a paid union official, may give her/his occupation simply as white-collar employee or office manager (for her/his union organization). While some problems of this sort exist for earlier German data from the monarchy through Weimar and into the Third Reich, in those times symbolism of class conflict in self-described occupations was not sidestepped with the same frequency, and at certain times and for certain parties it was in fact prized.

Organization of the Study

In the organization of the following chapters, I have tried to demonstrate the utility of longitudinal seminal-case analysis as a methodological approach to the study of social bases of political elite recruitment. While each chapter presents a distinct set of theses to be tested, the individual analyses have been grouped into two larger parts.

Part 2 emphasizes the application of seminal-case analysis for shorter (one-generation) timespans comparing all four polities. The first timespan, covering the period from 1900 to 1920, represents an era of revolution for Germany, Russia, and Mexico, in which all three nations experience revolutionary changes in their political systems. The United States serves here only as a nonrevolutionary control case against which to measure the extent of revolutionary elite displacement in the other polities. The second timespan, covering the interwar years of 1920 to 1940, represents for all four systems a time of trouble, of high system stress and tension, to which each political system must respond. The responses range from mild reform under FDR's New Deal to Cárdenas' agrarian populism to Stalin's Five-Year Plans and the Great Purge and finally to system collapse in Weimar and the establishment of the Nazi dictatorship. The third timespan includes the post-WWII (post-1945) years, a generation of general peace and at least relative prosperity for all four nations, a period of "normalcy" in which the political system is not under great stress.

Each chapter in part 2 examines the relationship between system-type and its response to a general political environment (revolution, high stress, low stress) in terms of change in the social composition of political elites. In this way, we shall examine propositions about the range of response and the response tendency (or typical response) in leadership recruitment to varying political stress levels in each system, as well as the varying elite displacements which occur when a political system cannot successfully respond to political stress.

In contrast to these four-nation comparisons covering one-generation timespans and controlling, very roughly, for stress level are the analyses of part 3. These chapters are single-nation studies, although some cross-national comparisons are included, and they utilize longitudinal data in greater depth than was possible in the four-nation analyses, generally covering several generations. In these chapters, country-specific phenomena provide the main theses for testing, although hopefully within a framework which allows for some generalization and elaboration of theoretically interesting propositions.

Chapter 5, for example, develops and evaluates four alternative hypotheses on the "revolution" in tenure in the U.S. House of Representatives since the turn of the century. This phenomenon is peculiar to the elite recruitment process in the United States and could scarcely be handled within the more general comparative framework of part 2. It also provides an opportunity to demonstrate the seminal-case approach covering almost two centuries of tenure development and utilizing correlation analyses more commonly found in cross-sectional studies.

Chapter 6 tests two competing sets of hypotheses—liberal democratic and Marxist—on class divisions in elite recruitment in Germany covering the period 1871 to 1972. Germany as a political culture has experienced four distinct system-types within one century, from monarchy (1871–1918) to the unstable (centrifugal) democracy of Weimar (1918–1933) to the fascist Third Reich (1933–1945) to the stable (centripetal) democracy of the Federal Republic. This single-nation study examines the social evolution of elite composition both within system and between system from the perspectives of liberal democratic and Marxist theses on class struggle and elite recruitment.

Related to the above analysis, but separated for the sake of clarity and presentation in greater depth, is a testing (chap. 7) of the well-known "end of ideology" thesis of Lipset and Bell in the area of elite recruitment, using the Federal Republic of Germany as a prime, perhaps the best, example of what the end of ideology process looks like in a particular polity. If the political development in the Bonn republic typifies the depolarization of class strife, how is this reflected in the social basis of leadership recruitment, both for the system as a whole and for individual parties? Here the advantage of complete time-series data for longitudinal or diachronic analysis is also illustrated, since important elite transformations occur within relatively short periods and without any overt crises or dramatic events to mark them.

The evolution in social composition of the Mexican political elite in the post-Cárdenas period (1940–1970) is the focus of chapter 8. Here the conservative development of economic policy and the institutionalization of the PRI regime are examined from a Marxist perspective on the state in capitalist society. Using a framework developed by Offe and by Gold, Lo, and Wright, modified to generate hypotheses on the effect of selective mechanisms on the composition of the political elite, the capitalist road of development pursued by the PRI is analyzed with respect to fulfillment of these (positive, negative, and disguising) selective mechanisms in the social basis of recruitment to the offices of deputy, senator, governor, and cabinet secretary.

The remaining two chapters (9 and 10) in part 3 deal with a generational interpretation of the Soviet political elite in its development, 1917 to 1971. These analyses view changes in the social composition of the Central Committee within a theoretical framework of political age cohorts developed by Lambert, Ryder, Cutler, and Mannheim and pose an alternative to four other schools of thought on the nature of both the Soviet elite and the Soviet system. Chapter 9 presents a critique of the Kremlinological and the rational-technical models of Soviet elite recruitment, two interpretations of the Soviet system dominant in Western political analysis. The following chapter deals with two neo-Marxist interpretations of the Soviet elite: the Trotskyite "bureaucratic stratum" model and the "new-class" thesis of Milovan Djilas. The generational approach is seen to offer additional explanatory power to the analysis of elite recruitment in the USSR and at the same time casts some doubts on several models commonly found in the literature on the Soviet system.

Part 4 provides a critical overview of the role of political ideology in the sociology of political elites. The debate among pluralists, radical democrats, and Marxists over the sociology of political elites is seen as part of a larger struggle within political science for ideological dominance or orthodoxy. Ultimately, political science itself is interpreted as part of the general struggle over the class order in the society at large.

Part 2. Four-Nation Comparisons

CHAPTER 2

Revolution and Elite Displacement: Social and Political Transformations

In the next three chapters, we shall be comparing elite recruitment in our four polities in an attempt to test some hypotheses relating to system-type as it responds to different environmental conditions (i.e., revolution, time of trouble, normalcy). In this chapter, we shall deal with the kinds of elite displacements which result from the Mexican (1910–1920), Soviet (1917–1921), and German (1918) revolutions in the first two decades of this century. This analysis will test hypotheses relating the nature of the revolution to the effect it exercised on elite composition and the process of elite recruitment. The United States serves here as a control case of nonrevolutionary or evolutionary elite development against which to measure the magnitude of revolutionary elite displacement in our other three polities.

Economic Development and the Political System: Some Comparisons

In some respects, our examination of the political elites of the kaiser's Germany, late czarist Russia, Porfirian Mexico, and the prewar United States does more than just establish a baseline against which we may test the nature of political revolution against elite recruitment in four seminal polities. It also provides a valid comparison of elite recruitment in four societies undergoing early industrialization, though of quite different intensities and extents and under different auspices. Yet it is clear that the prewar period for each nation was one of transformation of the economy from its agrarian and rural traditions to one ever more urban and industrialized.

In the forty years after the unification of the German state (1871) under the Wilhelminian monarchy and the leadership of Bismarck, Germany's economy had been rapidly industrialized and its population notably more urbanized into the growing new industrial centers. Similarly, the post–Civil War United States had by the outbreak of the Great War emerged as a primarily urban and industrial nation, although the pace of industrialization had been somewhat more gradual than in Germany (cf. Gershenkron 1962). By the second decade of the new century, capitalist development had proceeded to the point where these two nations represented the most powerful industrial economies in the world.

Mexico and Russia, while still largely agricultural and rural as of the early 1900s, were nevertheless experiencing important economic growth and definite breaks with their traditional modes of production. This development was more pronounced in its social and political impact than its statistical relationship to the entire economy might indicate. Under the dictatorship of Porfirio Díaz (1876–1910), and especially in the last twenty years of his regime, the Mexican economy underwent significant development in the mining and extractive sectors, and even some light-manufacturing (textiles, tobacco) sectors were experiencing considerable growth (cf. esp. Hansen 1971: chaps. 1–2). The Russian economy, especially during the decade of the 1890s under Finance Minister Witte (the Witte Plan) and again during the 1907 to 1913 lull between the abortive 1905 Revolution and World War I, had also achieved remarkable growth in selected areas, mainly mining, oil, railroads, and textiles, but with noteworthy progress in heavy industry (iron, steel, coke) as well (see Harcave 1959: chaps. 17, 21, for a good summary). This concentration of economic growth (in both economic activity and geographic location) was not the only reason for an increased social and political impact, however. Participation in and control of these growth sectors by foreign capital were extremely pronounced in both cases (cf. Hansen 1971: chap. 2). Thus, while the large percentage increases in nonagricultural production were made on relatively small initial bases in both Russia and Mexico in the general period of 1890 to 1910, the large-scale plant size, spatially concentrated industrial work force, and control by foreign capital magnified the total impact of this development.

Political System-Type and Definitions of Elites

The process of elite recruitment in our four polities differed significantly during this period. The United States still had multiparty competition within its basic republican framework, and it was just in this period that the last (to date) great challenges (from the Populists and Socialists) to the solidification of the two-party system were being made. For purposes of the analysis in this chapter, we shall take a sampling of House of Representatives membership (1906 through 1920) from both the prewar and the immediate postwar years as our American elite data base.

In Germany (at least after the dropping of the ban on the Social Democratic party in 1890) relatively unhampered multiparty competition was also the rule, and, although Reichstag majorities were not the basis for the forming of governments, at least in domestic policy Reichstag approval was required. After the 1918 Revolution, the National Assembly (1919) and the Reichstag (1920) became the basis of government and the formal locus of constitutional sovereignty in the new Weimar system. We shall be using the membership of the last (1912) Reichstag of the monarchy period and the memberships of the 1919 National Assembly and the 1920 Reichstag as the basic definitions of the national political elites in the German case. Data from Maxwell Knight's 1952 study of the German executive (cabinet) in the Kaiserreich and in Weimar are also available for selected comparisons.

In the late czarist period under Nicholas II, from 1905 through 1917, the Duma existed as an emasculated preparliament, without effective control over the actions of the autocrat. The electoral laws were unconstitutionally altered by the czar in 1906 and 1907 to gerrymander a Duma membership dominated by proczarist forces. Still, the Duma membership gives some systematic indication of the basic lines of elite recruitment for a national elective body and provides information divided along party or factional lines as well; for this reason we shall make use of Levin's 1973 analysis of the social composition of the third (1907–1912) Duma as our basic indicator of elite recruitment in the late czarist period. Data from a sampling of major figures in the czarist Council of State (cabinet) in the last decade of the autocracy provide information on the social composition in top executive posts. These data will be compared to the social composition of the Bolshevik Central Committee during the revolution and civil-war (1917–1921) years.

In Mexico, the regime of the aged Porfirio Díaz was, as Branden-berg (1964) has termed it, almost a textbook example of a corrupt political machine. The Mexican National Congress was packed with regime adherents and was as a body submissive to the will of the dictator. Nevertheless, the choice of Congress deputies is taken as an indication of those social forces which supported the regime (and benefited from it). These data are bolstered by additional analysis at the higher cabinet level of political elite composition under the prerevolutionary regime. This two-level analysis is compared to the background of deputies and cabinet secretaries throughout the suc-cession of regimes (Madero, Huerta, Carranza, Obregón) from the overthrow of Díaz in 1910 to the assumption of the presidency by Obregón in 1920, signaling a basic end to the revolution and civil war of the past decade.

Hypotheses on Elite Displacement: Political and Social Revolutions

Social and political revolutions are judged from many perspectives, and we must make clear that the present analysis focuses primarily on a single aspect, that of elite transformation. Nevertheless, if we have correctly identified in each polity leadership groups which ac-curately reflect the composition of the political elite, we will be able to test some working hypotheses about the nature and scope of the Mexican Revolution of 1910 to 1920, the German Revolution of 1918, and the Russian Revolution of 1917 to 1921 as they were reflected in the recruitment of a national political elite. We shall also say something about the American case as an evolutionary elite development process which does not go beyond the boundaries of liberal democracy in an advanced capitalist economy.

All three of our revolutions qualify as political revolutions (cf. Hagopian 1974: chap. 1) in that they bring into existence a new *political system*, a new *process* of establishing authoritative politi-cal power. The question to be addressed here is: what was the sub-stantive or social content of these political revolutions in the altera-tion of the political elite composition?

One feature commonly associated with political revolution (or counterrevolution) is generational renewal of elites (Quandt 1970; Merkl 1967: chap. 14). To the extent that in changing societies younger generations represent *as a whole* sociopolitical cleavages with respect to past older generations, sudden elite age cohort turnover may in itself represent a limited form of social revolution, even when the younger elites are drawn from essentially the same social origins and occupational-educational categories as the outgoing officeholders (cf. Lambert 1971; Cutler 1971; Inglehart 1971; Ryder 1965), since the concrete experiences of their social-class and educational cohorts may be strikingly different and they may develop different policy orientations from those of their elders. Still, we would posit that an elite displacement limited solely or almost solely to generational renewal, no matter how sudden or thorough, without alteration of class categories of elite recruitment, would represent only marginal social revolution though perhaps significant political reform within the boundaries of existing class structures.

Our major hypothesis is that basic social revolutions (or counter-revolutions) do not occur without *significant* and *qualitatively decisive* changes in the social composition of the relevant political elites. This is a working hypothesis, subject to falsification on the basis of the evidence to be adduced below. We are positing that, in those revolutions clearly judged as social, there will be such decisive and qualitative elite displacements as to basically alter the social categories from which political leadership is drawn. This also assumes that the social nature of the revolutionary process is revealed at the elite level through changes in the recruitment process. On the basis of this thesis, the following are expected:

1. Only gradual, evolutionary changes in elite composition should characterize the American political elite during this era. The United States had undergone its bourgeois political revolution over a century earlier, and, as the most stable and successful of the political systems through the first two decades of this century, the main social sources of elite recruitment of the prewar era would be expected to remain intact in the immediate postwar years.

2. Small quantitative and perhaps unimportant qualitative shifts in elite recruitment should be expected as a result of the 1918 German Revolution which, while establishing a liberal parliamentary system and an expanded set of governing (*staatstragende*) parties, did not, according to the consensus of scholarly opinion of various shadings (Bracher 1964; Zapf 1965; Kaack 1974; von Beyme 1973), loosen the grip of the dominant social strata on the military, the top civil service, the courts, or the economy. Rather, in fact, the SPD-led government, following a path of bourgeois liberalism, utilized the

intact aristocratic military command to put down the revolutionary workers' councils (*Räte*) which had been established and to crush the armed workers' uprisings (Berlin and Munich). With the assassination by the military of potential revolutionary leadership (Rosa Luxemburg and Karl Liebknecht), with the connivance of the Majority Social Democrats, the last act in the aborting of the social revolution was played.

3. Greater and perhaps important qualitative changes in elite recruitment should be expected as a result of the Mexican Revolution by some accounts (Brandenberg 1964; Scott 1964; Padgett 1965), especially in the aftermath of the brief liberal phase under Madero (1911–1913) and the temporary conservative setback under Huerta (1913–1914), when the "Revolutionary Family" began to institutionalize both the constitutional and popular bases of the new system. On the other hand, it is clear that the 1917 Constitution is a curious admixture of nationalist, capitalist, and socialist goals and methods, and other observers of the Mexican Revolution and its aftermath (Johnson 1971; González Casanova 1970; Eisenstadt 1966) do not consider it a successful social revolution but a betrayed one and an unfulfilled promise of social justice (cf. also Hansen 1971: chap. 4). To González Casanova and Hansen it is clear (also admitted by Brandenberg, Scott, and Padgett) that the basic pillars of the old order (Catholic church, large landowners, military, and both native and foreign capitalists) were still powerful social institutions in the immediate post–civil war era, and Eisenstadt (1966: 590) posits, though without empirical examination, that the new modernizing elites were also of at least secondary elite status in the Porfirian system. The expected effect of the Mexican Revolution on elite composition by these accounts should be primarily generational, without decisive social-class displacement.

Given the divided interpretations of the Mexican case as a *social* revolution, there are really two competing hypotheses: (a) the expectation of socially decisive elite displacement from the first school of opinion and (b) the expectation of primarily generational elite transformation from the second general line of thought.

4. The greatest quantitative and qualitative elite displacement should be found in the transition from the czarist system to the Bolshevik dictatorship of the proletariat, in which the privileges and sources of power of the previously dominant classes—nobility, Russian Orthodox clergy, large landowners (though not the kulaks), and both domestic and foreign capitalists—are eliminated and these so-

cial elements soundly beaten. This opinion is a basic consensus of Soviet scholars of widely divergent ideologies and judgments on the Revolution itself (cf. Churchward 1968; Lane 1971; Fainsod 1963; Conquest 1968).

The best indicators of class or social-stratification status are occupation, education, and social origin (either through father's occupation or through official designation, as in czarist Russia and imperial Germany). Most of the following analysis of elite-class composition rests upon the occupational variable and attempts to make the data as comparable as possible, but information on educational and social background will be included where it adds significantly to otherwise sparse occupational data or where these variables indicate trends divergent from the occupational data.

The Control Case: Generational Evolution within the Higher Stratum

The American example of elite development during this era is the least difficult to describe. As table 3 indicates, the age composition of the U.S. House, despite the trend toward higher tenure and the proliferation of "safe seat" districts, changes from one election to another in a smooth evolutionary pattern. The distribution of birth decades in the 1916 (or 1920) House is approximately the same as that in the 1906 (or 1910) House advanced by one decade. Gradual generational turnover has marked the long history of the U.S. Congress, with the average age in the House fluctuating generally between 47 and 53 over the last century.

In terms of social composition, the U.S. House at the turn of the century was overwhelmingly filled with lawyers, as it had been (and remains) since the founding of the republic. In fact, if we group other liberal professions (journalist, educator, doctor, engineer) together with lawyers, from 70 to 80% of House seats have generally been held by professionals of high education from upper- and upper-middle-class origins (cf. Matthews 1954). The 20 to 30% of representatives who were not professionals have been property owners, either business or farm owners. The only trend of note in this period is the beginning of a slight decline in the percentage of lawyers and a rise in the representation of other liberal professions among members of Congress (about which more later).

TABLE 3. Age and Occupational Structure of the U.S. House,
1906–1920

Birth decade	1906 %	1910 %	1916 %	1920 %
1820s	2	2	2	
1830s	5	2		
1840s	10	13	4	2
1850s	52	40	22	15
1860s	21	30	49	34
1870s	10	13	19	34
1880s			4	15
N	42	40	53	41
Occupation				
Lawyer	68	69	71	65
Business owner	20	18	19	15
Farm owner	2	5	2	5
Professional	10	8	8	15
N	40	38	52	40

The only notable difference between Democratic and Republican elite recruitment processes in terms of class composition has been the higher proportion of lawyers (and professionals generally) among Democrats and the higher percentage of property owners (capitalists) among Republicans. Almost no political elite recruitment even at the relatively modest national level of representative has come from the blue-collar or even the white-collar wageworking classes. The American political elite of this era represents, as Marx had foreseen in his description of the United States and the most complete victory of the capitalist ethic (Marx 1845–46), the total segregation of the wageworking class by both parties from the higher levels of political leadership. In terms of alternative, competing leadership groupings, the Democrats have been (relatively) the party of the liberal professions, the Republicans (relatively) the party of explicit property ownership. This is of course an oversimplification in the sense that many lawyers in Congress are also in business or are business partners, and a great many nonlawyers have an education in law.

The German Case: Liberal Democracy and Abortive Social Change

The membership of the last (1912) prewar Reichstag of the Wilhelminian Reich was a curious balance of social forces. On the one hand, there was the growing but yet underrepresented faction of Social Democrats, whose electoral strength had been rising steadily since the founding of the Reich in 1871; only the majority district system of 1871, which by the turn of the century terribly underrepresented urban and industrial districts, and thus SPD and working-class strength, kept the SPD from controlling that one-third of the parliament seats corresponding to its popular vote. Primarily associated with the SPD was a contingent of workers and unionists who held seats in the Reichstag (see table 4). On the other hand, despite the districting system which favored rural and small-town interests, the slowly declining fortunes of the political vehicles of the nobility (the Conservatives and the Reich party) brought about a decline in the percentage of titled deputies. The middle-class parties, mainly the more conservative National Liberals and the more liberal Progressives, accounted disproportionately for the recruitment of deputies from business and the professions, while the Catholic Center party accounted for most deputies from the clergy (and a goodly number of Catholic nobility, business owners, and professionals). While the various parties naturally nominated deputies from a range of occupations (for a more detailed account, see chap. 6), the level of association between party affiliation and occupation of deputies was quite high (Pearson's C = .69).

The net effect of the events of 1918 and 1919 (sailors' mutiny, collapse of the monarchy, workers' occupation of the factories, military suppression of the revolutionary socialists) on the social composition of the German political leadership in the 1919 National Assembly, a constituent assembly which was to write the new Weimar Constitution, was notable but certainly not decisive. Primarily as a result of electoral reform and the introduction of proportional representation, the number of wageworkers and unionists doubled from 15 to 30% of all deputies, although some of this notable increase must be suspect, since all the middle-class parties, even the reactionary German National People's party (DNVP), suddenly sprouted a "unionist" deputy faction. Important also was the decline of the aristocracy, the clergy, and the nontitled landowning class, all in good part attributable not to actual vote shifts but to a reformed

TABLE 4. Occupational and Age Structure of the 1912 Reichstag, the 1919 National Assembly, and the 1920 Reichstag

	National parliament		
Occupation	1912 %	1919 %	1920 %
Worker/unionist	15	30	26
Landowner	12	8	11
Business owner	7	6	7
Manager-administrator (private & government)	15	20	22
Professional	31	27	26
Landed nobility	7	0	0
Government nobility	6	2	3
Clergy	6	3	2
Military	1	0	1
Not classified	0	4	3
N	413	434	483
Birth decade			
1830s	1		
1840s	13	2	1
1850s	30	13	10
1860s	37	34	29
1870s	18	37	39
1880s	1	13	20
1890s		1	1
N	413	434	483

electoral system. Much of the former recruitment from titled government bureaucrats was displaced by recruitment from nontitled middle-class government bureaucrats.

The magnitude of the elite alteration described above was short-lived, however, for the elections to the first (1920) Reichstag of the Weimar republic brought severe electoral losses to the Left, reduced recruitment of deputies from working-class vocations and the bolstering of the social forces of the middle class, and thus began a reversal of the trend toward higher representation of the working class among deputies. At the same time, recruitment of deputies from business owners and landowners made a comeback to approximately pre-WWI levels, and even deputy representation from the aristocracy made slight advances (though still below its levels in the last years of the kaiser, the strictly monarchist parties having dissolved). In short, having adjusted to the new system of proportional representation and having put down the most serious attempts at socialist revolution, elite recruitment began a return to its previous pattern.

If the German Revolution of 1918 brought some quantitative though nondecisive shifts in the social balance of Reichstag recruitment, much of which was quickly reversed by 1920, the net effects in generational turnover were even less notable. Table 4 indicates that members of the outgoing prewar Reichstag were as a group not particularly old for a national parliament (vis-à-vis the U.S. House, for example), with the modal deputy born in the 1860s and thus in his forties or early fifties at election in 1912; over half of all deputies were under 50 years of age. In the 1919 National Assembly, the modal deputy was born in the 1870s (thus between 40 and 50 at election); just over 50% of all deputies were under 50 years of age. Elections to the 1920 Reichstag show some rejuvenation, quite marginal, however, and certainly not enough to represent a qualitative generational displacement vis-à-vis the prewar elite. One could say, in fact, that a decade after the 1912 elections, that is, midway through the first parliamentary session under the Weimar system, the age cohort structure had advanced in an evolutionary manner by one decade, certainly no more than is the usual case with the U.S. House of Representatives.

Generalizing from our data in both social and generational turnover, we might even say that this period as a whole only continued the gradual trend of declines in representation of the nobility and increases in representation of the working class (6% in 1893, 15% in 1912, 26% in 1920; cf. chap. 6), as well as the evolutionary change in age cohorts which had characterized the monarchy period (cf. Molt 1963). Figures on social and generational background of German cabinet members gathered by Maxwell Knight (1952: 25, 41) confirm these basic findings. Although the shift, in terms of social origin, from recruitment from the nobility (65% for 1890–1918) to recruitment from the middle class (78% for 1919–1933), as befits the establishment of a liberal democracy, is quite notable, the occupational shifting is not. Allowing for multiple occupations for several ministers, Knight calculates a continuing dominance of higher civil servants (65% in the monarchy, 48% in Weimar) and certain professions (lawyers down from 41% to 31%), with increases for journalists (mostly connected to party and union papers, up from 1% to 20%) and for business owners (up from 1% to 16%) and only minor increased participation for labor (from 3% to 11%). Very little in the way of generational displacement can be seen among cabinet members. Again we may confirm our working hypothesis that the Revolution of 1918 was, in terms of elite displacement (which is all we are considering here), a political revolution establishing a liberal democracy and continuing but not accelerating trends in elite recruitment which had been clearly established throughout the monarchy period.

Mexico: Elite Generational Upheaval and Social Stabilization

The Mexican case represents a complex picture of elite displacement for several reasons. The initial stage of the revolutionary process was begun by a liberal nonrevolutionary regime (Madero, 1911–1913), interrupted by a conservative or even a reactionary takeover (Huerta, 1913–1914), and only consolidated under praetorian auspices (Carranza, Calles, Cárdenas, Obregón; cf. esp. Brandenberg 1964) at the end of a decade of bloody civil war and mass suffering. The most radical revolutionary leaders (Villa, Zapata) were killed in the process of consolidation, although some with notably radical orientations (e.g., Cárdenas) remained to play important roles in later years. By all accounts the Revolution lacked centralized organization and above all theoretical direction and clarity, not to speak of consensus among the progressive forces, and this has been reflected in both the Constitution and the wide-ranging interpretations of it by leaders still broadly within the Revolutionary Family. In view of these circumstances, what forms of elite displacement characterize the Mexican Revolution?

Most apparent from a comparison of age structures of deputies in the Mexican National Congress as well as cabinet secretaries under Díaz and during the presidencies of Madero, Huerta, Carranza, and Obregón is that a generational revolution of great magnitude was under way. The elite of the late *porfirista* order was not only a repressive oligarchy, it was also an aged one, and this was not just limited to the dictator (born 1830) himself but to his entire cabinet, down to the level of deputy as well (see table 5). Within the decade

TABLE 5. Age Structure of the Mexican Political Elite, 1904–1924

	Cabinet secretaries				
Birth decade	1904–10 %	1911–13 %	1913–14 %	1917–20 %	1920–24 %
1820s	15				
1830s	15				
1840s	31				
1850s	31		28	7	11
1860s	8	60			4
1870s		40	43	29	33
1880s			29	57	33
1890s				7	19
N	13	10	7	14	27
	National Congress deputies				
1820s	2				
1830s	14	6			
1840s	22	9			
1850s	20	11		2	
1860s	20	22		6	5
1870s	18	33		20	11
1880s	4	18		50	38
1890s		1		22	45
1900s					1
N	85	103		102	87

1910 to 1920, the generational composition of cabinet secretaries advanced from a grouping born from 1820 to 1860, between the ages of 50 and 90 (92% of the last Díaz cabinet), to one born in the 1870 to 1890 period, ages 27 to 47 (86% of the 1917–1920 Carranza cabinet). The modal birth decade of secretaries advanced by three to four decades in ten years. At the level of deputy, the change is equally pronounced, with the modal birth decade shifting from the 1840s (22% of the last Porfirian Chamber of Deputies) to the 1880s by 1917 (50%) and the 1890s by 1920 (45%). In the last years of the old order, well over half of all deputies were over 50 years of age; by 1920, nearly half were under 30 years old, extremely young for any national parliamentary body. It is also apparent that the original Madero cabinet (and Congress) did not reflect the sharp generational revolution yet to come but, rather, indicated a more gradual evolutionary succession of political age cohorts.

With respect to displacements in social or class composition of the Mexican political elite (see table 6), we might first note that, at both deputy and cabinet levels in the Díaz period, leadership was drawn mainly from the liberal professions (especially lawyers, who accounted for approximately two-fifths of all deputies and secretaries), the Catholic clergy (over 10%), the military (19% of deputies, 8% of the cabinet), and, at the cabinet level, industrialists (15%). Only the large landowners (*hacendados*) of the dominant social classes were not personally represented in the basic officeholding *porfirista* coalition of the wealthy and powerful.

One social displacement which the Revolution does accomplish at the cabinet level at least is the disappearance of members from big business and the clergy (with one exception in the Obregón years, 1920–1924), although the clergy continued to hold about 10% of all seats in the Chamber of Deputies, and industrialists continued to hold a small number of seats as before. There is, of course, a rise in the representation of the military as the result of the civil war and the gradual piecing together of the Revolutionary Family from the various military leaderships (cf. Scott 1964; Brandenberg 1964). This trend was clearer and more consistent among the larger deputy grouping than at the cabinet level, but by 1920 it had arrived at about the same point for both (26% and 31% respectively). Representation of the professions remains high (45% to 70% of deputies; 55% to 70% of secretaries) throughout the Madero, Huerta, Carranza, and Obregón years, although there are some shifts toward greater recruitment from engineers and media specialists. Only small numbers of deputies and only one cabinet member were occupationally from the lower classes or were rural laborers, factory workers, and unionists, and functional representation by representatives of the lower middle class (white-collar employees, artisans, smallholders, and workers in the semiindependent trades) was also marginal. It must be said that occupational and social-origin information is missing for most deputies (though not for cabinet members), and it is possible that greater shifts in recruitment patterns are masked by a class bias in the availability of data. Yet it is also the case that, had a decisive social transformation in the elite recruitment pattern taken place, this would have been clearer, since as lower-class deputies rose further in the government hierarchy more information on their occupations, educations, and social origins would probably have become available. It is also possible that some larger proportion of the military within the Revolutionary Family had their social origins among the lower classes, so that

TABLE 6. Occupational Structure of the Mexican Political Elite, 1904–1924

	Cabinet secretaries				
Occupation	1904–10 %	1911–13 %	1913–14 %	1917–20 %	1920–24 %
Rural worker				7	3
Smallholder				7	
Landowner				7	4
Industrialist	15	20			
Clergy	15				4
White collar	8	10		14	
Military	8	10	29	7	26
Lawyer	39	40	57	36	37
Professional	15	20	14	22	26
N	13	10	7	14	27
	National Congress deputies				
Rural worker					1
Smallholder	1	1		1	
Landowner				1	
Worker/unionist	1			3	2
Industrialist	1	3		2	1
Clergy	11	9		13	11
White collar	1	1		6	3
Military	19	15		26	31
Lawyer	42	41		18	25
Professional	24	30		30	26
N	97	153		147	121

some greater elite displacement of the higher social stratum by people of lower- and lower-middle-class origins is mixed in with the filling of political offices with military leaders. Unfortunately, again the data on social origin are quite sparse (much more so than for occupation), and what data do exist on father's occupation for our elites do not particularly strengthen this line of argument. Some examples from Lieuwen's 1968 study of the Mexican military indicate that most leaders of the revolutionary armies were from the middle class, and Lieuwen himself emphasizes the middle class nature of this leadership (pp. 6–7, 21). Obregón was a *ranchero*, Calles a schoolteacher, Alvarado a druggist, Carranza a large landholder. Even Zapata, the most dedicated of the leaders for agrarian reform, was not a landless peasant but a smallholder who share-cropped on the side, and Cárdenas, still the major symbol of the fulfillment of the promises of the Revolution, was the son of modest property owners. A few military leaders clearly came from humbler backgrounds: Francisco Urguizo was an enlisted soldier in 1910, Pánfilo Natero an Indian peon, Pablo González a flour-mill worker. We must finally say that, even if most of the military leaders serving as deputies or cabinet secretaries were of lower-class origins, the Chamber of Deputies and the cabinet in 1920 would still be numerically dominated by the liberal professions (51 and 63% respectively), with lawyers still the strongest overall occupational source of elite recruitment. And we may safely assume that those who at the beginning of the century in Mexico were able to secure the higher education of the professions were not of lower social origins.

This leaves us with a picture of the Mexican Revolution as a thorough elite displacement in age cohorts but as a marginal movement or transition in the realm of social categories from which political leadership is drawn in the new system. The elimination of certain prominent big-business and Catholic church figures from high political office was not matched during this period by a qualitative or decisive reordering of elite recruitment patterns by the Revolutionary Family. To this extent, then, the data tend to confirm the second hypothesis on the nature of the Mexican Revolution, based on an interpretation of these years as a successful political but largely unfulfilled social revolution.

The Bolshevik Revolution: Generational and Social Elite Displacement

The third Duma was the only elected preparliament to live out its normal five-year term (1907–1912), and it is taken here as representative, with some reservations, of various political elites and as mainly supportive of the czarist system. Levin is undoubtedly correct (1973: chap. 10) in pointing out that many if not most of the "peasant" deputies among the rightist, moderate rightist, nationalist, and Octobrist factions were only front men for the local aristocracy and the government bureaucracy and thus do not represent the influence or strength of the smallholding peasantry but, rather, the opposite—its economic, social, and thus political dependence on the landed nobility. Even so, the data in table 7 give some indications as to the basic components of each party's leadership recruitment basis. The rightist, moderate rightist, and nationalist deputy factions were dominated, even without discounting for smallholder "proxies," by members of the nobility, both large landowners and government bureaucrats, and by clergy of the Russian Orthodox church, who were for the most part large landowners as well. As in prerevolutionary Mexico, the official church was not only the spiritual support for the autocracy but also a dominant economic class with its own immense landholdings and other investments. The Octobrist faction, basically supportive of the autocracy but opposing the czar on selected issues over the course of the third Duma, was also made up predominantly of the nobility but had a greater representation of business interests as opposed to the traditional agrarian orientation of the extreme right parties. The Constitutional Democrats, or Cadets, as the closest approximation to Western liberalism in the Duma, were also heavily weighted with (presumably enlightened) nobility, but the liberal professions were occupationally dominant. The Polish, Trudovik (Labor Bloc), and Social Democratic (Menshevik and Bolshevik) deputy factions, shrunken by the extreme gerrymandering of the electoral law of 1907 (see Harcave 1959: chaps. 20–22), give some sparse evidence as to the social bases of the more radical opposition groupings. Only the Trudoviki and Social Democrats nominated deputies from the lower classes in significant proportions (here discounting the clearly proxy nature of many rightist "peasant" deputies). We also note that, although the data on age structure have some gaping holes, the deputies of the rightist and Cadet factions tended to be older than those of the more radical opposition factions. With respect to social and age composition, the profile of the late czarist Council of State (cabinet) membership is even more pronounced. Drawn almost entirely from the nobility of landed interests and government high civil service, the council was dominated by an antiquated preindustrialization age cohort educated and socialized into a czarist Russia of the 1850s and 1860s.

Examination of the composition of the Bolshevik Central Committee leadership of the 1917 Revolution and the civil-war period (1918–1921) demonstrates that the elite displacement vis-à-vis the late czarist period was both generational and social. The top policy-making body of the Communist party (at this time) represented a modal generational advance of three to four decades over the

TABLE 7. Background Characteristics of Deputy Factions in the Third Duma, 1907–1912

| | Party faction | | | |
| | Rightist % | Moderate rightist % | Nationalist % | Octobris % |
Social class				
Nobility	45	32	77	60
Clergy	35	20	8	
Peasant	16	33	8	
Education				
High	45	36	30	55
Intermediate	35	28	50	35
Home	18			
Occupation				
Landowner	25	28	50	67
Smallholder	16	33	8	
Bureaucrat	}18		12	
Professional		4	16	
Clergy	35	20	8	
Worker			4	
Business owner				33
Age group				
Under 30				2
30–39		38	7	
40–49		38	46	}82
50–59		16	27	
Over 60				16
N	51	69	26	154

Source: Levin 1973: chap. 10.

age composition of the last czarist Council of State (see table 8).
It was also, according to some figures on other competing leadership groups in the 1917 Revolution (Cadets, Mensheviks, and Socialist Revolutionaries), the youngest of the possible successor elites.

Socially, the initial revolutionary Central Committee reflects only the first break with the czarist past. The top Bolshevik leadership at this time still rested with the cosmopolitan, well-educated

	Party faction		
det	Polish %	Trudovik %	Social Democrat %
	82	7	21
	9	64	58
	91	29	26
		7	16
		64	58
	45		5
		50	11
		7	
	36	29	37
		14	47
	9	7	
	27	64	
	54	29	
	9		
	11	14	19

"revolutionary modernizer" generation cited by Huntington (1968) and Kautsky (1968). In the course of the War Communism struggle against Western military intervention and the White armies, greater percentages of workers and peasants with mainly secondary educations and lower-class origins advanced to Central Committee membership, so that by the 10th Party Congress (1921) two-thirds of all members were from lower-class occupations, and approximately the

TABLE 8. Age and Background Characteristics of the Russian Political Elite, 1912–1921

	Czarist ministers	Bolshevik Central Committee				
Birth decade	1912–17 %	1917 %	1918 %	1919 %	1920 %	1921 %
1830s	6					
1840s	18					
1850s	35					
1860s	35			5		
1870s	6	43	40	48	32	33
1880s		52	53	37	58	59
1890s		5	7	10	10	8
N	17	21	15	19	19	24
Occupation						
Rural worker					12	11
Factory worker		20	33	50	63	56
Other worker			33			
Professional		80	33	50	25	22
Military						11
N		5	3	6	8	9
Education						
Low					8	
Secondary		42	44	50	54	64
High		58	56	50	38	36
N		12	9	10	13	14
Social origin						
Peasant		27	25	27	47	41
Worker		13	25	18	13	35
Middle class		13				
Intelligentsia		33	42	46	33	18
Nobility		13	8	9	7	6
N		15	12	11	15	17

same proportion had attained no more than secondary education. In terms of social origin, the evolution of the Central Committee over these early years of the Soviet system shows a growing influx of members from peasant origins and, especially in 1920 and 1921, a decrease in those from intelligentsia family backgrounds. The 10th Party Congress shows sharply increased recruitment from worker origins (up from 13% to 35%), so that by the end of the civil war over two-thirds of Central Committee members were of lower-class social origin. On the basis of these data, the expectation of thorough qualitative turnover in the Russian political leadership along both generational and social lines is fulfilled.

Summary: Revolution and Elite Displacement

In the testing of our general working hypothesis relating the nature of the revolution, as broadly judged by scholarly opinion, to the scope and extent of transformations in elite recruitment, we find a good deal of support from each of our four seminal cases. The American political system, despite the social transformations of urbanization and industrialization progressively changing the society at large, continues to recruit political elites from very much the same social strata and occupations and provides for gradual age cohort turnover within these elite strata. The German Revolution conforms in terms of elite displacement to its generally accepted reputation as a failure in social change, as the establishment of a new political system without lasting qualitative shifts in leadership composition. Even in terms of generational turnover, the German experience was not a decisive break with the past. In age cohort displacement, the German case ranks with the American non-revolutionary example rather than with the massive generational upheavals of the Mexican and Soviet revolutions. The Mexican Revolution, however, appears to have been, in terms of elite displacement, first and foremost a generational transformation, with some social shifts in leadership recruitment of lasting but secondary magnitude. The level of missing data for the Mexican elite during this period provides room for doubt on the question of social change in elite composition, but not enough doubt to negate our basic findings. Of interest in the Soviet case is the transformation of the top Bolshevik leadership through the civil-war years from the well-educated revolutionary modernizers of higher social origins prevalent in the 1917 Central Committee to the final confirmation of the party's proletarian roots in the Central Committee elected at the 10th Party Congress.

The above analysis should provide motivation for further testing of several related propositions on revolution and elite transformations. For future research, we might posit that strictly political revolutions, those revolutions which bring about a new system or process of elite recruitment but which leave the social order relatively intact, or fail to make decisive alterations in class structure, would seem to have little (Germany, 1918) or only transitory effect on elite composition. Socially dominant classes may well be able to adjust to strictly political revolutions in terms of keeping the social basis of elite recruitment intact. The experience of Weimar as a weak republic, though by no means doomed from the start, may indicate the superficiality of a new political system established without social transformations.

Revolutions of a mixed nature or incomplete revolutions, which firmly establish a new political system but which make only partial transformations in the social order, may evidence notable generational displacement of political elites (Mexico, 1910–1920) but only marginal and nondecisive social-class displacement among political elites. Only a full-blown social revolution would be expected to produce a decisive alteration in the social basis of leadership recruitment, both generationally and in class background (Russia, 1917–1921).

From the American case, as a nonrevolutionary control case in a revolutionary period, one might posit for future testing that one measure of a stable liberal democracy is the almost complete exclusion of elite recruitment, by all viable parties, from the lower or working classes.

CHAPTER 3

Political Systems under Stress: Interwar Elite Developments

The present chapter seeks to compare patterns of elite transformations in the period between the two world wars, as each political system responds (or fails to respond) to a series of economic crises. The baseline for comparison in elite development is the composition of the leadership in the early 1920s, for each system a period of relative calm following a decade of revolution, civil war, and world war.

The interwar period affords an opportunity to examine four basic system responses to stress, as reflected in the composition of the political elite. In the United States, the system is challenged by the Great Depression. In Weimar Germany, the young liberal democracy is overwhelmed by the economic collapse of the Depression and is overthrown by a counterelite, establishing a new fascist dictatorship in the 1930s. In Mexico, unrest from years of unfulfilled revolutionary promises and predatory militarism forces the Revolutionary Family to react. And, in the Soviet Union, crisis in economic development in the late twenties brings the industrialization debate on the future of the Revolution to a head.

The American case represents a successful program of reform capitalism (New Dealism) within a well-established liberal democracy. The German case represents an unsuccessful struggle of the new "system" elite against two emerging counterelites: the revolutionary socialist KPD and the counterrevolutionary middle-class NSDAP. In Mexico, a program of agrarian reform and demilitarization of politics succeeds in stabilizing and institutionalizing the Revolutionary Family without major system changes. And, in the Soviet case, a second (industrial) revolution accompanied by the massive party purge of the thirties produces a new social and economic order.

America: Return to Normalcy and the New Deal

In the United States, the return to normalcy and relative prosperity under Harding and Coolidge was rudely interrupted during the Hoover presidency by a massive contraction of the capitalist economy, which led to a basic electoral shift, a new Democratic majority party, and a program of reform capitalism linked to social-welfare advances (Roosevelt's New Deal). Although the New Deal program did not bring the return of economic prosperity (most economists now agree that only the massive deficit spending for World War II accomplished that), it did serve to maintain the integrity of the two-party system and the economic order. Given the severity and duration of the economic crisis and the magnitude of electoral shifting in the 1930s, one might expect that significant changes in the social bases of elite recruitment would be noted during this era, with perhaps some recruitment from working- or lower-middle-class occupations, although also perhaps more recruitment from business and farm owners in a generally more polarized political atmosphere. On the other hand, given the long tradition of class-homogeneous elite recruitment which both major parties had established, and given that both parties strongly supported the existing economic and social orders, we might hypothesize that New Deal reformism, as a strictly nonsocialist defensive program, would not involve major changes in the social sources of elite recruitment but might involve some rejuvenation among the political elite associated with the interparty personnel turnover in Congress. While we can pick out some working-class individuals who made their way into the House of Representatives during the Depression era, our expectation is that these would be isolated examples not representative of any major shifts in elite-class composition.

The evidence from our random sampling of representatives from the Sixty-seventh (1921) to the Seventy-ninth (1945) Congresses generally favors the second (no-change) thesis. In terms of age structure, the House samples indicate no generational displacement of greater than usual proportions involved in the sweeping Democratic victories of 1930, 1932, and 1936 (see table 9). In fact, there seems to have been some aging of House membership during the Depression years and a greater than usual representation over the period 1924 to 1944 of the birth decade of the 1880s, perhaps as a result of the general lengthening of House tenure (cf. chap. 5), with this generation being the first to fully benefit from that trend. However, the period of clear numerical dominance by the generation of House deputies

TABLE 9. Age and Occupational Structure of the U.S. House, 1924–1944

Birth decade	1924 %	1928 %	1932 %	1936 %	1940 %	1944 %
1840s	2					
1850s	2	3				
1860s	31	23	9	5	2	2
1870s	38	33	24	22	13	11
1880s	25	33	47	48	46	33
1890s	2	8	18	20	27	33
1900s			2	5	10	16
1910s					2	5
N	45	39	45	40	48	45
Occupation						
Lawyer	61	59	62	50	52	53
Business owner	20	24	18	20	21	16
Farm owner	2	3	2	8	6	2
Professional	11	8	11	20	19	18
White collar/ blue collar	2	2				4
Military, manager, other	4	2	7	2	2	7
N	45	39	45	40	48	45

born in the 1880s still runs only for about a decade (1930 to 1944) and never reaches majority proportions. From the data on age structure of the House, one could not plausibly differentiate the twenties as an era of conservative dominance from the New Deal reformism of the thirties.

The occupational background data on representatives tell a similar story. To be sure, the trend toward lesser recruitment from lawyers (65% in the 1920 House vs. 53% in 1944) continues, as does the concomitant shift toward higher recruitment from other liberal professions (15% in 1920, 18% in 1944). But, in line with the no-change thesis of reform capitalism as a system stabilizing the class order and offering no change in the elite composition, there is no evidence of any elite displacement along social-class lines. Out of several hundred representatives who fell into our sample of this period, a scant three show up as blue-collar or white-collar employees. Additionally, the few House members from lower occupational strata appeared in 1924, 1928, and 1944, not during the Depression years, so even these tokens could not be related to the New Deal reform program. In short, while the American political elite does show evolutionary shifts in occupational composition over time, these gradual changes are limited to the upper social strata and may be conceived of as integrative (cf. Kirchheimer 1966) within the gradually changing occupational composition of the dominant social class but, however, in no way integrative of elements, even growing elements (such as white-collar employees), of the wageworking classes and in no way representative of the occupational structure of the society at large.

It may be argued that, while the U.S. political elite *as a whole* showed no class or generational displacement during this era, there may still have been greater elite polarization between the two system parties along either age or occupational lines, which may be disguised by considering the elite without considering the party divisions. But a check on the level of association of both age and occupation with party affiliation (see table 10) shows again no coherent pattern of change during the interwar period and generally low levels of interparty elite differentiation over the entire period. The generally low and negative gamma figures indicate that the Democratic party representatives had been somewhat younger than Republican House members, both before and after the Great Depression, but the Depression era itself shows no pattern of generational polarization beyond the normal range of the twenties or early forties. Nor do the figures for occupational cleavage between parties (Pearson's C) indicate any clear change in the interwar period which could be related to the Depression and the New Deal. It is true that the peak for occupational differentiation (.46) falls with the 1930 House, at the outset of economic collapse, but this is marginal and on closer examination is due to an entirely (93%) lawyer-dominated Democratic House sample, while the Republican House sample includes a greater than usual recruitment from nonlawyer professions and corporate management.

Weimar and the Third Reich: Demise of Democracy under Stress

Weimar Germany, in contrast to the American case, represents an embattled liberal democracy which had averted a socialist revolution in 1918 to 1919 but which paid the high price of bolstering reac-

TABLE 10. Correlation of Occupation
and Age with Party Affiliation in the
U.S. House, 1922–1944

Year	Occupation (Pearson's C)	Age (Gamma)
1922	.25	−.30
1924	.41	−.16
1926	.41	−.11
1928	.39	+.09
1930	.46	−.15
1932	.40	−.05
1934	.32	+.24
1936	.34	−.11
1938	.32	−.08
1940	.32	−.18
1942	.43	−.29
1944	.41	−.24

tionary and often antirepublican forces (in the military, civil service, and courts) of the Right in the process, as well as splitting the labor movement into the prosystem reformist Social Democratic party (SPD) and the antisystem socialist revolutionary Independent Social Democratic party (USPD) and later the Communist party of Germany (KPD). Threatened from both Left and Right, the main forces of liberalism (Social Democrats, Catholic Center, and Democrats) were able, in the relatively calm reconstruction period from 1924 through 1928, to maintain the integrity of the system and even to reduce antisystem electoral support on the Right to manageable proportions (see Lipset 1963). In 1928, at the peak of Weimar's postwar recovery, the new German republic had every prospect of supporting a multiparty system capable of forming center-right, center, and center-left coalition governments (much as post-WWII Italy had done), with the Communist (11% of the vote in 1928) and the Nazi (only 3%) parties as permanent antisystem oppositions. As Bracher (1970) has pointed out in his multi-causal account of Weimar's development, the republic was not so weak as is often supposed, nor was it doomed from the start for a Nazi revolution. But the strains of the Depression quickly undermined the fragile electoral support of the Protestant middle-class parties (see Lipset 1963: 139), and within four years, riding a tide of scared middle-class voters, the NSDAP vote had ballooned from 3% to 37%. On the Left, the SPD lost some ground to the Communists but remained basically whole, and the Catholic Center party (and the regional Catholic Bavarian People's party as well) retained its electoral strength to the very end. Finally, the reactionary Nationalists (DNVP) under Hugenberg, the party of big business, formed a coalition with the Nazis which in a short time sealed the fate of Weimar (see esp. Bracher 1970 for an excellent description of the last stages of Weimar). The Nazi victory has been variously described by liberal democratic observers as a basically petit-bourgeois antimodern revolt of the lower middle classes, which were being squeezed out by both big labor and big capital in the continuing modernization of the economy (see Lipset 1963; Bell 1964). To these observers, the Nazi revolution was anticapitalist as well as antisocialist in nature. Others of liberal persuasion (Friedrich and Brzezinski 1966; Arendt 1951; Kornhauser 1959) have viewed the Nazi phenomenon (usually compared to the Stalinist Soviet system) as a new form of totalitarian state which had no firm relationship to the economic order or to class society. Socialists (Sweezy 1942; Neumann 1942; Kuehnl 1971) have basically analyzed the Third Reich era as a counterrevolutionary coalition of corporate and finance circles of capitalism with the middle-class mass following of the Hitler movement. While earlier Marxist interpretations tended (Dutt 1934) to see fascism as a necessary stage in the development of the state under capitalism, it has now been largely accepted by Marxists of various persuasions that the Nazi dictatorship was a contingent rather than an inevitable occurrence, an emergency resort to violent suppression of the workers' organizations and the relinquishment of political power by the capitalist class, in return for the safeguarding of the rights of property and the reestablishment of worker discipline and subordination under bourgeois management. Baran and Sweezy (1966: 155), for example, thus consider liberal democracy to be the "normal" political system for capitalism, and fascism to be one possible but deviant alternative.

We may try to develop some consequences from these competing interpretations of the fall of Weimar and the rise of the Third Reich for the question of elite development. Most research on the Nazi elite has concentrated on certain sectors (military, police, propagandists, administrators) or has tried to pick out differences within the Nazi leadership (see esp. Lasswell and Lerner 1965) without comparing this group to the political elite it superseded (one clear exception for cabinet ministers is, of course, Knight 1952). The only common-ality stressed by the Lerner and Pool sample, drawn from the 1934 *Führerlexikon,* was that of "marginality," but this concept was so loosely defined (Lasswell and Lerner 1965: 304–305) as to be of min-imal utility. By their definition, nearly all Center deputies were marginal by virtue of being Catholic, whereas the great majority of SPD deputies as well as KPD deputies were marginal by virtue of professing no religious affiliation, having lower education, and hav-ing been enlisted men (not officers) in terms of military service.

On the other hand, it is not easy to draw any clear consequences for elite development or composition under Nazism from the "to-talitarian" school of thought, since it says so little (see Hobsbawm 1973; Fleron 1968; Gregor 1973) about the class or even interest group relations which attached themselves to the NSDAP move-ment. As several critics have correctly pointed out, the totalitarian interpretation, whether applied to Stalinist Russia or Nazi Ger-many, is primarily a data-lacking psychological interpretation of "mass society," which denies a priori the continuance of class or interest group relations within the totalitarian state. Lipset's and Bell's views on the Nazi revolution and on right radicalism in gen-eral are clearer in their implications of elite composition. Lipset (1963) draws on ecological correlations of NSDAP vote and proprie-torship to bolster his thesis that it was the small business owners and small farmers who were most supportive of the Nazis. He adds that Nazi propaganda in the 1920s (note: before the seizure of power) contained both antifinance capitalism and antisocialist rhetoric (both in connection with anti-Semitism) and was thus aimed against the large-scale forces of modern industrial society under capitalism (pp. 143 ff.). Bell (1964) has widened this basically antimodernist interpretation of the radical Right to include all sorts of "dispos-sessed" in the category of those threatened with status or economic loss by the continuing modernization of urban industrial society in the West.

On the whole, if the Lipset-Bell interpretation of the Nazi move-ment is correct, we should be able to detect a preponderance in the NSDAP leadership of petit bourgeoisie (small entrepreneurs) as symbols of those occupational groups most threatened by modern big business and big labor.

Marxist and neo-Marxist interpretations of the Nazi movement, unlike liberal models, focus more heavily on what the Nazis actu-ally did after they came to power, as well as which interest groups collaborated with and most benefited from the Nazi takeover. No competent observer (not even Lipset or Bell) could deny that it was the banking and industrial interests which, after the Nazi elimination of its Strasser–Brown Shirt adherents in the 1934 Blood Purge, were able to reap the rewards of close alliance with and support of the regime, even if they did not hold political power. The anticorporate and antifinance slogans of the 1920s were dropped from Nazi literature, while, of course, all independent labor organizations were smashed and their leaders jailed, killed, or forced into exile. Sweezy (1942) and Neumann (1942), in their still relatively early analyses of fascism in Germany, emphasize that the economic crisis threatened the whole middle class, not just the smaller entrepreneurs. Neumann in particular (pp. 14–16) notes that several of the largest corporations were severely hit by the Depression, while many of the largest banks went under in 1931 and were taken over by the state. And it is clear, even from Lipset's analyses of the electoral data, that the mass base of the Nazi party in the early 1930s went far beyond the bounds of the small propertied classes to embrace the civil-service and white-collar sectors as well (Gerth 1952). Within the Nazi elite, Marxists would expect to see a preponderance of middle-class occupational backgrounds of all types, as a reflection of the threat the Depression posed to the social position of the middle class *as a whole*.

In our analysis of the changing elite structure of Weimar between 1920 and 1932, the most apparent feature of the data is the growing generational cleavage between deputies of the radical antisystem parties (KPD and NSDAP) versus deputies of nonradical parties (or system parties, although the DNVP was not really a supporter of the system but was not about to attempt an overthrow on its own). Even during the most stable period in Weimar's history—from 1924 through 1928, when Nazi representation was formally outlawed (although a shadow group, the National Socialist Freedom party, held a few seats)—the age cleavage between Communist deputies and either Socialist (cf. Hunt 1964) or all other deputies (cf. Hobsbawm 1973: chap. 7) was enormous (see table 11). In 1928, still before the Depression, nine-tenths of all KPD deputies were under 50, and over half were under 40, while three-fifths of non-KPD deputies were over 50. With the deepening economic contraction from 1929 through 1932, the non–radical party deputy factions as a whole maintained a gradual generational turnover, and the antisystem radicals recruited over one-quarter of their deputies to the second 1932

Reichstag from those still under 30. The younger generations of NSDAP and KPD deputies were those born after 1890, the front generations of World War I (especially the Nazi faction), those who had suffered economically from the Depression at the outset of their work careers (especially those born after 1900, for both KPD and NSDAP).

The elites of the *nonradical* parties by no means compare in age to the prerevolutionary *porfirista* lower house in Mexico, and in fact (for the second 1932 Reichstag) they have an age distribution quite similar to that in the 1932 U.S. House of Representatives. The political elite culture of Weimar's liberal democracy was, however, from the outset one of relative class balance (Sweezy 1942) as opposed to the traditional and, even during the Great Depression, still quite intact upper-middle-class dominance in the United States. In Weimar, the generational cleavage among parliamentary elites was in very large measure also a system/antisystem cleavage, which by 1932 had made the functioning of a classic liberal democracy all but impossible.

This cleavage in age cohorts among the political elite was over time increasingly congruent with the occupational divisions which existed among all deputies, regardless of party. The correlation between occupation of deputies and their generation (born before or after 1890) rises from .32 in the second 1924 Reichstag to .39 by 1928, .41 by 1930, and peaks at .46 for both 1932 Reichstags.

Compared with the parliamentary memberships of 1924 and 1928, during the era of economic reconstruction and partial rapprochement under Stresemann between Germany and the West, the Depression brings with it an acute class polarization within the political elite (see table 12). Although, interestingly, there was already some increasing representation of blue-collar workers in the Reichstag prior to the economic collapse, an effect of the "proletarianization" or "bolshevization" of the KPD in the mid-twenties (cf. Hobsbawm 1973: chap. 7), it is after the economic crash that deputy recruitment from factory and service workers (not including unionists) begins to climb noticeably. Just as notable are the rises in recruitment, during 1929 to 1932, from an array of lower-middle- and middle-class occupations (white-collar employees, lower government officials, the military, and engineers). A breakdown for the last freely elected Reichstag of deputy occupations for KPD, NSDAP, and the system parties indicates the sources of the shifts in elite recruitment and the contrasts in the composition of the two

TABLE 11. Age Structure of the Reichstag, 1924–1938, for System ▾

Birth decade	1924II[a]		1928	
	System %	Anti-system %	System %	Anti-syste[m] %
1840s	1		1	
1850s	3	2	2	1
1860s	23	4	17	1
1870s	42	2	42	5
1880s	27	58	32	38
1890s	4	34	6	53
1900s				1
1910s				
N	437	50	422	61

[a] "II" indicates the second election in a given year. In 1924, 1932, and 1933 there

counterelites, which were generationally rather similar. The KPD leadership is composed of quite young men and women of the blue-collar class (64%), with some white-collar employees (8%) and unionists (5%), all predominantly of lower education—in short, a profile of the young radical proletariat. The Nazi parliamentary elite is somewhat more complex but consists overwhelmingly of middle-class elements, and in contrast to the system party elites those elements are somewhat lower in status (with the exception of doctors) than the prestige professions (lawyers, professors, judges).

It is clear that the influx of lower-prestige middle-class deputies into the Reichstag after 1928 comes mainly through NSDAP recruitment. The 1932II (II indicates the second Reichstag elected in 1932) NSDAP faction is especially heavily weighted, in comparison with both system and socialist revolutionary elites, with white-collar employees (10%), the military (8%), farm owners (16%), small business owners (3%), lower government officials (5%), teachers (4%), and engineers (5%). Among top prestige professions, only doctors (still only 2% of all Nazi deputies) seem to have been recruited more often by the Nazis than by the more respectable system parties. It should be observed that the Nazi counterelite also recruited a considerable percentage of its deputies not just from farm owners (mostly small- and middle-sized holdings, compared to the wealthier landowners recruited as deputies by the middle-class system parties in the twenties) and small business owners but quite tisystem Parties

		1933II[a]	1938
tem	Anti-system %	All NSDAP %	All NSDAP %
	1		
	1	1	2
	5	6	5
	18	19	16
	48	45	42
	27	29	33
			2
	284	698	858

e two national elections.

frequently from industrialists and corporation owners (5%). A sizable element of the Nazi elite was drawn from the working class (15%), from the unorganized and antiunionist workers. But, compared with both the KPD leadership of the young revolutionary proletariat and the leadership of the system parties, the NSDAP deputy recruitment symbolizes quite well the vanguard of the counterrevolutionary middle class, not just the petit-bourgeois entrepreneurs but a wide range of middle-class (and relatively well educated) elements.

The effects on elite composition of the Nazi ascendancy are also highlighted if we look at the Reichstag membership in the single-slate elections of 1933II and 1938 (the Gross-Reichstag after the annexation of Austria and the Sudetenland). Eliminated from the political elite are the elements of organized labor (unionists); somewhat diminished are the typical representatives of bourgeois democracy (the liberal professions). The professions, which had accounted for nearly 30% of the pre-Depression parliamentarians, now accounted for less than 20% of Reichstag seats in the Third Reich, even though certain professions (engineers and teachers) enjoyed markedly higher representation. Normally 10% of Reichstag seats in the twenties had gone to the top prestige professions (lawyers, professors, judges), but this had dropped off to between 2 and 4% under the Nazi dictatorship. The top state, party, and interest group functionaries of the Weimar system had, of course, largely been dis-

TABLE 12. Occupational Composition of System Party, NSDAP, and KPD Deputies to the Second 1932 Reichstag

Occupation	System %	NSDAP %	KPD %
Blue collar	1	15	64
White collar	1	10	8
Military	1	8	
Industrialist	5	5	
Landowner	10	16	3
Small business	1	3	
Clergy	2	1	
High civil servant	15	5	
Lower civil servant	1	5	
Party manager	7	5	5
Interest group manager	6		
Business manager	4	4	
Writer	15	6	7
Publisher	1	2	
Professor	4	1	
Lawyer	4	3	
Judge	1		
Teacher	3	4	2
Doctor	1	2	
Engineer	1	5	1
Union leader	15		5
Housewife	1		3
Other		1	2

placed, as had the reporters and writers connected to non-NSDAP newspapers and journals.[1]

The collapse of Weimar is thus associated with the inability, either socially or generationally, of the system parties to widen their bases of leadership recruitment. Even before the Depression, Weimar had developed a radical socialist counterelite both generationally and socially distinct from the system elite. The Weimar party system was already bifurcated and, compared to the American

1. For a more detailed analysis of the Nazi political elite along occupational lines, as part of a more systematic test of competing models of elite recruitment, see chapter 6.

case, highly polarized; the primary effect of the Depression was to add another radical middle-class counterelite on the Right, also generationally and socially distinct from the system elite. With such an elite recruitment process, the chances for a within-system reform program dwindled. As Neumann points out in his 1942 analysis, given the unwillingness of the Western powers to aid the republic and the unwillingness of the ruling economic interests to voluntarily make concessions to the middle and working classes, the clear choice was either socialist revolution or imperialist expansion of the economy through remilitarization. The latter course was, however, incompatible with free public debate and also with independent unionism. Given this dilemma, the corporate and banking interests clearly gave the Nazis a helping hand in undoing the liberal democracy and smashing the labor movement, thus giving up the normal political form of capitalism (and many important liberties) but preserving the capitalist economic order.

Interwar Mexico: Institutionalization of the Revolution

The problems facing the new political leadership of Mexico in the early 1920s were manifold. A decade of civil war had torn the fabric of the old order without producing a distinct victory for a new society, without much agreement within the Revolutionary Family as to what the new society should look like (for a good description of the internal splintering of the revolutionaries on goals, see Womack 1969). Closely related to this situation was the dominance of the political system by the leaders of the revolutionary armies which had risen in the course of the civil struggle. Lacking any ideological consensus and a decisive breaking with the old order, the idealism of many former amateur soldiers, now turned full-time generals, quickly degenerated into corruption and self-enrichment. Although Carranza tried to control this "predatory militarism" (Lieuwen 1968: 37 ff.), by the end of his term of office the military share of the federal budget was still 66%, and by most accounts local military leaders continued to operate a degenerated system of semiautonomous warlord states. From Lieuwen's analysis, the interwar period of Mexican political development revolved around the problem of getting the military under control and out of the business of political king making. Lieuwen considers the armed *cristero* revolt of the latter twenties, plus the overcoming of the military revolts of 1920, 1923, 1927, and 1929, as major events in the institutionalization of the political system and the establishment of civilian control over a professional military. The machinery of the revolutionary party, set up by Calles in 1929, is seen as reaching the point of no return under Cárdenas, the first president to serve out a six-year term without major military violence (see also Brandenberg 1964: viii–ix), a precedent which has now held firm for over thirty-five years. By the end of Cárdenas' term of office, the military share of the budget was down to 21%.

In terms of social policy, the Obregón (1920–1924) presidency was the first to engage in significant land distribution to the landless rural workers, creating the beginnings of a new smallholder class. Calles, as president from 1924 through 1928, was most known for his anticlerical campaign, which in turn was met by the *cristero* uprising of rightists and the church. During the *maximato* period (1928–1934), when Calles was still the undisputed head of the Revolutionary Family, ruling through the puppet presidencies of Portes Gil, Ortiz Rubio, and Rodríguez, his social program became more and more conservative, virtually abandoning agrarian reform, dropping the antichurch campaign, and favoring foreign (especially American) investment. This conservatism of the *maximato* period, in part influenced through U.S. Ambassador Dwight Morrow and his close relationship with Calles (cf. Brandenberg 1964: 72–74), meant the suppression of labor unions and the denigration of local capitalists to the advantage of American and other foreign investors.) This conservative trend was then reversed under the presidency of Cárdenas (1934–1940), leading to a break with Calles (as head of the Revolutionary Family) in 1935 and the inception of large-scale agrarian reform, this time taking the form of semicollective *ejidos* rather than small private holdings. Cárdenas also gave his blessing to organized labor, including the right to strike, though there continued to be strife between the Stalinist, Trotskyite, and noncommunist union factions. Foreign investors were warned that an overbearing presence would not be tolerated, and in 1938, supported by a wide spectrum of Mexican opinions (including the church), Cárdenas nationalized foreign oil-company holdings. Anticorruption campaigns in the civil-service sector are credited with reducing graft under Cárdenas, and he maintained a reputation for personal honesty unmatched by other presidents. But, above all, the Cárdenas land reforms, continued into the regime of Avila Camacho

(1940–1946), finally made good one of the promises of the Revolution and broke the power of the hacienda (although cf. Johnson 1971 on the continued existence of certain "untouchable" landowners), one of the social mainstays of the *pax porfiriana*. In 1940, opposition to Cárdenas' reformism, especially competition from communists within the labor movement, led to the election of the moderate Avila Camacho, who would consolidate some of the social gains yet drop attempts to continue and would mainly hold the Revolutionary Family and the Party of the Mexican Revolution (PRM, forerunner to the PRI) together.

The Cárdenas presidency represents for most observers, both sympathetic and critical toward the PRI, a key turning point in two respects: (1) the development of the political system, an end to predatory militarism; and (2) the first fulfillment of the social-justice aspect of the Mexican Revolution, especially in the distribution of land to the landless agricultural workers. Yet most observers also note a certain continuity of Cárdenas with the Obregón-Calles beginnings of political institutionalization and agrarian reform and make clear that Cárdenas' reform policies did not permanently shift the Revolutionary Family to the Left, since, after the wartime presidency of Avila Camacho, what followed was a very conservative probusiness administration under Alemán. That is, the Cárdenas reforms were not decisive in the sense of permanently weakening the conservative wing of the Revolutionary Family but, rather, the conservative elements of the party were able to stop further reform efforts.

The interwar trends in occupational composition of the Mexican political elite give some affirmation of the demilitarization of the political system. At the deputy level, there is a steady decrease in recruitment from the military (see table 13), so that, by the 1940 inauguration of Avila Camacho, the proportion of deputy seats held by the military had been cut by half the 1920 figure (15% vs. 31%). At the higher cabinet level, however, it is also apparent that military men were a usual contingent of every cabinet, with no steady pattern of decrease. This should not be too surprising, since, as Lieuwen (1968), Brandenberg (1964), and González Casanova (1970) all point out, it was military political leaders like Calles, Cárdenas, and Avila Camacho who promoted and presided over the professionalization and depoliticization of the armed forces during this period. Only later would demilitarization in terms of elite recruitment be apparent at the higher officeholding levels.

TABLE 13. Occupational Structure of the Mexican Political Elite, 1924–1946

	Cabinet secretaries			
Occupation	1924–28 %	1928–34 %	1934–40[a] %	1940–46 %
Rural worker	8			
Landowner			3	
Worker/unionist	8	2		
Industrialist		4	4	
White collar		6	8	4
Military	8	18	15	22
Lawyer	8	27	35	39
Other profession	58	39	31	31
Clergy				4
N	12	49	26	23
	National Congress deputies			
Rural worker	1	1	1	1
Smallholder		1	1	3
Landowner				2
Worker/unionist	4	3	4	4
Industrialist	1	1	1	2
White collar	7	3	4	3
Military	26	27	22	15
Lawyer	26	28	22	36
Other profession	27	32	36	29
Clergy	8	7	9	3
N	74	176	101	88

[a] Only those cabinet secretaries who served with Cárdenas after his break with Calles in 1935 are included, since this begins the actual composition of the Cárdenas cabinet.

The data on elite occupational background attest also to the continuing middle-class dominance of the Mexican leadership, even throughout the Cárdenas reform years. The main beneficiaries of the decline in recruitment from the military are members of the liberal professions, especially lawyers and engineers, who by 1940 account for nearly half (47%) of all deputies and over half (52%) of the cabinet membership. At one point, during Calles' presidency, engineers alone accounted for nearly half of all secretaries, but this seems to have been an anomaly; generally, a lawyer's background has been the most favored occupational category.

Minor trends which also appear in table 13 deserve mention. One is the fall-off, between 1934 and 1940, in the proportion of deputy seats filled by the clergy. This is interesting because it does not come at the time of Calles' antichurch crusade but, rather, a decade later, at the moment when a presidential candidate (Avila Camacho) professed to be a believer and when there had developed a sort of dé-tente between the church and the Revolutionary Family. Given the continuing (even increasing, cf. González Casanova 1970: 38–48) strength of the church and its still generally traditional and conservative, if not reactionary, nature, this decline can hardly be interpreted as the defeat of the Catholic hierarchy as a political influence, although it may appear as a sign of the clergy's decreased need to engage in actual office seeking.[2]

Another minor trend in elite recruitment categories is the appearance, starting with Calles and strengthening under Cárdenas and Avila Camacho, of deputies (and a few scattered secretaries) drawn from rural worker/smallholder and industrial worker/unionist vocations. The percentages are of course small, a combined total of only 9% of all deputies in 1940, but perhaps are still indicative of the limited social reforms of the Cárdenas era. At the same time, we should note the appearance of some industrialists and large landowners at both cabinet and deputy levels during these same years of reform. What we might conclude is that the demilitarization of elite recruitment during the interwar period, while primarily strengthening representation of the middle-class professions, also spread some greater representation to both working and propertied classes.

If the Cárdenas agrarian reform of the thirties does not qualify as a major or qualitative change in the social bases of elite recruitment, save for the decline in military representation at the deputy level, neither does it represent a generational upheaval in the Revolutionary Family. As table 14 illustrates, the pattern of age cohort turnover in the interwar period was gradual at both cabinet and deputy levels, during both the more conservative as well as the reform presidencies. In fact, the pace of rejuvenation did not prevent a certain aging

2. To fully and substantively analyze this trend toward lower recruitment from the clergy, which continues into the postwar period, it would be necessary to research the political orientations of individual clerical deputies, since there are modernist as well as traditionalist factions in the Catholic church in Mexico. However, this is beyond the scope of this study.

TABLE 14. Age Structure of the Mexican Political Elite, 1924–1946

	Cabinet secretaries			
Birth decade	1924–28 %	1928–34 %	1934–40 %	1940–46 %
1860s	17	2		
1870s		11	4	
1880s	58	37	31	4
1890s	25	50	61	70
1900s			4	26
N	12	49	26	23
	National Congress deputies			
1850s	2			
1860s	2			
1870s	6	5	3	1
1880s	34	23	14	6
1890s	56	55	48	22
1900s		16	34	52
1910s		1	1	19
N	54	134	85	80

of the political elite: by 1940 only 70% of deputies were under 40 compared to 83% in 1920, and only 26% of cabinet secretaries in 1940 were under 40 compared to 52% in 1920. Yet, given the extreme youth of the political elite in 1920 (as in the Bolshevik case), some aging would seem inevitable in any stabilized nonrevolutionary situation, and the Mexican political elite of the mid-thirties was still quite young by international comparison. The age distribution in the Chamber of Deputies under Cárdenas (83% born 1890–1910) is much more similar to the counterrevolutionary all-Nazi Reichstag of 1933II (74% born 1890–1910) or the postpurge 1939 Soviet Central Committee (70% born 1890–1910) than the New Deal U.S. House of 1936 (only 25% born 1890–1910, 70% born 1870–1890).

The above analysis has described an evolution of the interwar Mexican elite which can best be summarized as an institutionalization of the political system through a decline in military influence (though by no means complete elimination) and a strengthening of other, mainly middle-class professional, elements. The data on occupational and age characteristics of the political elite indicate no sharp discontinuities but, rather, a gradual shifting of what were from the start dominant middle-class recruitment values within the Revolutionary Family system.

The Second Soviet Revolution: Industrialization and Purge

The interwar evolution of the Soviet system following consolidation of the Revolution follows a dual path. In the years (1921–1928) of the New Economic policy (NEP), reconstruction of the war-shattered economy to prewar levels of production was achieved with a mixture of state ownership of the "commanding heights" of finance—heavy industry, transport, and wholesale trade—but re-privatization of retail trade and the growth of the middle class (kulaks) in the countryside. New entrepreneurs (NEPmen) and a prosperous rural bourgeoisie coexisted with state-run enterprises in industry, and virtually no collectivization of agriculture or long-run state planning for agriculture existed during these years. At the same time, within party ranks, especially after Lenin's death in 1924, a long and heated debate on the industrialization question (cf. Ehrlich 1960) was going on, which was to end with the political defeat of the Left and the Trotskyites (and later the Zinovievites and the United Opposition; cf. Daniels 1960) and the victory of the Stalinist faction of the party. However, it was the basic Trotsky-Preobrazhensky Five-Year Plan for collectivization of agriculture and rapid industrialization and urbanization, with concentration on heavy and defense industries, which Stalin adopted in response to the "scissors crisis" of 1927 to 1928, just after the ouster of the leaders of the United Opposition (Trotsky, Zinoviev, and Kamenev) from the Politburo and the Central Committee at the 15th Party Congress in December 1927. Having made the economic program (though in extreme form) of his beaten opponents his own, Stalin then turned against those who still advocated continuation of the NEP, with further concessions to the kulaks, who increasingly held control over the grain trade with the cities, and a slow industrialization of the economy. This Right Opposition, led by Bukharin, Rykov, and Tomsky, though holding originally strong positions in state and union organizations, was overwhelmed by events and was substantially defeated by the 16th Party Congress (1930), so that, by the end of the first Five-Year Plan, an internal peace of sorts seemed to exist within the party for the first time in over a decade. The kulaks had been violently eliminated as a social class, agriculture had been completely collectivized, and a decisive industrial mobilization process had been set in motion, all at high cost in human terms and against no small resistance in the countryside. At the "Congress of Victors" (1934), Stalin announced that there was no longer anyone left to fight, and certain defeated and repentant oppositionists of both Left and Right, including Bukharin, Rykov, Piatakov, and Tomsky, regained their Central Committee seats, although usually as candidate members only.

The Great Purge of 1936 to 1938 seems therefore all the more puzzling, and indeed unnecessary, in light of Stalin's already firm control of the party leadership. As Khrushchev later related, at the 20th Party Congress (1956), in his denunciation of Stalin's crimes, between 1934 and 1939 over 70% of all Central Committee members were purged, most of them imprisoned or executed, all the result of Stalin's growing paranoia and the "cult of personality" (see Khrushchev 1956), since, according to Khrushchev, there was no conspiracy or organized opposition to Stalin within the party leadership. If, however, we view the change in the Soviet economy wrought by the frantic pace of the first two Five-Year Plans (1928–1938), summarized in table 15, we might theorize that the Stalinist purge of top party leadership should also be taken in the context of the second Soviet (industrial) revolution, designed, apart from the dictator's possible paranoia, to bring the political elite into line with that economic revolution (see Unger 1969 on changes in the rank-and-file party membership during this period).

The period of intraparty struggle against Trotskyite, Left, and Right Opposition (1921–1930) is marked by gradual turnover in the age cohort which made up the Central Committee (see table 16), albeit with some aging of its membership. The average age of the party elite rises from 39 in 1921 to 45 by 1934. Still, by the Congress of Victors, following the intraparty struggle, the modal birth decade had advanced from the 1880s to the 1890s, and nearly 90% of all Central Committee members were under 55. In other words, by our international comparisons the newly victorious Stalinist coalition was quite young. Given the extremely youthful character of the Bolshevik leadership in the revolution and civil-war years, one would, as in the Mexican case, have expected some aging to occur, both within the party leadership and the rank-and-file membership. What

TABLE 15. Results of the Industrial Revolution under the First and Second Five-Year Plans, 1928–1938

Product	1928	1938
Pig iron (million tons)	3.3	14.6
Steel (million tons)	4.3	18
Rolled steel (million tons)	3.4	13.3
Electricity (billion kwh)	5	39
Locomotives	478	1,626
Tractors	1,200	80,000
Motor vehicles	700	211,000
Occupational fields (%)		
Agriculture	77	55
Industry	10	25
Public administration/social service	3	10
Social services		
Students in elementary and secondary schools	12,068,000	31,517,000
Students in higher schools	177,000	603,000
Public libraries	28,900	77,600
Movie houses	9,700	30,900
Hospital beds	247,000	672,000
Doctors	63,000	110,000

Source: Harcave 1959: 602–604.

occurs between 1934 and 1939 is therefore a generational revolution in an already youthful political elite. The recent allies of Stalin, the proletarian cadres who rose in the party apparatus during the twenties, are decimated. That group of first-generation Stalinist leaders born predominantly in the 1890s, who by 1934 accounted for a numerical majority (56%) of the Central Committee, was suddenly replaced by an age cohort born in the 1900s, an age group which had come to maturity (age 21) after the Revolution had been initiated and defended, a generation which had neither theorized nor led the armed struggle for Soviet power. Interestingly, though, the oldest (a relative term for the Soviet elite at this point, to be sure) age cohorts of Bolsheviks (born in the 1870s and 1880s), which included of course Stalin, Kalinin, and Voroshilov at the top of the Stalinist

TABLE 16. Age and Background Characteristics of the Soviet Central Committee, 1925–1939

Birth decade	1925 %	1930 %	1934 %	1939 %
1860s		1	2	
1870s	23	15	10	12
1880s	54	43	29	18
1890s	23	41	56	26
1900s			3	44
N	57	61	59	61
Occupation				
Agricultural worker	4	4	6	4
Factory and other worker	76	80	82	68
Professional	10	7		7
Military				14
Office worker	7	4	6	
Technician	3	4	6	7
N	29	29	22	28
Social origin				
Peasant	34	28	32	31
Worker	42	40	43	45
Middle class	10	9	10	13
Intelligentsia	11	17	13	11
Nobility	3	6	2	
N	38	47	47	45
Education				
Low, secondary	58	67	72	34
Technical	8	4	8	37
Teachers, medical institute	11	17	8	19
Party School				2
University	23	12	12	8
N	26	24	25	47

leadership, were less affected by the purge as an age grouping, and so the average age of the Central Committee remained stable (at 45 years) between the prepurge 17th and postpurge 18th Party Congresses.

Just as important, the elite transformation during the Great Purge represents a skills revolution in the top Bolshevik ranks, though not (as yet) a shift in terms of social class or occupational background. Throughout the NEP period and up to the Congress of Victors, the occupational backgrounds of the political elite continued the proletarianization trend, with some further increases in worker backgrounds from 1921 (56%) to 1934 (82%), accompanied by declines in professional and military backgrounds and by the appearance of a few members from office-worker and technician vocations. Even allowing for ideological bias in the reporting of occupational career, the Bolshevik leadership was definitely of the working class, with real experience in the factories and mines as wageworkers. In terms of social origin, the pattern is much the same, with minor increases in those from worker families and some decreases in those from peasant families. The educational profile of the party leadership up to 1934 showed some further declines in the proportions of those with university educations (only 12% by 1934) as well as the appearance of a few workers with educations at technical institutes. Despite high personnel turnover between Central Committees in the gradual consolidation of power by Stalin and his allies during the prepurge period, the class-origin, occupational, and educational composition of the party remained overwhelmingly proletarian, and in certain respects it became even more so. The effect of the Great Purge on this composition represents a qualitative and immediately decisive displacement only in the educational sphere. There is a shift in modal educational achievement from secondary school (60% in 1934) to technical institute (37% in 1939, or 56% if we add medical and teachers institute training). The percentage of members with some form of higher education jumps from only 28% to 66% in the five-year span between the 17th and 18th Party Congresses. This educational displacement or skills revolution, representing the vanguard of a new generation who had just passed through the recently established agronomical and polytechnical institutes in great numbers, did not, however, coincide with a similar displacement in social and occupational origins. The newly established educational standards for party leadership would of course have an effect over time (see next chapter) on occupational experience patterns, but the immediate effect on occupational composition was quite marginal, the addition of a contingent from the military (14%) being the most notable change from 1934.

The above analysis indicates that the elite development of the Great Purge era was primarily a skills revolution among a party elite which had already made, in the winter of 1927–28, the basic decision on the rapid industrialization of the economy. An earlier, though by no means old or long-entrenched, age cohort of Stalin's party allies, predominantly of low or secondary education and of proletarian origin, was replaced by an even younger age group of technically trained leaders of similar class origin, capable of directing and planning for the new urban-industrial Soviet society.

Summary: Political Systems under Stress

We may now draw some conclusions from our interwar data on elite development in systems undergoing crisis. First, we may pair the experiences of the two liberal democracies and note that the well-entrenched upper-middle-class elite of the American two-party system, even under the stress of the Great Depression, underwent no significant generational or occupational displacement associated with the New Deal program of reform capitalism. We would offer our opinion that reform capitalism in general does not aim at a reordering of class elite recruitment priorities but, as a system-maintaining program, is directed at strengthening the status quo, and its success should be judged in this light. Thus, while there may have been some ethnic shifts in the American elite to include more Italian-, Irish-, Polish-, and other hyphen-Americans through the New Deal coalitions, this was done only within the boundaries of upper-middle-class integration. On the other hand, the political elite of the Weimar republic, bifurcated from the start by the suppression of the socialist revolution and the related necessary maintenance of reactionary social elements, was briefly able to move toward a more "typical" liberal political elite, but the consequences of economic depression proved overwhelming. Two counterelites, highly differentiated in occupational, class, and generational profiles from the leadership of the system parties, quickly made the operation of the liberal democratic state all but impossible. As Marx predicted in his account of the protofascist regime of Louis Bonaparte (1852), the propertied classes opt for loss of political power and liberty rather than risk the overthrow of the economic order. The Nazi elite, already predominantly middle-class in composition (if from lower status levels) and laced with a sizable contingent of industrialists as well as an array of propertied and nonpropertied middle strata, quickly shucks off its social-fascist wing and settles into a pattern of close collaboration with the capitalist class.

We may also pair the experiences of our two one-party systems to see how they responded to developmental crises in the first decades of revolutionary power. In the Mexican case, the semipopulist revolution carried out by a middle-class elite succeeds in gradually subduing the predatory military leadership and (under Cárdenas) begins to fulfill some of the social-justice promises of the Revolution. This is accomplished through an agrarian reform which, though widespread in scope, does not involve a thorough reorganization of the economic order or a direct threat to more modern (nonfeudal) propertied interests. In so doing, the middle-class political elite strengthens its own position within the marginal changes, in the social bases of officeholding recruitment. The ability of the Revolutionary Family to provide (in international perspective) young leadership, a striking feature of the Mexican one-party system, appears already in this interwar era. The Soviet leadership, after the period of economic reconstruction in peaceful coexistence with private retail trade and the rapidly growing kulak rural bourgeoisie, makes a collective decision about the future course of Soviet economic development. The Stalinist faction, victorious over a series of intraparty oppositions, opts for centralized Five-Year Plans involving rapid collectivization of agriculture (the liquidation of the kulaks as a social class), development of heavy industry, and equally rapid urbanization; within a single decade, this decision and its execution fundamentally changed Soviet society. The Great Purge of the 1930s can be seen, apart from its unforgettable features of terror, as a generational and skills revolution among the Soviet political elite, providing for an early dominance of a generation risen from the working classes but, unlike the still youthful incumbents they displace, possessing the higher technical education enabling a more direct planning and knowledgeable oversight of the new urban industrial complex.

In a more general perspective, the above analyses illustrate the several possible responses to system stress in terms of elite recruitment. One proposition for further testing would be that the more stable political and social systems (here the U.S.) are best able to withstand political stress without transformations in the social basis of elite recruitment, although perhaps not without some policy reform. The weight of political tradition and deep-seated institutionalization as an independent variable affecting leadership recruitment should not be underestimated.

On the other hand, there are several response alternatives for newborn political systems under stress. For a young and only weakly institutionalized democracy (Weimar), a second proposition might be that the system elites must either widen their social or generational base of leadership recruitment or run a high risk of being overthrown by counterelites, revolutionary or counterrevolutionary.

For a young one-party system under stress, the road to an initial political institutionalization would also seem to involve transformations in the base of elite recruitment, particularly with respect to age cohort. This might occur through purge or some rotational ("no reelection") agreement, or perhaps some combination of the two, and we might hypothesize that the basically generational displacement of elites under stress serves to reaffirm (in the Soviet case) or consolidate (in the Mexican) the social order of the new system.

CHAPTER 4

Elite Recruitment under Normalcy Conditions

The post–World War II era for each of our four polities is a prolonged return to normalcy, for each an absence of the great wars and revolutionary upheavals which marked the first two decades of the century and the great economic crises and transformations which erupted in the interwar years. To be sure, the more than a quarter century of postwar history is not without its political unrest and crisis points (the civil-rights movement, the Vietnam War and Watergate, the denunciation of Stalin, the 1968 massacre of students at Tlatelolco, the Berlin confrontations). Yet, in each country, economic growth has been relatively steady and sufficient to ameliorate popular demands; politics has grown more tame and less hazardous (at least within the system parties); the political systems, by a variety of measures, have become more stable, with antisystem groups small and ineffectual. In short, this has been an era of *relative* peace and prosperity, in which political problems, while sometimes insolvable within the system (e.g., Vietnam policy, a failure for both major U.S. parties) or only partially solvable (e.g., the question of destalinization), did not basically threaten the foundations of the social or political order itself. By the latter sixties, political leaders of all four systems could (and did) with some justice proclaim to their people, "You never had it so good." That this overlooked the atrocities a prosperous America was committing in Vietnam, that it avoided the misery of millions of squatter poor in Mexico City living within sight of luxury and plenty, that it brazenly rationalized the Soviet suffocation of Socialism with a Human Face in Czechoslovakia, that it concealed continued class inequities and growing inequalities in West Germany, all this is not denied. And, although, in the mid-seventies, it now seems to many (including myself) that this interlude free from major system-shaking events is coming to a close, the years of postwar development provide once again an environmental control in which to compare the evolution of political elites.

In this respect, this chapter will deal with "politics as usual" in four seminal political systems, a situation in which, to a great extent, the system recruitment process is operating under historically minimal pressure. Especially after the early postwar years of reconstruction, a massive effort in the Soviet Union and a considerable effort in West Germany, the experiences of this period should provide a four-nation comparison of elite recruitment when the system has its "druthers." By the mid-sixties, we may posit, elite composition should represent a "typical" value pattern for each system at its best and thus offer some further insights into the core values of the system itself.

Postwar America: Liberal Professions Forever

If we had not already looked at the composition of the U.S. House for both the World War I and interwar years, we might reasonably expect to find some important shifts in the social bases of elite recruitment as the United States moves into the postindustrial society of mass consumption. After all, most historians have generally characterized the Eisenhower years (1952–1960) as conservative, quiescent, the Silent Generation of American youth. By contrast, the sixties are filled with traumatic issues (civil rights and Vietnam) which politicize blacks, student youth, and the Wallace backlash constituency. The presidential elections of 1960, 1964, 1968, and 1972 seem to polarize the two-party system when compared to the elections of 1952 and 1956. The Republican party appeared to many (mostly journalistic) observers as irrevocably splintered and fundamentally changed by the Goldwater nomination, with the Democratic party also undergoing stress during the 1968 and 1972 divisive primaries and national conventions. One might have concluded that, with the victory of insurgent Goldwaterites over Rockefeller-Scranton moderates and the bitter defeat of antiwar McCarthy partisans at the hands of labor and regular organization (Humphrey) Democrats, there would be some movement in the occupational-generational patterns of Congressional recruitment. Certainly, with the unexpected and, for labor and party regulars, distasteful McGovern nomination (the radic-lib vanguard of antiwar sentiment), we might expect some unusual happenings in Congressional nominations.[1] In terms of legislation affecting civil rights for black citizens, social programs for medical aid to the elderly, and generally improved welfare benefits, the Johnson administration's Great Society reforms represented a long-overdue and serious extension (some would say the final act) of the New Deal program.

However, the analysis of political elite composition in the U.S. House throughout the early years of this century as well as during the interwar period has been nothing if not an indication of the strength of the upper-middle-class bias in recruitment through thick and thin. With this perspective, there is no reason to expect any difference in the present analysis. If New Deal reformism in the face of the Great Depression did not imply either a generational or an occupational shift in the basic values for officeholding, either in the Democratic or the Republican parties, then one could hardly expect the calmer situation of the postwar fifties or sixties to produce any qualitative displacements or upheavals.

The data confirm again the no-change hypothesis. Generational turnover (see table 17) has been moderate and gradual throughout, even for the 1964 Johnson landslide, which produced lopsided Democratic House majorities (295 to 140). Throughout, the bulk of representatives are between 40 and 59 years of age (67% in 1951, 59% in 1957, 61% in 1961, 66% in 1967; see *Statistical Abstract 1968*: 366); as was true for our earlier periods of analysis, the birth-decade profile of 1972 (1968) is basically that of 1952 (1948) advanced by two decades. If the decade of the 1960s (or at least the Kennedy-Johnson years) was a reform era, it certainly did not produce any sort of qualitative rejuvenation of House membership (or Senate membership).

The occupational sources of Congressional recruitment remain remarkably stable throughout the postwar period. Generally, about one-half of all representatives are lawyers by profession (with 1968 standing out as an exception without apparent explanation); the drop-off in the proportion of lawyers in the House, evident in the earlier periods under study, had by the early fifties reached a stable plateau, which has been maintained. Another 20 to 30% of members of Congress have been business or farm owners, but, although the percentages fluctuate considerably from one sample to the next

1. There were, to be sure, some unusual happenings in individual Congressional races (e.g., the contests involving Loewenstein, Dow, and Abzug in New York State), but the question here is whether this alters the archetypal profile of the American political elite along occupational/generational lines.

TABLE 17. Age and Occupational Structure of the U.S. House, 1948–1972

Birth decade	1948 %	1952 %	1956 %	1960 %	1964 %	1968 %	1972 %
1870s	3	2	1	1			
1880s	16	10	8	3	1		
1890s	31	30	24	15	6	3	2
1900s	36	34	32	30	22	17	6
1910s	14	20	25	31	34	35	30
1920s	1	4	9	20	32	37	38
1930s					5	8	24
N	38	45	47	31	50	50	50

Occupation							
Lawyer	58	51	49	48	52	66	52
Business owner	13	22	21	23	20	12	16
Farm owner	5	7	9	3	6	2	4
Manager		2	4		4	6	8
Professional	16	13	13	26	10	10	14
White collar	2	2	2		4	2	2
Other	5	2	2		4		4
N	38	45	47	31	50	50	50

(from 18% in 1948 to 29% in 1952), there is no clear trend toward decline or rise in the general representation of this group. A third occupational category finding some regular representation is that of nonlawyer professions (engineers, teachers, professors, journalists, doctors), which vary from between 13 and 26% in our postwar representative samples, again without a distinct pattern. One minor trend in our data, which, however, may well be due entirely to sampling error, is the increase over 1960 to 1972 in House recruitment from managerial occupations, rising to 8% of our 1972 House sample. In any case, this is of minor significance. More important is the continued exclusion of blue-collar and white-collar employees from American political leadership, even at the modest national level of representative.

As with the data for earlier American Congresses, we have checked the possibility that there are periods of greater and lesser polarization between Republican and Democratic representatives along occupational or generational lines, but this is once more belied by the data. The level of association (Pearson's C) between party and occupation hovers around a moderately low .40 throughout the postwar period, with the Republican party still more inclined to recruitment from business and the Democratic party more heavily lawyer-oriented. As for age cohort cleavages between the parties, the relationship is always slight, and the direction of the relationship (i.e., whether Democratic or Republican House members tend to be younger) is unstable. We may infer from our analysis of American political elite development over seven decades of this century that, as long as the present two-party system remains intact, there is not likely to be any change in the class bases of recruitment to Congress. Furthermore, periods of reform capitalism (New Deal, Great Society), while representing some extensions of civil (i.e., bourgeois) rights and welfare benefits, do not imply any reordering of recruitment values along class lines, do not widen the social bases of officeholding to the wageworking classes, and have not even involved significant (qualitative) age cohort displacements in the officeholding elite. In terms of elite composition, these findings are substantially in agreement with Matthews' (1954: 30) and Clapp's (1963: 9) data from the House of Representatives and can be generalized with some confidence to cover, from Matthews' data, U.S. senators, cabinet officers, and state governors as well. At lower elite levels (state legislators), Matthews indicates greater representation of farm owners and fewer lawyers. Davidson (1969: 37–49) includes a short section on Congressional occupations which also substantiates our analysis, both in terms of composition and trends in lawyer dominance. Additionally, his survey of occupational backgrounds of 87 members of the Eighty-eighth Congress (1963–1964), which allows for multiple naming of occupations, clearly shows the overlapping of legal and business–farm owner experience and interests. Moreover, Davidson notes some important regional differences in occupational background, especially in the South, which account for much of the apparent nationwide differences between Democratic and Republican Congressional profiles. For the non-South regions taken together, there is almost no difference between the social bases of recruitment by the two major parties. With the economic and political development of the South, and the rise of the Republican party in that area, we might expect that over time the nationwide occupational profiles of the two system parties will become even more similar. In terms of elite recruitment, reform capitalism is what its name implies: reform within the boundaries of the present system which affirms the existing social and political hierarchy.

The analysis of American elite recruitment over three eras illus-

trates two important points. First, even within a given social order
(feudalism, capitalism, and socialism) there exists political debate
(i.e., politics) within the ideological confines of that system (see esp.
Miliband 1969: chaps. 6–7). This within-system politics is often
heated and involves intense personal rivalry for political office, for
power. Yet in retrospect the New Deal and New Frontier/Great Society reform programs, despite some right-wing charges of "creeping
socialism," have maintained rather than undermined the social
basis for elite recruitment.

Second, social-class background analysis of political elites is limited in not being able, at least in the American case, to distinguish
periods of reform from periods of conservative policy, because
neither goes beyond (or even approaches, in my opinion) the boundaries of political debate acceptable to the present social order. This is
a serious limitation to the application of elite background analysis
to within-system policy alternatives, which are of course the stuff of
day-to-day politics within political systems not undergoing revolution. It would be a serious error to claim that elite background
analysis can predict policy positions of individual actors within a
system where the political elite is derived so overwhelmingly from
the upper social strata. This is, however, not the purpose or the
claim of this study; rather, we are interested in the much broader
connections between system and succession, which involve policy
alternatives, but policy alternatives writ large.

Bonn: Elite Evolution in the Development of a Stable Democracy

The development of the postwar *Bundesrepublik* (Federal Republic)
is one of the legitimate success stories in the construction of a stable
liberal democracy upon the ruins of a fallen, not internally overthrown, dictatorship. No doubt the early reintegration of West
Germany into the Western anticommunist alliance, the sizable
Marshall Plan aid, the success of Konrad Adenauer's diplomacy in
the West, and above all the economic miracle (*Wirtschaftswunder*)
of the new republic contributed greatly in the early years to the viability of the system. In its first decade, the Federal Republic
achieved the remarkable feat of assimilating over ten million Ger-
mans expelled from former eastern regions of the Third Reich as
well as refugees from East Germany. And yet during these same

years the right-radical Socialist Reich and German Right (SRP, DRP), revanchist refugee League of Refugees and Expelled (BHE), and regional right-wing German (DP) parties were electorally defeated and their considerable voter following won over by the conservative Christian Democrats (CDU/CSU) under Adenauer (see Nagle 1970: chap. 2). On the Left, the Communists (KPD), despite an exemplary record of resistance to the Nazis, were able to muster only a decreasing fraction of their prewar voting strength and were outlawed (1956) in the heyday of Cold War anticommunism. As the Marxist historian Hobsbawm has pointed out (1973: 52–53), the Hitler regime seems to have effectively pulverized the KPD, in the early 1930s the strongest communist party in the West, as a mass movement. In this sense, fascism fulfilled its purpose in destroying the revolutionary vanguard of the proletariat.

Between 1949 and 1961, the three system parties (Christian Democrats, Free Democrats, and Social Democrats), increased their combined share of the vote from 72 to 94%, squeezing out all splinter parties, left and right, from Bundestag representation.[2] This was predominantly a period of political conservatism, as Adenauer's Christian Democrats increased their electoral support from just 31% in 1949 to a full majority of 50% in 1957, while the left-of-center SPD remained right around 30% (29% in 1949, 32% in 1957). Only in the second decade of the republic, from 1961 through 1972, as the German economy passed the stage of reconstruction and was able to develop a mass-consumption society to a high level (in early 1975, by measures of gross domestic product per capita among the wealthiest in the world), did the political development of the Social Democrats, under Willy Brandt and after the adoption of a non-socialist (Godesberg) program, convert the party system into one of conservative-liberal parity. The SPD, making a strong appeal to middle-class employees, to Catholics, to professionals, and to the young, rose steadily from 36% of the vote in 1961 to 46% in 1972, for the first time topping the CDU/CSU (45%). The Free Democrats (FDP), after a falling-out with the conservative Erhard government in 1966, became more liberal under the new leadership of Walter Scheel. In 1969, they went into coalition with Brandt's SPD, resulting in the first SPD-led government, the first time in twenty years that the Christian Democrats were in the (loyal) opposition. By the

2. In an electoral law change specifically designed to deny representation to small splinter parties, the Bonn Basic Law requires that a party get at least 5% of the national vote to be eligible for a proportional share of seats in the Bundestag. Most state parliaments have a similar law.

latter sixties most observers had concluded that the Bundesrepublik now qualified as a stable liberal democracy increasingly resembling the American system (cf. Heidenheimer 1971: x; Edinger 1968: 286–287; Merkl 1965), with alternation in power by the two major parties (the FDP perhaps providing the swing vote or eventually being eliminated), both strongly committed to the existing social order. After a minor scare in the recession of 1966 and 1967, when the rightist National Democratic party (NPD) suddenly appeared to claim 5 to 10% of the vote in several state elections (cf. Nagle 1970), most survey evidence shows increasing high levels of system support (Verba 1965; Boynton and Loewenberg 1973; Conradt 1974). Even the hotly contested 1972 election, which seemed to produce a polarization not visible in earlier elections (and a record 91% voter turnout), is seen by Conradt and Lambert (1973) as a sign of system-supportive behavior reinforcing the new politics of major party parity. Of the four major postwar reconstructed liberal democracies (France, West Germany, Italy, and Japan), West Germany by scholarly consensus represents the outstanding success story. We might interpret the evolution of political elite recruitment in the 1949 to 1972 period as a reflection of the achievement of a stable liberal democracy in an advanced and prosperous capitalist economy. We should expect, by way of comparison, qualitative differences vis-à-vis Weimar (and the Third Reich) and some greater similarities (though it would be foolish to expect complete congruence) with the classic American standards of elite recruitment values.

Both expectations are largely borne out by the empirical evidence. The Federal Republic, unlike the Weimar system, has been able to provide for gradual generational elite turnover without encountering, at least within the Bundestag, a young radical counterelite from antisystem parties. As table 18 indicates, the age composition of Bundestag deputies has, after the American fashion, progressed quite smoothly, with the age structure of 1969 a close approximation to that of 1949 advanced by two decades. A comparison of Bundestag age structures to those in the contemporary U.S. House illustrates a striking similarity. This should not be surprising, however. The age composition of system party deputies (i.e., excluding KPD and NSDAP) in the Weimar Reichstag was already similar to that of U.S. representatives; in fact, the age distribution of the 1932II system party deputies was quite similar to that of the 1953 Bundestag deputies with a two-decade lag. Bonn's economic recovery and continued growth into prosperity, plus its successful military-political

TABLE 18. Age and Occupational Structure of the German Bundestag, 1949–1972

Birth decade	1949 %	1953 %	1957 %	1961 %	1965 %	1969 %	1972 %
1870s	1	0	0	0	0		
1880s	15	7	4	2			
1890s	34	30	23	15	5	1	0
1900s	34	38	38	35	27	13	3
1910s	14	22	26	30	33	31	21
1920s	2	3	9	17	29	40	45
1930s			0	1	6	15	26
1940s						0	5
N	400	483	506	527	509	497	496
Occupation							
Worker/employee	49	39	25	13	13	13	15
Landowner	8	8	9	11	8	6	4
Business owner	6	6	7	8	6	5	4
Manager- administrator	14	20	28	35	40	38	34
Professional	18	21	26	28	29	33	38
Other (includes housewives)	5	6	5	5	4	5	5
N	400	483	506	527	509	497	496

integration into the Western bloc, have prevented a generational bifurcation of elite recruitment.

The trends in occupational background of deputies over the 1949 to 1972 period also support our basic theses (for a more detailed test of the "end of ideology" thesis with respect to occupational/ educational deputy backgrounds over this same timespan, see chap. 7). The most apparent change is the rapid withering away of elite recruitment from the worker/employee category. This occupational grouping, the largest among deputies in the earliest (reconstruction) years of the Federal Republic (49% of all deputies in 1949), quickly drops off to only 13% by 1961 and has remained at that low level ever since. This accords well with the American pattern of an all-party exclusion of any significant recruitment from wageworking groups, although the German process has not gone quite so far. One might also note that, as in the American case, an office worker gets a party nomination more often than a factory worker—generally two-thirds of the worker/employee deputies in each Bundestag have been white-collar, not blue-collar.

While recruitment from occupations directly identifiable as capitalist (business and farm owners) increased somewhat in the ascendancy of Adenauer and the Christian Democrat/Free Democrat governments of the 1950s, the changes were minor and were more than reversed over the succeeding years, so that by 1972 capitalists, like workers, enjoy only marginal direct representation in the federal parliament. Christian Democrats, like U.S. Republicans, have recruited 20 to 25% of their deputies from business and farm owners (the FDP, in its earlier conservative alliances with Adenauer, drew even more frequently from business circles). However, Social Democrats, who have shed about every other heritage as a Marxist party, still nominate very few (never more than 4%) entrepreneurs, whereas American Democrats nominate members of Congress from such strata with greater regularity. Except for this difference, the postwar parallelism between American and West German political elite recruitment from working and capitalist classes is quite strong.

The greatest increases in elite recruitment are from the managerial and professional categories. This rising trend toward recruitment of managerial talent, both corporate managers and union business executives (*Geschäftsführer*), falls in the Adenauer era and levels off at a plateau comprising around one-third of all deputies. The trend toward higher representation of the liberal professions is more gradual and is spread out over the entire history of the Bonn republic, and there is no sign that it has peaked yet, even though liberal professions (combined) represent the modal occupational grouping and account for nearly two-fifths (38%) of 1972 Bundestag deputies. This latter trend, overriding all three system parties, is another area of Americanization of the German political elite and is still more evidence of the most desired or "typical" composition of political elites in durable liberal democracies. We need not try to oversimplify this convergence, for there are still some clear differences. The law profession, while well represented (12% of 1972 deputies), is still nowhere near as much a "pathway to parliament" as in the American setting, and, on the other hand, there is presently much greater recruitment from such professions as professor (9%) and engineer (5%) than in the U.S. House. It should be noted, however, that many of those deputies from administrative civil-service positions have educations in law but have never entered private practice. Comparatively more value is placed on managerial talent, and there are still traces of skilled-worker recruitment (although any knowl-

edgeable observer will remark that these few "worker" deputies
have long since parted with their factory experience and now drive
to the Bundestag in their Mercedes like the other deputies). Even
without the above qualifications, the postwar German case shows
the evolution of a political elite homogeneous across party lines (see
chaps. 6 and 7), as in the United States, and evidencing many of the
background features of a "typical" bourgeois democratic leadership.

Mexico: Economic Development and Social Disparity

Postwar Mexican industrial development was launched by a sharp
reversal, by President Miguel Alemán, of the Cárdenas reforms. Although originally elected with the backing of Cárdenas and Avila
Camacho, Alemán used the immense powers of the presidency to
shift government far to the Right. During his years in office (1946–
1952), both rural worker organizations (*ejidatarios* and the landless)
and union leadership were effectively closed out of the political-
influence system. Alemán's overriding goal was industrialization,
and to this end he did all in his power to aid both foreign and domestic entrepreneurs. In addition, a new and growing group of "public
entrepreneurs," who ran government-owned enterprises, was benefited by his industrialization drive. This latter group of close
Alemán associates was noted for its corruption and its unabashed
pillaging of public funds, especially during the last year of Alemán's
term. Running roughshod over other PRI factions, the *alemanistas*
abolished constitutional restrictions on the size of landholdings,
making possible new large-scale commercial landholdings, and ig-
nored the 51% Mexican ownership formula in business and industry
to attract American capitalists. Even by Brandenberg's account, relatively favorable to the PRI along the spectrum of scholarly opinion,
Alemán succeeded in advancing capitalist economic development at
great expense to the majority of Mexicans:

> Capital accumulation, forced savings, and foreign capital be-
> came the new gods. Agriculture was squeezed, driven harder,
> and crudely exploited to provide surpluses for export. . . .
> Meanwhile prices soared and denied the popular masses milk,
> meat, and fresh fruits—everything, in fact, but corn and beans.
> Conspicuous consumption by these new "Revolutionary Con-
> servatives" and others exacerbated critical balance-of-payments
> problems. (1964: 103)

A clear idea of the relative political balance of popular versus capitalist interests, which marks the postwar era of Mexican development, can be drawn from Brandenberg's description of the confrontation of *cardenistas* and *alemanistas* in late 1951, over the question of choosing a presidential successor to Alemán:

> Meeting the crisis was uppermost. If Cárdenas had openly broken with Alemán, he probably could have counted on the support of a majority of the nation's teachers, soldiers, trade unionists, civil servants, and *ejidatarios*. On the other hand, Alemán probably could have found strong backing from many bankers, industrialists, merchants, foreign capitalists, and "small" [i.e., no longer small under the new landholding provisions] farmers. Through a process of back-scratching and log-rolling . . . a modus vivendi emerged: Alemán would remain President (long live constitutionalism); all factions, including the *alemanistas*, would lend support to the candidacy of Adolfo Ruiz Cortines, a non-controversial civil servant; the major economic programs of the Alemán administration would continue into the regime; and the masses would receive greater attention. (1964: 107)

In other words, in a showdown the reform forces, representing the overwhelming majority of the population, essentially capitulated before the representatives of the foreign and domestic bourgeoisie, representing a small minority of the people. Brandenberg himself concedes that the Ruiz Cortines regime did little to honor its pledge to pay greater attention to popular needs; rather, most workers, outside of a few favored places like Monterrey and the Ruiz Galindo industries in Mexico City, suffered from inflation and declines in real income, and the amount of land distributed dropped even further from the level of the Alemán regime. Ruiz Cortines' main effort in agriculture was to shift from agrarian reform to capitalist development (Brandenberg 1964: 110). However, the Ruiz Cortines administration is generally credited with purging the government bureaucracies of the most corrupt Alemán cronies (Johnson 1971: 32; Brandenberg 1964: 110) and with generally ameliorating the *cardenista-alemanista* split in the PRI.

The succeeding presidency of Adolfo López Mateos (1958–1964) marks in many ways and is judged by most scholars (see González Casanova 1970; Brandenberg 1964; Johnson 1971) the high point of postwar political stability and popular contentment in Mexico. López Mateos, in an easing of the conservatism of the previous two regimes, once again turned government attention to large-scale land distribution to the landless and extended socialized medical services to rural and poorer urban areas. But the government of President Gustavo Díaz Ordaz (1964–1970) was not able to act as an effective compromiser of interests within the Revolutionary Family. His regime is most noted for its initially inept and then brutal handling of the student uprising at the National University in Mexico City in September to October 1968 (see Johnson 1971: chap. 6), which Johnson, in a liberal critique of the Mexican system, sees as the decline of the "revolutionary axis," the weakening of the system of control through coopting interests into the PRI umbrella organization, a weakness also evident under the presidency (1970–1976) of Luis Echeverría Alvarez.

This system of cooptation of various group leaders is the basis for the continued stability necessary for economic growth in its present (capitalist) format (cf. Anderson and Cockcroft 1969), which along with public welfare and Mexicanization is seen as the major system-goal of the postwar era. The political stability and industrial growth achieved during this period coincide with what Horowitz terms the "development of a strictly middle-class vision of what the Mexican Revolution was all about" (in González Casanova 1970: xi).

It must be said that the victory of the middle-class interpretation of the Revolution (perhaps the only possible outcome, given the early defeat of socialist and radical popular elements during the civil-war years) has helped create a more modern industrial society. Production per capita doubled from 1940 to 1964, and the rate of economic growth, while fluctuating considerably, averaged over 5% for the 1945 to 1965 period. Industrial workers accounted for 20% of employment in 1964 as opposed to 13% in 1940, while the agricultural work force declined from 65% to 53%. More than half the population is now urban (towns of 2,500 or more). On the other hand, González Casanova points out that the range of inequality is severe and much greater than in other developed nations. At the same time that a new middle class is emerging (estimates vary greatly; see González Casanova 1970: 112–113), there is growing cleavage in living standard between classes and regions (pp. 105 ff.), as well as growing influence from American capital (pp. 57 ff.), which rose from 62% of all foreign investment at the end of Cárdenas' presidency to 74% by 1957, after which date the Bank of Mexico has refused to publish this information. Of the 400 largest corporations in Mexico in 1962, 232 are either foreign-owned (p. 161) or have strong foreign investment (p. 71).

We expect that political elite evolution will reflect this victory of the middle-class vision (or version) of the incomplete Mexican Revolution, so that elite composition should increasingly reflect a "normal" middle-class pattern of recruitment values. Occupational sources of deputies and secretaries confirm this (see table 19). Deputy recruitment from military leaders continues to decline from 15% in 1940 to 1946 to a quite nominal 1% by 1970. Cabinet recruitment from the military, with 1952 an exceptional case, also drops off sharply from the general interwar level to something under 10% of all secretaries, and this includes the Ministries of Defense and Marine/Navy. At both deputy and cabinet levels, lawyers are the most favored occupational category, although media specialists (journalists, publishers, and professionals in film, radio, and television) were quite heavily recruited during the Alemán, Ruiz Cortines, and López Mateos regimes (1946–1964). The liberal professions have formed the social basis for the bulk of recruitment from officeholders, both before and since the Revolution, but this relationship solidifies even further after World War II—by 1970, nearly nine-tenths of all secretaries and seven-tenths of all deputies are drawn from these callings, which as a group account for less than 3% of the economically active population. Yet, while this confirms our general thesis, we should pay attention to the differential between cabinet and deputy levels, which says something about the cooptation and control strategy of the PRI as capitalist development of the economy progresses. While there is little representation of anything but the liberal professions at the cabinet level, there is rather steady growth at the lowest national elite level of contingents from factory workers, unionists, white-collar workers, and semiindependent (public and private sector) employees. These occupational elements of a modern economy, which had gained footholds in the value structure of PRI recruitment under Cárdenas and Avila Camacho, now hold slightly over 20% of all deputy seats. On the other hand, the smallholders, who had been allotted a small but growing proportion of seats in the 1930s, have all but disappeared from the Chamber of Deputies over the postwar years (only 1% in 1970). This also reflects this era's emphasis on industrialization and economic modernization. This deputy/secretary differential is an indication of two elements of PRI strategy: (1) the general PRI policy of coopting leaders from the new and growing work-force sectors of the economy and (2) the relegation of these leaders from the wageworking classes to minor offices only. In this sense, the PRI has not yet fully consolidated a bourgeois political revolution, for it still

TABLE 19. Occupational Structure of the Mexican Political Elite, 1946–1976

	Cabinet secretaries				
Occupation	1946–52 %	1952–58 %	1958–64 %	1964–70 %	1970–76 %
Rural worker			5		
Smallholder	3		5		
Landowner					3
Industrialist	3				
Military	7	20	10	9	10
Lawyer	50	38	40	47	48
Professional	36	42	40	43	39
N	32	22	21	29	31
	National Congress deputies				
Rural worker	1		1	1	1
Smallholder	1	1	3	2	1
Landowner	2	1	1	1	1
Unionist/worker	8	7	11	11	12
White collar	4	7	4	11	10
Military	8	11	8	4	1
Lawyer	36	19	16	30	32
Professional	34	53	49	33	38
Clergy	3		4	4	2
N	100	135	236	362	161

feels obligated (at least at the deputy level) to attempt cooptation of a certain increasing number of wageworker representatives, and, even though these may be a pliable vanguard of the working class, there is still an upper limit, now being approached, on the number of deputy seats that can be allocated to labor and popular leaders from the wageworking classes. It is difficult to imagine that the higher offices could continue to be exclusively reserved for the liberal professions without protest. At some point, it would seem, the segregation process would become too blatant and the situation could get sticky. There is also the potential danger that some of these lower-level leaders may, as in the 1968 national strike action and massacre of students at Tlatelolco (cf. Johnson 1971: 151, 154), become radicalized and desert the official PRI policy line (see chap. 8).

Another area of change in postwar Mexican elite recruitment has been that of age structure (see table 20). Generational turnover has

TABLE 20. Age Structure of the Mexican Political Elite, 1946–1970

	Cabinet secretaries				
Birth decade	1946 %	1952 %	1958 %	1964 %	1970 %
1880s	6				
1890s	22	55	14	3	
1900s	56	27	57	31	13
1910s	13	18	29	24	19
1920s	3			35	45
1930s				7	23
N	32	22	21	29	31

	National Congress deputies				
1870s	1	1			
1880s	7	1	1	0	
1890s	19	12	7	3	1
1900s	40	25	28	15	8
1910s	31	44	42	40	27
1920s	2	15	19	27	29
1930s		1	3	15	34
N	85	73	168	383	191

continued to be gradual and evolutionary, a quality of elite recruitment which Huntington (1968), for example, does not expect in developing nations. Clearly, this is one of the distinctive features of Mexico as a one-party system and is more often associated with stable liberal democracies in advanced capitalist nations. But there has been some further aging of the Mexican leadership over the last 30 years, which means that by the 1970 to 1976 sexennium only 34% of all deputies (vs. 70% in 1940) and 23% of all secretaries (vs. 26% in 1940) are under 40 years of age. The change, especially among deputies, while occurring gradually, has moved the age structure much closer to that of members of the U.S. House or the West German Bundestag. In the López Mateos years (1958–1964), for the first time since the Revolution, less than half of all deputies were under 40, and since then the majority of deputies have been between 40 and 59 (56% in 1970). At the cabinet level, officeholders continue to be somewhat younger than their American or West German counterparts, although there was notable aging (dejuvenation) in the changeover from Alemán to Ruiz Cortines in 1952, as well as a ten-year rise in the average age of cabinet members from 1946 to 1958. If the present trends continue, by the end of the 1970s there should not be much difference between elite age distributions in Mexico and in the two leading capitalist democracies, and, in this respect as well as in the gradual turnover in age cohorts and the dominance of liberal professions, the Mexican political elite may have developed "typical" liberal democratic recruitment values.

After Stalin: An Aging Leadership in Modern Socialism

The first several years of the postwar era in the Soviet Union were devoted to massive economic and social reconstruction. The population (20 million estimated killed) and material (two-fifths of total assets destroyed) losses suffered by Soviet society were greater than those suffered by any other nation, except perhaps Poland. Only in the early 1950s did the Soviet economy begin to move beyond reconstruction, and this coincides with the political development of the post-Stalin era. Two general features characterize the more relaxed and less troubled recent decades of Soviet evolution: (1) a gradual but, over time, sizable expansion of consumer goods production relative to producer (heavy industrial) goods output and (2) a qualitative downgrading of state coercion and police control as a basic feature of Soviet society.

Both broad tendencies surfaced very quickly after Stalin's death in 1953. Within weeks amnesty had been decreed for hundreds of thousands of labor-camp prisoners, and a potential new purge (the so-called Doctors' Plot), which had been brewing in the last year of Stalin's one-man rule, was denounced as a hoax. Beria, chief of the secret police since 1939, was arrested with his top associates and, after a secret trial, executed—the last major Soviet politician to be violently eliminated. All defeated or unseated political leaders since 1953, including Malenkov, Molotov, Bulganin, Khrushchev, Shelest, and most recently Shelepin, have been given lesser posts or have been pensioned off but have never been imprisoned or even brought to trial. In the two years after Stalin's death, the special tribunals of the Bureau of State Security (MVD, formerly NKVD) were abolished, many security forces were reassigned to regular military control or abolished, the economic empire (mostly mining, lumber, and infrastructure projects) of the labor-camp organization (GULAG) was dismantled, and party control was reasserted over the secret police.

The labor camps have remained a minor fixture since the mid-fifties. Within the party, debate over policy has become more open and frank, with various interest groups (see Lodge 1968; Skilling 1971) contending for influence without having to fear draconian consequences. Especially after Khrushchev's 1956 denunciation of Stalin's crimes, there was a period of cultural-political liberalization (1958–1962), which, if somewhat restrained under Brezhnev and Kosygin, still has not been undone. The treatment of extraparty opposition, such as that accorded Solzhenitsyn (deportation), Amalrik (public trial and conviction), and Sakharov (public criticism), all open opponents of the Soviet system, cannot be compared to what would have happened to them in the 1930s. Public demonstrations (e.g., by Jews wishing to emigrate or by opponents of the invasion of Czechoslovakia), while leading to harassment or arrest, would have constituted an act of instant martyrdom under Stalin.

On economic policy, Malenkov's "New Course" of 1954 to 1955 recognized the backlog of unfulfilled consumer desires by emphasizing light industry. Khrushchev, first concentrating on expanding agricultural output (Virgin Lands program, amalgamation of collectives into state farms, introduction of corn varieties), later initiated programs for increased consumer production of a wide range of goods. Many of his campaigns for greater output were later criticized as "harebrained" and "goulash communism," but Brezhnev and Kosygin, typically with more caution and less fanfare, have continued the trend toward greater attention to consumer desires, even lifting the restrictions Khrushchev had placed on mass production of private passenger cars. The motivational emphasis in Soviet economic growth has increasingly shifted from coercion under Stalin through normative or moral exhortation under Khrushchev to utilitarian (monetary/material) incentives during the last decade's collective leadership. Soviet society has continued to industrialize and urbanize at slower rates, and by the early 1970s it represented a predominantly urban-industrial society (55% of the population lived in urban areas in 1967), though with an agricultural work force still considerably larger than that in the United States or West Germany. Per capita GNP in 1964 ranked above that of Japan and Italy but below that of the U.S., West Germany, France, and Britain. Production of consumer durables (televisions, refrigerators, cars, washing machines, etc.) increased fivefold between 1950 and 1964, although the gap between American and Soviet consumption patterns is still great (cf. Lane 1971: 288–293). On the other hand, in provision of social (including health) and educational services, the Soviet

Union now compares favorably with the United States, with better doctor/capita and student/teacher ratios and a markedly more equitable distribution of both medical facilities and educational opportunities among all segments of the population. And, while social stratification among manual, nonmanual, and farm workers persists in income differential and educational attainment, a conscious post-Stalin incomes policy much reduced high pay differentials introduced during the first two Five-Year Plans (cf. Osborn 1970, 1974: chap. 3). After thirty years of peace and steady economic growth, the modern Soviet system presents a picture of political stability and internal social peace unprecedented in its history.

In terms of elite recruitment, we would expect to see a recognition of the changes in vocational structures in the economy, as well as a further call for the higher educational backgrounds needed for comprehensive and informed economic and social planning. This would be a logical extension of the industrial revolution set in motion in the 1928 to 1938 period and continued after the wartime hiatus. The data on educational background of Central Committee members for the 19th through the 24th Party Congresses (there was no election of a Central Committee at the special 21st Congress in 1959) indicate the thoroughness of the skills revolution in recruitment values (see table 21). The proportion of members with some form of higher technical education (polytechnical, agricultural, military, teachers, or medical institutes) rises from 68% in 1952 to 82% in 1971, and the proportion of those with technical educations specifically related to economic areas (polytechnical and agronomical institutes) increases from 39% to 62%. Especially apparent is the effort under Khrushchev to recruit people with expertise in agriculture, a field long neglected under Stalin. The share of members with university educations remains stable and distinctly minor compared with the American and West German cases (see chap. 7). There is a small contingent with educations at the Party High School, a special college for training party leaders; and the number of those with only primary or secondary educations drops from nearly one in four to less than one in ten. This represents a complete reversal of the situation in 1934, when nearly three-fourths of all members had no higher education of any sort.

Occupational composition of the Central Committee has reflected work-force modernization in a planned socialist economy: technical workers, engineers, office workers, and factory managers, hardly represented at all among 1939 Central Committee members (only 7%), account for increasing shares of seats (22% in 1952, 35%

TABLE 21. Social and Age Structure of the Soviet Central Committee, 1952–1971

Occupation	Central Committee				
	1952 %	1956 %	1961 %	1966 %	1971 %
Agricultural worker	2	2	5	5	4
Factory, other worker	53	51	36	30	26
Office worker	4	2	4	5	4
Technician	7	9	16	19	17
Professional	22	21	28	32	37
Manager	5	6	2	2	5
Military/police	7	9	9	7	6
N	55	81	137	153	181
Education					
Low/secondary	24	15	10	9	7
Technical	39	52	57	60	62
Military inst.	5	9	10	9	10
Teachers/med. inst.	24	15	12	12	10
Party School	3	4	5	5	5
University	5	5	6	5	6
N	76	105	169	189	224
Birth decade					
1870s	1				
1880s	6	2	1	1	
1890s	20	15	6	5	3
1900s	56	59	47	39	27
1910s	16	23	40	46	50
1920s	1	1	5	8	19
1930s			1	1	1
N	96	123	172	190	232

in 1961, 45% by 1971). Organized another way, occupations with professional status (teachers, engineers, doctors, professors) have, mainly as a result of strongly increased recruitment of engineers, increased from 22% of Central Committee membership in 1952 to 37% in 1971. One segment of the work force, the *kolkhozniki* (collective farmers), deliberately neglected and distrusted by Stalin, began to find some increased Committee representation under Khrushchev, but still of minimal proportions. Throughout the postwar period, there is a steady contingent from the military of 6 to 9%, but there is very little recruitment from the police apparatus. The sharp decline in factory-worker occupational background, from a peak of 72% in 1930 to 40% in 1952 and 15% in 1971, corresponds closely to the skills revolution. During the Revolution, the factory worker was both in Marxist-Leninist theory and in fact the proletarian core of the party leadership, but in the postwar era political leadership is more heavily drawn from technical and white-collar strata. If we combine all wageworking vocations, excluding managers, professionals, and military/police, we find that the total declines slightly over the postwar years (down from 65% to 55%) but that the factory-worker share of this combined wageworker bloc sinks from 61% to only 28%. One other point worth mentioning is the general tendency toward occupational diversification of leadership recruitment categories: in 1952, for the first time since 1919, factory-worker backgrounds did not account for a majority of the Central Committee membership. Unlike political recruitment under advanced stable capitalist systems, the growing diversity of the work force finds a response in elite recruitment values which covers the entire range of occupational strata, that is, including the wageworking class. In terms of family social origins, the recruitment process reflects the increased social mobility from the peasantry into the urban work force and into the party in the post-Stalinist period, as well as some greater recruitment from middle-class and intelligentsia origins. On the whole, however, the class origins of the Central Committee in the postwar period are not all that different from those in the interwar period, at least beginning with the latter 1920s. Broadly, these figures illustrate the point, conceded even by severe critics of the Soviet system (cf. Djilas 1961; see also chap. 10), that, throughout the process of educational upgrading and occupational diversification, the elite recruitment process has kept its roots in the working classes.

But, if Soviet elite recruitment emphasizes technical training and reflects the growing work-force complexity of an advanced urban industrial society, it certainly has not placed much value, since Stalin's death, on age cohort rejuvenation. Average ages of Central Committee members have risen steadily, from 44 in 1939 to 58 in 1971. The modal birth decade has advanced only from 1900–1909 to 1910–1919. The top leaders in the Politburo and the Secretariat are, as of 1977, all in their late sixties or seventies (Brezhnev is 70, Kosygin 72, Podgorny 73, Suslov 74). In comparison with the U.S. House and the West German Bundestag, the Central Committee membership since the early 1950s has lagged behind in the advancement of younger age cohorts (those born 1920 and after); this prolonged period of generational ossification has reversed the age-structure relationship between Soviet and Western parliamentary elites which existed during the interwar period. Indeed, the blockage of generational elite turnover is so striking as to call for a specific and detailed generational interpretation of the Soviet system from its inception (see chaps. 9 and 10 for an examination of a generational model of the Soviet elite compared with totalitarian, rational-technical, Trotskyite "bureacratic stratum," and Djilas "new-class" critiques). For now, we can conclude that one of the difficulties in elite recruitment for a stable Soviet socialist system, in contrast to the Mexican PRI regime, is that of generational succession.

System-Typical Elites: A Summary

The prosperity and relative calm of the postwar era have afforded an opportunity to gauge the "politics as usual" recruitment values of four seminal political systems. With these analyses as a basis, further theses may be developed and tested on other nations with similar political systems, although the comparison among these four major systems is in itself instructive. Each system presents a potential model for other polities, and general propositions raised here should be tested and refined through other studies. Any simple attempt to claim validity for all systems of type X on the basis of our findings would of course violate the original intent of the longitudinal seminal-case method (see chap. 1 again), namely, to keep the historical record straight as to what has factually occurred in terms of elite evolution in these important polities.

We have seen, however, that American political leadership has maintained its classic (quite dogmatic) profile of recruitment from predominantly liberal professions, to the exclusion of worker/ employee vocations, while undergoing evolutionary age cohort turnover. The Bonn Federal Republic, as it has developed a stable democratic system, has experienced elite transformations which, as the Weimar system was unable to do, have brought political elite composition more into line with the American pattern. The victory, after World War II, of the middle-class interpretation of the Mexican

Revolution has also meant a strengthening of the liberal professions as the dominant social basis for officeholding recruitment and an elite age cohort recruitment more similar to the West German and American, rather than either the Mexican interwar or Soviet postwar, patterns. Mexican political recruitment, however, also shows a continuing cooptation of leaders from the growing industrial and white-collar work-force strata, but this is limited to minor posts and may eventually conflict with overall middle-class control of Mexican politics. Changes in Soviet elite composition, while reflective of the growing industrial complex of the society at large and the technical expertise needed for concrete problem solving in a state-planned economy, have not, in the absence of either purge or other institutionalized (e.g., "no reelection" in Mexico) mechanism, provided for significant generational turnover since the Great Purge. While the present age cohorts must soon pass from the scene, it would appear that the more placid collective leadership coalitions after Stalin have not placed much value on youth recruitment, an apparent anomaly in a revolutionary party officially committed to building a new society.

Two general propositions may be suggested here. First, there seems to be a modal age cohort distribution for political elites in systems not under stress, a distribution already found in the United States and West Germany, gradually approached in Mexico, but conspicuously absent in the Soviet Union. A corollary to this proposition would be that, in the absence of democratization within the Soviet (and perhaps other one-party) system, or some other mechanism for age cohort renewal (purge or mandatory rotation), there will be a tendency toward generational oligarchy. Chapters 9 and 10 explore the basis for this generational stagnation in the Soviet elite and examine the possible consequences for the Soviet system.

In three of our polities a trend toward higher representation of the professions was evident. There are very significant differences here, of course. In Mexico the percentage of professionals in elite offices has reached the American level, with lawyers present in exceptionally large numbers. In West Germany, the trend is also strong, although many deputies with educations in the professions, especially law, have entered parliament by way of higher civil-service careers (a possibility prevented in the United States by the Hatch Act, prohibiting officeholding by civil servants). The increased representation of the professions among Soviet leadership is predominantly from engineering fields, not law. Yet a second general thesis might be that the liberal professions *as a whole*, perhaps because of high social status in both capitalist and socialist systems, will be more heavily represented in times of prosperity and peace, regardless of system-type. Here one might suspect that the American case would prove to be a deviant example of the dominance of the liberal professions among elite occupations in all circumstances.

Part 3. Single-Nation Studies

Tenure in the U.S. House: Longitudinal Analysis of Four Alternative Explanations

The American political elite, as the previous chapters have shown, has long been characterized by an evolutionary transition of age cohorts and by occupational dominance of the liberal professions, primarily lawyers, with some representation of business and farm owners and almost total exclusion of wageworkers. Nevertheless, there have been many developments worthy of study in the career patterns of national-level officeholders. One of these developments, which has interested observers of the Congress for some time, has been the "revolution" in length of tenure among House representatives since the turn of the century.

The longitudinal seminal-case approach would seem to be particularly appropriate here, given the availability of data covering a quite considerable timespan (1789–1970). The analysis of the revolution in Congressional tenure should also demonstrate the potential use of correlation analysis with single-nation time-series (as opposed to cross-national) elite data (cf. chap. 1).

Throughout the nineteenth century, between 50 and 90% of all House members in any given period served only one or two terms (four years or less); few representatives made membership in the House a long-run career (ten years or more). But this began to change in the early 1900s, so that by the 1950s the tenure pattern of representatives had been reversed, with less than one-fourth serving only one or two terms and well over half serving ten years or more.

The purpose of the present chapter is explicitly to spell out hypotheses formulated to explain the increased tenure in the House of Representatives, to operationalize empirical indicators with which to test these hypotheses, and then either to confirm or modify the original theorized relationships through empirical tests using a random sample of 1,000 representatives covering the period 1789 to

1970. If long tenure in office is a major prerequisite for what has been called the institutionalization of the House (Polsby 1968; Price 1965) in its present state, it may be productive to analyze alternative explanations of increased tenure.

The first hypothesis to be tested is one relating the seniority system within the House to tenure: namely, the seniority system is directly related to increased tenure in the House. This positive effect of seniority on officeholding expectations is formulated by Huntington as follows:

> The longer men stay in Congress, the more likely they are to see virtue in seniority. Conversely, the more important seniority is, the greater is the constituent appeal of men who have been long in office. The current rigid system of seniority in both houses is a product of the twentieth century. (1965: 9)

While Huntington speaks of seniority as a "product," he is also clearly positing the seniority system as a causal variable in the patterns of long tenure which characterize the House in this century. Similarly, Polsby, Gallaher, and Rundquist (1969: 807), in their speculation about a causal model to explain the durability of the seniority system, describe a feedback loop of causation leading from the seniority system through job security and greater attractiveness of House service to low turnover and a large corps of veteran representatives. And Price (1965: 23), in his discussion of the professionalization of the House career, considers this development to be the result of two causes: the seniority system and the growth of safe districts.

Our second hypothesis might be called the solidification of the "party-system" thesis; it relates to events which took place in the 1890s involving the realignment and stabilization of the two-party system. The watershed point is usually taken to be the election of 1896, with the fusion of the Populist and Democratic parties in support of the candidacy of William Jennings Bryan. The major proponent of this thesis is Schattschneider (1956), who posited a basic solidification of the party system following the 1896 Bryan debacle. According to Schattschneider, this stabilization of the two-party system, carrying with it the elimination of the Populist party, which had been a growing threat to the two major parties in the late 1880s and 1890s, led to a situation of one-party dominance in individual states and districts, with the Republicans predominant outside the South and the Democrats without challenge in the Southern states. Whereas in 1892 a competitive party situation existed in 36 states, by 1904 only 6 states could still be labeled as equal in strength of the two major parties, and in 29 states the relative strengths of the two major parties were so unbalanced as to offer no interparty competition (see also Durden 1965; Rogin 1967). We are explicitly interested here in the relationship between the stability over time of the two-party system, *not* in the competitiveness of the two parties within each district. As conceived by Schattschneider, with the elimination of viable third parties, the noncompetitiveness within districts follows directly, although not tautologically. Thus, our measurement for this hypothesis will focus on the ability of the two major parties to hold down third-party strength.

Still a third hypothesis, which might well be termed the "frontier thesis," notes that the United States had (with the exceptions of Hawaii and Alaska) reached its Manifest Destiny by the first decade of the twentieth century. Sometimes this thesis relates the addition of new seats in the House to high rates of turnover (Fiorina et al., n.d.), and it is true that, by the second decade of this century, the House had reached its present size. Simply stated, the "frontierness" of the United States is inversely related to the length of tenure of House members. Only as the society matures or stabilizes does the role of the representative increasingly become a career occupation (Witmer 1964: 530–531).

Another variable which has been related to the length of tenure is the mode of communications between constituency and the member of Congress, the "communications thesis." Both in means of transportation for the representatives to and from Washington and in the possibilities of communication with one's constituency from Washington, there has been a series of developments, dating back to the construction of a nationwide railway system, which has steadily, but seemingly at an accelerated pace in the last few decades, increased the capacity of members of Congress to conduct their business in Washington as professional House members while maintaining grass-roots contact with their perhaps far-distant home districts.

The Sample

In order to test the above hypotheses, a random sample of 1,000 representatives was drawn from the *Biographical Directory of the American Congress, 1774–1961*, of which 895 had served in the

House of Representatives from 1789 through 1961. A stratified sample of 24 names was drawn from the *Congressional Directory* for the Eighty-sixth through the Eighty-eighth Congresses as a supplement to be used in certain cases for purposes of extension of analysis into the 1960s. The data set was grouped into periods of decades by combining five consecutive Congresses and by including each member of Congress according to the first House in which he/she served. The intent here is to deviate from the practice of looking at the total membership of each House and calculating the mean tenure, or percent turnover; rather, we intend to concentrate on the achieved career tenure of *newly elected* representatives. We shall argue not that this procedure is any more accurate or correct but that it serves to illustrate different aspects of officeholding.

In particular, we shall be able, at an earlier date, to detect *changes* in the ability of representatives to maintain themselves in office if we concentrate on the total longevity in office of newly elected members of the House, rather than on the mean tenure of the total membership in a particular Congress.[1] Thus, for example, we shall look at the newly elected members of the first five Congresses (1789–1799) to give us an estimate of the tenure patterns for members of Congress in the decade of the 1790s. Newly elected representatives, we shall assume, have to face reelection in the same environment in which they are first elected. Thus, if a representative is first elected in 1908, before the introduction of radio, it is assumed that he faces reelection throughout his career in the House without benefit of radio as a means of communicating with his constituents, despite the fact that his career may in fact extend into the era of radio communication. This assumption is, of course, rather crude, but it may be justified on two grounds: first, the assumption is clearly stronger in the course of the first few tries at reelection and only gradually distorts the capabilities available to the representative; second, it may be argued that, after several successful reelections, an incumbent has established a mode of operation less adaptable to new conditions than is true of newly elected members.

If we are concerned with changes in the tenure pattern of newly elected members, it is also important that we look primarily not at

1. There is also, of course, the factor of desirability, which is intertwined with ability, but, beyond the difficulties of measurement of this factor over time, it lies beyond the scope of this study. See Schlesinger 1966 for an exposition of ambition theory as an input to career patterns. Thus, for purposes of the analysis here, no distinction is made between representatives defeated for reelection and those who voluntarily did not seek reelection.

statistics of central tendency, although this might also be helpful, but rather at the distribution of career tenures for each time period. Clearly visible from the data is the general curvilinear trend in the percentage of one-term representatives, rising from 38% in the 1790s to a peak of 61% among newly elected members in the 1840s, remaining at a high plateau through the latter half of the nineteenth century, and declining throughout the twentieth century to a low of 17% by the 1960s. More instructive perhaps are the same data, grouped by differing lengths of tenure, presented in table 22, in which attention is focused on two groups of members—those serving up to three terms, or six years, and those serving at least five terms, or at least ten years. Although the choice is clearly arbitrary, six years or less in the House do not seem long enough to warrant calling a member a career representative, whereas ten or more years of service will be taken as a partition defining a House career.

Analysis of Hypotheses—Seniority

Difficulties arise in the operationalization of independent variables in each of our four hypotheses. How are we to measure the seniority system? Basically, there are two choices: a dichotomous dummy variable dividing the pre-1911 and post-1911 Congresses or an interval scale variable measuring percentage of violations of seniority in selection of committee chairs in the House, by decades. It is clear that the seniority system had its origins as a concept long before the 1910 House "revolution" against Speaker Cannon (Hinckley 1971). In fact, it is clear that seniority prevailed in about 80% of chair assignments in the House during Cannon's speakership (Chang 1928: 11). And, conveniently, Polsby, Gallaher, and Rundquist (1969: 792–794) have calculated the percentage of uncompensated violations of the seniority rule, by decades, from the 1880s through the 1960s, showing the rather steady decline in violations of seniority from 33% of all chair assignments in the 1880s to 0% in the 1950s and 1960s. On the other hand, it is also clear that the House revolt of 1910 was a watershed in the development of the seniority system. Before this revolt, a newly elected Speaker started out in office with a "honeymoon" period, in which he could more easily afford to violate seniority while building a coalition of supporters. After the Speaker had built his coalition, however, the costs of ignoring seniority began to rise, and reliance on seniority became a means of avoiding conflict. After the revolt of Democrats and insurgent Republicans against Cannon, this honeymoon period was denied the Speaker, so that one could reasonably divide the history of the House into an era (post-1911) in which the seniority system was present and an era (pre-1911) in which the seniority system was absent. This produces a dummy variable for seniority which produces values (0 or 1) covering all eighteen decades, as opposed to just nine decades for our interval scale seniority index. As one test of the seniority hypothesis, we shall correlate both indexes of seniority with several indexes of tenure. Table 23 gives the matrix of zero-order correlation coefficients for our dichotomous seniority index (X_1) and our interval scale seniority index (X_2), with four indexes of tenure expectation, taken from Table 22.

While both indexes of seniority correlate at fairly high levels with all four indexes of tenure for newly elected members, with the interval scale variable doing somewhat better except for correlations with Y_1 (percentage of newly elected members serving one term only), a closer examination of the data in table 22 should caution us against any causal interpretations from the correlation results. We should note, especially in the post–Civil War era, that the first noticeable drop in the percentage of one-term representatives and the first notable rise in the percentage of career representatives occur between the 1870s and 1880s, at a time when seniority was more regularly violated than followed. The decade of the 1890s, marked by the severe Depression in 1893 and by several subsequent recessionary fluctuations, presents a partial reversion to the pre-1880s pattern, and the first decade of this century then resumes the upward trend of tenure.[2] Taking into account the weakness of seniority, measured by percentage of violations during these two decades (60% in the 1880s, 49% in the 1890s), it would seem that the rise in tenure precedes the strengthening of the seniority system; that, if anything, the hypothesized causal sequence may have to be reversed. That is, the early seniority system could well be seen as the result of the development of new tenure patterns in the House.

2. The possibility that sampling error within each decade may account for the recorded differences in tenure between the 1870s and 1890s is of some concern here. The confidence intervals around the recorded percentages range from 6% to 9%, depending on sample size for each decade and the sample proportion around which the confidence interval is constructed. While the "true" proportions may be closer than the sample proportions, and the differences thus fewer from decade to decade, there remain differences in the posited direction which are statistically significant.

TABLE 22. Cumulative Distribution of Career Tenure
for Newly Elected Representatives

Decade elected	Number of terms served in the House			
	One %	Up to two %	Up to three %	Five or more %
1790s	38	62	81	19
1800s	44	50	78	11
1810s	53	66	76	17
1820s	28	44	72	25
1830s	43	82	90	3
1840s	61	89	94	2
1850s	50	78	89	8
1860s	51	81	86	9
1870s	52	75	86	9
1880s	28	62	67	25
1890s	44	73	80	15
1900s	22	41	57	33
1910s	39	54	61	32
1920s	36	44	56	37
1930s	23	44	67	29
1940s	40	44	58	41
1950s	19	25	28	56
1960s	17	29	38	50

On the other hand, time-lagged correlation analysis of tenure with
each of the seniority indexes, which might be taken as an indicator
of the time sequencing which produces the maximum correlation
levels, proved inconclusive. For X_1, covering all eighteen decades,
correlation levels varied rather slightly and nonuniformly when the
four indexes of tenure were lagged ahead or behind seniority by one
to three decades. With the interval scale variable X_2, covering only
nine decades, the highest correlation levels more clearly occurred
with a *zero* time lag, and the fall-off was more uniform when positive and negative time lags were introduced. This might support a
thesis of a seniority relationship of mutual reinforcement between
tenure and seniority, once the seniority system was well established
in the House.

The suspicion arises that perhaps the increase in tenure in the
1880s is a regional phenomenon related to the "redemption" period

TABLE 23. Correlation of Seniority and Tenure Indexes (Zero-Order)

	Y_1	Y_2	Y_3	Y_4	N
X_1	−.52	−.69	−.76	.80	18
	(.014)	(.001)	(.001)	(.001)	
X_2	−.19	−.70	−.53	.63	9
	(.313)	(.017)	(.073)	(.036)	

Note: Figures in parentheses indicate level of significance.
X_1 = Dichotomous dummy variable for seniority.
X_2 = Interval scale variable (percentage of uncompensated violations of seniority) for seniority.
Y_1 = Percentage of newly elected members serving one term only.
Y_2 = Percentage of newly elected members serving up to two terms.
Y_3 = Percentage of newly elected members serving up to three terms.
Y_4 = Percentage of newly elected members serving five or more terms.
N = Number of decades for each seniority variable.

in the South, the suppression of voting rights for blacks, and the development of a one-party monopoly in most Southern districts. If this were the case, then it could be argued that the above findings represent only the "special case" of the South, not a nationwide development. However, this seems not to be the case. While the drop in the percentage of one-term Southern representatives (a difference of 36%) from the 1870s to the 1880s is greater than the change for non-Southern representatives (20%) during the same period, the trend is clearly a nationwide phenomenon. Similarly, while the percentage of new members in the House who served for ten years or more rises dramatically from 9 to 41% for the South, it doubles (9% to 18%) for the areas outside the South as well. For both Southern and non-Southern members, there is a temporary reversal in trend in the 1890s (stronger outside the South) and a resumption of the original trend begun in the 1880s. The data thus indicate a similar sequence of changes for both regions, although with differing intensities.

As a partial check on the above findings, and also to help in the testing of other hypotheses, a complete census was taken of the representatives of four states: Massachusetts, Kentucky, Texas, and California. Correlation analysis between indexes of tenure and indexes of seniority strength gives approximately the same results as were achieved for the nationwide sample, with especially high correlation levels for California and somewhat weaker correlations for Kentucky. An examination of the trend of tenure in the last three decades of the nineteenth century shows very divergent patterns, with Texas and Kentucky closer to the pattern of the national sample, Massachusetts reversing the 1880s and 1890s nationwide trend despite the Depression of the 1890s, and California displaying a delayed development of longer tenure for its representatives.

At the level of bivariate analysis, then, seniority would seem to be closely associated with length of tenure, but there are serious questions regarding the direction of any posited causal relationship.

Analysis of Hypotheses—Solidification of the Party System

Measurement of the extent of stability in the two-party system involves many assumptions, all of which can be questioned, and in the end we must arrive at an index which is a rather crude amalgamation of different sets of local and state environments. The great bulk of literature on American party politics concludes that there are not one but fifty Democratic and Republican parties, whose span in terms of issue orientation, organizational forms, and competitiveness reaches across the spectrum of American politics for each national party. The measures suggested here, then, are clearly intended only as rough approximations, and improved indexes may be needed for more detailed analysis.

The operationalization of this hypothesis lays particular importance on the disappearance of the Populist threat to the Republican and Democratic parties in the establishment of safe seats in the House. No third-party force has arisen since the 1890s which has, in terms of Congressional voting, so disrupted the organizational coherence of the two major parties. As Durden (1965: 165 ff.) makes clear, even in the "redeemed" South, the strength of populism and its attempt to regain the franchise for the black citizen necessitated a second "redemption" in several Southern states. In this regard, the South need not be viewed as a regional exception but, rather, as an integral part of a nationwide development during this period. The declining ability of third parties to effectively challenge the party system (again at the Congressional level) in the twentieth century is thus seen as a factor increasing the tenure expectations of members of the House. This would seem to hold in spite of the basic shifts in relative strength within the two-party system during the 1930s, which, despite producing what some have termed a more competitive national system, have not hindered the continued decline of district-level competitiveness (see Schattschneider 1960; Jones 1964).

The purpose, then, of the proposed indexes of system solidification is to measure the extent to which third parties are able to compete with the two major parties or, conversely, the extent to which the two major parties are able to prevent (by whatever means) third-party development as a viable alternative to the established party system. We shall take as our indexes the percentage of minor-party vote for representatives (X_3) in each Congressional election since 1896 (the earliest date for which data are available in *Historical Statistics of the United States*) and the percentage of representatives in each Congress not affiliated with either the Democratic or the Republican party (X_4), starting with the decade of the 1880s.[3] Both indexes, averaged over each decade, show clearly the declining strength of third-party movements at the Congressional level in the last eighty years, and the percentage of minor-party representatives reflects the rise of the Populist threat in the 1880s and 1890s and its sharp decline thereafter.

The correlation analysis of these two indexes $(X_3$ and $X_4)$ with our dependent variable reveals a strong relationship between party-system stability and percentages of House members serving ten years or more (Y_4), up to six years (Y_3), and up to four years (Y_2). Weaker, and statistically not significant at the .05 level, are the correlations between indexes of two-party solidification and percentages of members serving only one term (Y_1) in the House (see table 24).

Our interpretation here might be that the "solidification of the party system" thesis does well in "explaining" the development of safe seats in areas where third parties (e.g., the Populist party in the South and in some Midwestern and Western states) might have afforded the only viable opposition, but it does not do as well in "explaining" the continued existence of marginal seats where competition between the two major parties still exists.

Once again, a look at table 22 raises doubt about the direction of causality of the hypothesized relation, since the party system, ac-

3. The rationale for starting with the 1880s is that party affiliation in periods prior to and just after the Civil War becomes too problematic for decent operationalization. Even here, the choice was made to exclude Progressive Republicans involved in the Bull Moose revolt (63d and 64th Congresses) from the category of third-party representatives but to include Progressives (9 in the 63d Congress, 3 in the 64th) as third-party members of the House.

TABLE 24. Correlation of Party-System Stability and Tenure Indexes

	Y_1	Y_2	Y_3	Y_4	N
X_3	.47	.83	.78	−.85	6
	(.176)	(.020)	(.033)	(.017)	
X_4	.54	.94	.86	−.92	9
	(.067)	(.001)	(.001)	(.001)	

Note: Figures in parentheses indicate level of significance.
X_3 = Percentage of vote for minor parties in Congressional elections since 1896.
X_4 = Percentage of House members not affiliated with the Republican or the Democratic party starting with the 1880s.
N = Number of decades for each party-system variable.

cording to Schattschneider and Durden, among many others, entered a period of intense challenge in the late 1880s and 1890s. It may be that the party system was aided in its solidification through the ability of incumbents, still primarily from the two major parties, to gain reelection, even if at the same time this meant, as has been pointed out, a drastic decline in interparty competition at the district level. Contrary to the opinions of some (Burnham 1965), who perceive the development of the present party alignments as active manipulation of the electoral system emanating from the party organizations (i.e., viewing the party machine or leadership as the exogenous variable), one may argue that, from the temporal sequence of two trends—one toward greater tenure in office and one toward stabilization of the present two-party system—the stability of party alignments may depend on environmental variables rather than on any manipulative ability the party system possesses and undoubtedly does *try* to utilize.

Analysis of Hypotheses—Frontier Thesis

If one defines a frontier as an area in which heavy immigration from outside accounts for a large increase in population, with little or no outmigration, then one can take as an index of "frontierness" the change in population from one period to another. The rationale for this operationalization shall be that a more rapidly growing population creates a whole series of problems for the representative seeking reelection. In a rapidly growing constituency, the representative is likely to be faced with a changing configuration of interests reflecting an increasingly diverse and complex social structure. In such an environment, the representation function becomes more difficult in terms of adaptation to constituency desires, whether in terms of issues, personality, party affiliation, or other identification factors. Conversely, in a more stable population, members of Congress, once elected, can, so to speak, grow old in office with their electoral coalition (see Snowiss 1966). The presumption is that in postfrontier America such rapid changes in constituency makeup, despite some still notable internal migrations, have decreased. By this standard, areas (states) with larger population increases for a certain time period (decade) are ranked higher on an index of frontierness, and areas with a more stable population or with population decline are at the lower end of the scale. For purposes of testing the frontier hypothesis, we shall look at our index of frontierness (X_5) for the United States as a whole and for the states of Kentucky, Texas, California, and Massachusetts. These four states were chosen in the belief, a priori, that three of them (Kentucky, Texas, and California) were at one time frontier areas within the context of the whole republic, whereas Massachusetts, presumably a more settled and stable society even at the time of the first Congress, could act as a control group at the state level.[4]

The correlation matrix in table 25 shows the greatest strength of relationship for the United States as a whole, with our index of frontierness doing progressively better in explaining percentages of longer terms of House service. At the state level, only the correlations for Texas and our control state of Massachusetts approach the nationwide levels of correlation, and for Kentucky there seems to be little or no relationship at all between population growth rates and length of tenure for that state's House delegation.

The case of California is interesting in that only in the 1960s and 1970s is California losing its status as a new frontier of settlement and heavy immigration. Unfortunately, the tenure expectations for the group of California representatives newly elected in the Eighty-seventh through Ninetieth Congresses are far from complete, but if

4. One of the findings of this research is that absolute rates of population growth clearly misjudge the turnover in population in such states as Massachusetts in the historical context. One has only to read the names of representatives from that state around the turn of the century and note the departure of the Crowninshields and Adamses, replaced by the Fitzgeralds, Kellihers, and Connerys, to understand the extent of Irish immigration and Yankee outmigration from particular districts.

TABLE 25. Correlation of Frontier and Tenure Indexes

	Y_1	Y_2	Y_3	Y_4	N
National sample					
X_5	.59	.59	.68	−.72	18
	(.005)	(.005)	(.001)	(.001)	
Massachusetts					
X_5			.53	−.59	18
			(.015)	(.006)	
Kentucky					
X_5			.15	−.08	18
			(.280)	(.381)	
Texas					
X_5			.60	−.59	11
			(.019)	(.021)	
California					
X_5			.38	−.37	11
			(.112)	(.119)	

Note: Figures in parentheses indicate level of significance.
X_5 = Rate of population change by decades.
N = Number of decades for each frontier variable.

we look at just the newly elected members of the House from California in the Eighty-seventh and Eighty-eighth Congresses, who have had the opportunity of holding office for (up to 1972) ten years, nearly 70% (11 of 16) have achieved ten years of service, and 75% are still members of the Ninety-second Congress. It would seem that the California delegation, as the state loses its frontier status, is developing tenure expectations similar to other states and to the nationwide pattern.

If we turn from the correlation matrix to the temporal sequence in population and tenure trends, nationwide, the decline in population growth rates began during the Civil War, when the growth rate first dropped below the 30% level. The steady declining trend continues through the 1960s, with minor aberrations caused by the Great Depression and the post-World War II baby boom. Since the upward trend in tenure does not appear until the 1880s, it is plausible, from the temporal sequence of events, to regard population growth as the causal variable.

At the state level, however, it would appear that for the state of Kentucky, in particular, the frontier thesis does not hold. From a perusal of tenure patterns of states in the nationwide sample just after entry into the union, with an admittedly small number of cases, we may nevertheless venture the guess that in some states, at the time of statehood, "first families" dominated the political scene and, despite a rapidly growing and thus unstable electoral base, could gain reelection with somewhat greater ease, relying on their reputation. The same may hold in part for the revolutionary political leadership in its ability to gain reelection, if desired, to the House in the first decade of Congresses. Alternatively, we may be faced here with an ecological fallacy, namely, that certain *districts* in a state with a rapidly growing population may still have a relatively stable electorate and that it may be these districts in which turnover is lower.

Analysis of Hypotheses—Communications Thesis

Several scholars of the House have touched on the communications thesis. Price (1965: 48–49), for example, mentions the role of radio and television, of mobile trailer offices, and of airplane travel in enabling representatives to communicate effectively with their constituents. Bailey (1970: 4–11), in his description of the advantages of the incumbent, includes a section covering the various modes of communication open to members of Congress. Stokes and Miller (1971: 14–18), in their study of the saliency of Congressional candidates, demonstrate the tremendous advantage to a candidate of being known and point out the greater exposure possibilities for incumbents through radio and television. A general communications thesis would include radio and television, the earlier development of a nationwide railroad passenger service, and automobile travel, besides the most recent introduction of civil air transportation. Each new mode of communication and their combination over time should, according to this thesis, increase the tenure of members of Congress.

The number of possible indexes available to test a communications thesis of House tenure is probably unlimited, but for now we shall limit our research to indexes which attempt to measure the development of three modes of transportation (railroad, automobile, and airplane) and two modes of mass communication (radio and television). There is, for each of these five variables, a wide choice of available statistics to reflect the introduction of each technological advance, and most are highly intercorrelated. For the development of the railroad system (X_6), we have taken the railroad-track mileage operated; for the introduction of the automobile (X_7), the number of auto registrations; for the development of commercial air passenger service (X_8), the air revenue passenger mileage; and, for the development of radio as a mass communications system (X_9), the number of radios in the United States. The introduction of television as a communications medium (X_{10}) was so rapid that, within the decade of the 1950s, the overwhelming majority of households had access to a television set, if not actual ownership of one. Therefore, X_{10} is posited as a dichotomous dummy variable, with a value of zero for the pre-1950 era and a value of one for the 1950s and 1960s. Finally, a composite index (X_{11}), reflecting the addition of each new mode of communication as an important capability for representatives, was formed on the assumption that these new capabilities have had an additive effect in increasing the ability of the House member to pursue a career in the House. The further assumption was made that each development would be treated as equally important—obviously a crude assumption but one which allows us to test the overall communications hypothesis at the level of bivariate analysis.

As our correlation matrices for the national sample and for our four state delegations show (see table 26), there is considerable variation from state to state in strength of correlation for each mode of communication, as well as for our composite index. In general, our indexes do better in explaining percentages of career House members, and in general our composite index does better than any single component. A notable exception is Texas, where the index of railroad development has much greater strength than any other component and is also higher in correlation than the composite index. Railroad development (X_6) is most highly correlated with tenure for Texas and California, the two states most distant from Washington, which seems to support the notion of our communications hypothesis. And the composite index (X_{11}) also does best when applied to the most distant state, California. On the other hand, our correlations for the state of Massachusetts are also very high, with automobile travel (X_7) most closely associated among the individual indexes. Also of some interest are the lower levels of correlation of

TABLE 26. Correlation of Communications and Tenure Indexes

National sample (N = 18)

	Y_1	Y_2	Y_3	Y_4
X_6	−.61	−.67	−.77	.80
	(.003)	(.001)	(.001)	(.001)
X_7	−.62	−.70	−.78	.78
	(.003)	(.001)	(.001)	(.001)
X_8	−.53	−.53	−.65	.60
	(.012)	(.011)	(.002)	(.004)
X_9	−.57	−.67	−.78	.77
	(.006)	(.001)	(.001)	(.001)
X_{10}	−.57	−.59	−.75	.68
	(.007)	(.005)	(.001)	(.001)
X_{11}	−.66	−.75	−.85	.87
	(.002)	(.001)	(.001)	(.001)

	Massachusetts (N = 18)		Kentucky (N = 18)		Texas (N = 11)		California (N = 11)	
	Y_3	Y_4	Y_3	Y_4	Y_3	Y_4	Y_3	Y_4
X_6	−.75	.76	−.70	.68	−.88	.85	−.87	.84
	(.001)	(.001)	(.001)	(.001)	(.001)	(.001)	(.001)	(.001)
X_7	−.85	.90	−.52	.60	−.63	.54	−.81	.86
	(.001)	(.001)	(.017)	(.005)	(.018)	(.043)	(.001)	(.001)
X_8	−.69	.75	−.45	.58	−.41	.43	−.66	.67
	(.001)	(.001)	(.036)	(.007)	(.107)	(.095)	(.013)	(.012)
X_9	−.82	.87	−.43	.55	−.57	.44	−.74	.78
	(.001)	(.001)	(.042)	(.011)	(.035)	(.088)	(.005)	(.002)
X_{10}	−.62	.68	−.46	.58	−.34	.42	−.61	.61
	(.004)	(.001)	(.032)	(.007)	(.154)	(.099)	(.024)	(.023)
X_{11}	−.87	.91	−.68	.72	−.83	.76	−.93	.96
	(.001)	(.001)	(.001)	(.001)	(.001)	(.003)	(.001)	(.001)

Note: Figures in parentheses indicate level of significance.

radio (X_9) and television (X_{10}) for Kentucky and Texas, when compared to the nationwide sample for California and Massachusetts.

Many questions are raised by an examination of the communications thesis. What are the differential effects which various technological innovations have had in different regions of the nation? Have radio and television played a more important role for House members in states like Massachusetts and California, as opposed perhaps to Southern or border states of the Civil War Confederacy, and why? We can also pose some further speculative questions. Will, for example, the deterioration of rail passenger service have any effect on the transportation capabilities of House members from certain districts (e.g., rural districts without regular or nearby air passenger service), or has the need for some mode of passenger service, enabling more frequent and less tiring trips to and from Washington, been effectively superseded by the development of long-distance modes of mass communication?

These questions cannot be answered in the context of our data, however. The communications variables we have chosen can serve only to confirm the general notion that there does exist a high correlation between the advances made in the area of communications technology in the past century and the development of longer tenure patterns for House members.

Analysis of Hypotheses—Partial Correlation

In addition to testing each of our hypotheses individually through bivariate correlation and examination of the temporal sequence of events, we can also, without going so far as to offer a causal model for House tenure, develop a series of partial correlations which will test the strength of each hypothesis, controlling for the effects of other variables. Our original hypotheses still maintain a high correlation level, and we can be more sure that our original correlations were not just examples of spurious correlation, at least with respect to the controlled variables.[5]

Unfortunately, data limitations on certain variables restrict our ability to use partial correlation analysis to the fullest. First, the interval scale index of seniority goes back only to the 1880s, so that in order to cover the period prior to 1880 we must use the less exact dummy variable for seniority. Second, both indexes of stability of the two-party system are limited in their timespan; the best we can do is to use percentage of third-party representatives, and this carries our data coverage back only to 1880. This means that our third-order partials, covering only nine decades for our national sample, will

5. An attempt to present a causal model of tenure in the House would be completely inappropriate here, since we are testing individual hypotheses and have not developed any theory linking these hypotheses, and since I am sure that there is no clear unidirectional and temporal sequence of causality necessary for such an attempt. We can of course never be sure that spurious correlation is not present, since there may always be outside variables which we have not taken into account.

omit analysis of the pre-1880 era.[6] It also means that the zero-order correlations from which the third-order partials are calculated will in general be different from the Pearsonian correlations used in our bivariate analysis of our four hypotheses. One way to get around this limitation for partial correlation analysis of the seniority, frontier, and communications theses is to omit the party-system solidification thesis and calculate second-order partials, for which the data will span all eighteen decades.

Finally, for each of our four state delegations, second-order partials can also be analyzed, since we have individual state indexes for our frontier thesis, and we can assume that our nationwide indexes for mode of communications and seniority hold at the state level as well. We could not make the assumption that the index of party-system stability is equally distributed over the fifty states, so we are more or less forced to drop that index from consideration for partial correlation analysis for Massachusetts, Texas, Kentucky, and California.

The seniority thesis comes off very poorly in the second- and third-order partial analyses of the national sample. For all indexes of tenure, the level of strength of relationship indicated by the partial correlation coefficient, controlling for the effects of other theses, declines to insignificance or reverses the direction of the originally posited relationship. This would indicate that seniority accounts for little or nothing of the variance which could not be accounted for by other hypotheses, and this is confirmed at the state level through examination of the second-order partials between tenure indexes and seniority. For Massachusetts, Texas, and California, the strength of the seniority thesis is statistically insignificant and at a level which would in any case account for generally less than 10% of the remaining variance (the only exception being the second-order partial of seniority with tenure of ten years or more in the House). Only for the Kentucky delegation does the seniority thesis continue to be both statistically significant (at about the .1 level) and at a level which would account for somewhat more than 10% of the remaining variance for both state indexes of tenure (−.32 and .36).

The frontier thesis fares even worse than the seniority thesis when analyzed through partial correlation. At the national level, for

6. With only four degrees of freedom for third-order partials, levels of significance will suffer even for rather high third-order correlations. Using the SPSS PARTIAL CORR routine as installed at the Syracuse University Computing Center, any data pairs with one or more missing items are omitted entirely from calculation of partials.

both second- and third-order partials, even the direction of the relationship remains seemingly random. However, the third-order partials do not afford a very good test of the frontier thesis, since the data on which they are based do not include the period prior to 1880, and thus they do not reflect the great decline in rates of population growth from averages of 35 to 36% per decade, covering the first half of the nineteenth century, but the rather more uneven pattern of population change from levels of 21 to 25% in the last three decades of the 1800s. This is reflected in the much weaker zero-order correlations used for calculations of third-order partials compared to the zero-order correlations used for the second-order calculations. However, even if we restrict ourselves to the second-order partials, it is clear that the frontier thesis cannot account for any substantial portion of the variance unaccounted for by the seniority and communications thesis.

Once again, at the state level, the second-order partials confirm this judgment, with a slight exception for Texas, for which the frontier thesis is at least near the border of substantive if not statistical significance. It may be that the operationalization of the frontier thesis has been poor, that we must construct other indexes of population instability, which would include the effects of internal migration and the total of in- and outmigration, at both the state and national levels. The simple frontierness measure of rate of population change, however, does not add to our ability to account for variance in tenure expectations.

Alternative operationalizations of this thesis might attempt to measure total turnover, that is, in- and outmigration, births and deaths, as an improved indicator of population stability/instability. The problems of making such estimates over any extended period of time, even for a few urban areas, are well documented by scholars from many disciplines. Excellent work by Thernstrom (1969, 1970) and Knights (1969) on residential mobility and persistence patterns has shown the possibility that total population turnover was as great for both small and large urban areas of the East and Midwest as for the newly settled areas of the West in nineteenth-century America. This is a field in which large gaps in our knowledge still exist, however, and in which the range of estimate and speculation is still rather broad.

Two theses emerge from this analysis relatively unscathed and in fact strengthened. Nationwide, for all measures of tenure and for both orders of partial correlation, the communications thesis remains strong, able to account for up to 94% of the remaining variance and statistically significant in all cases. Taken by states, the communications thesis would seem to be vindicated by the examples of Massachusetts and California but somewhat weakened by the results for Texas and Kentucky. Even for the Texas and Kentucky data, however, the partials are still in the direction of the originally posited relationship, although they are much lower in magnitude and statistically insignificant.

Even with the limitations in terms of timespan covered by the index for solidification of the party system, the original thesis would seem to be strengthened through the related third-order partials, which remain high and maintain their statistical significance. The party-system hypothesis, as operationalized here, can account for most of the remaining variance, controlling for all other theses.

We had stated earlier the objection to using the index of party-system solidification at the state level, since this would entail the assumption that the development of the two-party system proceeded evenly throughout the United States during each time period. Nevertheless, in order to provide perhaps some further evidence on the party-system thesis, the calculations of third-order partials for each state were made. For Massachusetts and Kentucky, it was not possible to include data on tenure for newly elected members of the House for the 1960s, and therefore all third-order partials are automatically statistically insignificant with such a limited data base. For Texas and California, however, very high partials can achieve statistical significance.

The third-order partials at the state level present a variety of patterns. For Texas, the original thesis would seem to be sustained by the high (.71 and −.60) partials, both significant at about the .1 level. The Massachusetts data show a decline in the levels of third-order partials (to .59 and .50), and there is no possibility of statistical significance, while for California the partial for the index of tenure up to six years, weakened from the level of the original zero-order relationship (down from .88 to .53), is still close to being significant. Only for the Kentucky delegation does there seem to be essentially no explanatory power left to the solidification of the party-system thesis after controlling for the other three theses, but we must note that Kentucky is the unit of analysis for which, at all levels of correlation, all our theses are weakest in ability to account for tenure patterns.

The above results may do nothing more than indicate the weakness of the equal-distribution assumption under which third-order partials were calculated at the state level. That is, they may serve to confirm the common wisdom about the great variation between states in the nature and development of the present party system. They do not, at least, disconfirm or refute the results of our analysis using a national sample of representatives.

Several notes of caution are in order at this point regarding the interpretation accorded partial analysis findings. When testing the strength of a posited relationship while at the same time controlling for the effects of outside variables, we are in effect giving these outside variables a collective "first shot" at accounting for the variance in our dependent variable. We should not necessarily conclude that weak partials indicate either no relationship or a spurious zero-order relationship for a particular thesis. What we are examining is the extent to which our theses overlap, statistically, in ability to account for total variance in dependent variables.

In addition, we are not able to posit a clear time sequence and unidirectional nature of causality among our independent variables and cannot therefore carry the analysis over into causal modeling. Our partial correlations are useful primarily in the negative sense of disconfirming the strength of a particular hypothesis when the partials are near zero. On the other hand, hypotheses for which partials are high are not necessarily thereby confirmed as strong causal factors, since at higher orders of partial correlation a decreasing portion of the original variance remains to be explained.

Summary, Conclusions, and Speculations

Our analysis of tenure patterns in the House has served to develop some new aspects of a well-studied trend toward longer careers in the House. Primarily, by looking not at mean tenures, which for the period of the 1880s and 1890s show only a slight and unsteady rise (2.56 terms for the Forty-seventh Congress, 2.79 terms for the Fifty-sixth Congress), but rather at total career tenures of newly elected House members, we can see the beginnings of higher tenure in an earlier period (the 1880s) than mentioned in most theses on the causes of this development. This again illustrates the importance of how one chooses to structure the data in determining what conclusions will follow.

From this analysis, it appears that seniority should be mainly viewed not as a prime causative of higher tenure patterns but as a result and perhaps as a mutually reinforcing factor at a later date. One need not argue that the seniority system was a necessary result of longer tenure or of the phenomenon known as institutionalization (cf. Chaffey 1970). We have found that seniority cannot explain the development of higher tenure for House members if we also choose to posit alternative explanations involving environmental variables (communications technology, frontierness, the party system) external to the House. This should say something to those who would peg restructuring of the House to higher percentages of newcomers: Davidson, O'Leary and Kovenock (1966) speak of the "economy of change" in Congress as being associated with greater turnover; Hinckley (1971: 7) posits that if change comes it will be through the gradual election of new members of Congress with new views on the proper role of Congress. But what will produce greater turnover, not just on a one-shot basis as in 1964 but as a long-term development? In what factors external to the House must the reformer hope to find salvation? The present study offers several possibilities for future speculation, as well as several suggestions for further research.

First, and most significant, one should ask whether abolition of seniority would make much difference without changes in the external environment in which members of the House are chosen. Our own opinion is that it would not, even if it could be done, which in all likelihood it cannot.

Second, although the solidification of the party-system thesis held up well under analysis, it will be noted that our operationalization of the thesis was in terms of the viability of third-party organizations, not directly in terms of the viability of the organizational structures of the two major parties. Nor did we directly posit anything about the nature of the two-party competition in each district. . . . Given the undoubted increase in the percentage of safe seats in the House during this century, reformers should be (and apparently are) working to provide viable competition (either through the major parties or through third-party candidacies). This requires, of course, much work, often with little payoff, but the "cheap" solution of convincing the House to reform itself on the basis of "logic" or "intellectual acumen" does not have much prospect for success. Still, to say this is not sufficient, for the reformer must have some notion of what factors are crucial to an incumbent's reelection chances and what factors are thus crucial to changing the composition of the House.

Huntington (1965: 7) has said that crisis develops "when an institution loses its previous sources of support or fails to adapt itself to the rise of new social forces." Has the House been losing its past bases of support? Where are the new social forces which might be marshaled by potential reformers?

The frontier hypothesis, to the extent that it has any validity, would have the reformer look to areas of high immigration as a sign of a shifting electorate perhaps more open to a change in representatives. To be more useful, we might revise our index of population change to include in- and outmigration and to examine the displacement of social groupings by other groupings. This would not necessarily determine the direction of possible change, only the increased possibility for personnel change in the House. Thus, one might look to urban districts with large immigration of blacks (or simple outmigration of whites) or to Southern districts, where new registration and voting possibilities in the 1960s essentially amount to large immigration of a new electorate. One might also look to districts and states in the Southwest and Florida, which are still, in the Southwest at least, closer to the traditional image of the frontier. Finally, one might regard certain rapidly growing suburban areas as frontier possibilities. All this, however, should be done within the historical context of migration levels, for there will always be relative differences in population changes, which may or may not be large enough in absolute terms to afford an increased chance for turnover.

Clearly, however, our present operationalization of the frontier concept has proved relatively weak as an explanatory variable, and improvements in operationalization of the frontier thesis, as well as a reworking of the original thesis, would seem to be called for.

The communications thesis emerges as the strongest input into accounting for changes in tenure, substantiating what others have said about the advantages of the incumbent in this field. Insofar as our communications variable is a surrogate of the more diverse and complex phenomenon of industrialization, we should be cautious of overreliance on the communications aspect of this broader development. Our justification here rests on the purpose of this research: to state explicitly, to operationalize, and to test hypotheses relating to tenure as implicit and untested in the literature on the House of Representatives.

One might speculate, however, on the indirect effect which modern communications (especially television) may have in altering the behavior of representatives or the roles they adopt. Several scholars (e.g., Price 1965; Jones 1964; Burnham 1965; Bailey 1970) have examined the "segmental" or "provincial" attitudes of representatives or the tendency toward "localism" through self-selection out of more cosmopolitan types. This tendency has been linked to the communications process between constituency and representative, continually expanding the importance of local issues to the detriment of consideration of problems of national or international scope. If, on the other hand, McLuhan and others are correct in their "global village" speculations, then the localism of representatives may be changed through increased saliency of national and transnational events at the district level. The developments in communications technology may serve to bring the world to members of Congress without greater physical mobility on their part.

The above commentary should not exclude the possibility that entirely new developments may come into play in altering or maintaining the present role and structure of Congress, nor can we be certain that the relationships examined here will hold for future Congresses. But our speculation would be that new variables or new relationships affecting tenure (and thus the form of institutionalization of the House) would be environmental, external to the House.

CHAPTER 6

Marxist and Liberal Democratic Models of Elite Recruitment: German Parliamentary Deputies in Kaiserreich, Weimar, Third Reich, and Bonn

German political development over the last century (1871–1972) provides an extraordinary example for the application of the longitudinal seminal-case approach to elite analysis. Germany, as a modern nation-state—that is, within recent history— has experienced four distinct political systems: the monarchy (Kaiserreich) from 1871 to 1918; the unstable (centrifugal) democracy of the Weimar republic from 1919 to 1933; the Nazi dictatorship of the Third Reich from 1933 to 1945; and the (increasingly) stable (centripetal) democracy of the Federal Republic since 1949.

Here longitudinal seminal-case analysis is based on a longer timespan than was possible for use in the four-nation comparisons of part 2. Rather than comparing four political systems in a given era, this chapter is concerned with four political systems which characterize recent German experience and, more specifically, with elite transformations during and between each of these four systems.

Germany also represents a case of rapid and advanced industrial development over the last century, an economic development which contains several cyclical highs and lows for analytic purposes. From an unindustrialized, predominantly rural society at mid-nineteenth century, Germany underwent rapid industrialization during the Kaiserreich, to the point of being the leading economic power in Europe by the turn of the century. It suffered especially in the wake of defeat in World War I and in the worldwide Depression of the early thirties. Economic recovery through military rearmament under Hitler was followed again by economic ruin at the end of World War II. Finally, the postwar economic miracle (*Wirtschaftswunder*) has brought the Federal Republic to new heights of material prosperity.

Germany offers the possibility of examining the relationship of economic and state structures to political elite composition within one general political culture, even granted that that culture has undergone significant change, with significant carry-over in economic definitions, institutional structures, and elite personnel at boundary points from one system-type to another.

Class Conflict and Political Elites

Both Marxist and liberal democratic theorists are interested in the relationship between economic system and state system and, in more specific terms, between economic order and the political elite (or state elite; see Miliband 1969). Marxists in general view the role of the political elite as that of guarantor of the established economic order and the interests of the dominant social classes as a whole. They do not argue that the socially dominant class in society must rule in person (see Kautsky 1903: 13), only that the state governs in its interests. A main task of the state would seem to be to prevent the emergence of a state elite recruited from the nondominant, under capitalism, working class. Particularly under capitalism, as an unplanned economy with a multitude of individual entrepreneurs, it would be impossible for the state to act in the interests of each capitalist, since what is in the interests of one property owner is not necessarily in, and in fact must be opposed to, the interests of others. Rather, it must be the role of the state to maintain the boundary conditions, the rights of property, necessary for the survival and reproduction of the existing class order.

Liberal democratic theory, on the other hand, holds that in a contemporary development of a pluralist democracy the state acts as a neutral compromiser of social interests; that all groups, free to organize and enter the political arena, can influence the state; and that the state does not necessarily favor one set of interests, most notably business interests, over others. Obvious deviations from this norm are seen as transitory and irrational exceptions or as minor flaws which do not negate the general argument. Theorists admit that in the early stages of industrialization class conflict was mirrored in government action in favor of the new bourgeois elite, but they

argue that in mature, or postindustrial, capitalism the basis of political decision making shifts to more neutral, technocratic, or
managerial-professional grounds. This, they would argue, is in fact
the difference between the unstable newly industrialized liberal
democracy, polarized by the strain of recent transformations in economic and social structure, and the stable high-mass-consumption
societies of the post-WWII Western democracies.

Although there are a multitude of studies on backgrounds of political elites in various nations at various points in time, only a small
minority are intended as explicit tests of class-based recruitment
from either liberal democratic or Marxist models. Most have tended
to focus on such topics as revolutionary elites (e.g., Lasswell and
Lerner 1965), communist elites (Fischer 1968; Donaldson and Waller 1970), and political decision makers in general (cf. Marvick 1961;
Knight 1952; Matthews 1954). A favorite topic, though confined to
the theoretical arena of more conservative versus participatory liberal democrats, has been the debate over power elites and elite
pluralism (Mills 1956; Hunter 1963; in part Jaeggi 1969; Zapf 1965;
Dahrendorf 1967; von Beyme 1971; Dahl 1961). Cross-sectional
works (e.g., Quandt 1970) have resulted in a series of interesting if
questionable individual findings only loosely related to theoretical
perspectives.

Only in recent years have some scholars tried to integrate empirical evidence on class recruitment of political elites into explicitly
Marxist or liberal democratic theories of the state. Miliband (1969),
Domhoff (1967), and Jaeggi (1969) have most notably done this from
a Marxist or at least a Marxist-oriented perspective; from the liberal
democratic persuasion the works of Bell (1973) and Edinger et al.
(1975) and the earlier work of Molt (1963) are probably most worth
noting, among many others. These works, while of greater theoretical import, still tend to use data on elites from a single era and do
not cover the entire time system or the entire variety of state systems offered by the German case. This chapter hopes to begin filling
the gap for this one important case.

Class Polarization, Elite Recruitment, and System Stability

While disagreeing on the role of the state in capitalist development,
both Marxists and liberal democrats converge on the notion that the
most stable political order is one that is not polarized along salient

class-cleavage lines (in our case here, of course, religious, sectional, racial, and other cleavage lines may also be of relevance).

Marxist theorists in general expect elite formation to reflect the level of class polarization in economic development. They posit that (1) in periods of relative class depolarization, or low class struggle—a cyclical occurrence in capitalism—there will be less emphasis on direct rule by the socially dominant class, and the state will present itself as a neutral lawgiver above civil society (Marx 1845–46); (2) during periods of high or increasing class strife, the state must present itself more clearly as the supporter of the rights of property; (3) in extreme crisis (class balance; see Sweezy 1942; Engels 1884; Marx 1852), the capitalist class may turn political power over to a counterrevolutionary (fascist) elite of the lower middle class in order to stave off socialist revolution.

Liberal democratic theorists, on the other hand, expect (1) the state elite to reflect clearly the class strain of early industrialization in which the state forcefully intervenes in favor of capital over labor (see Bell 1973); (2) in an era of "mature," "mass-consumption," or "postindustrial" capitalism, the state elite will reflect a shift toward managerial and technocratic (knowledge as property) bases of decision making and away from worker-owner symbols of class division (Lipset 1963); (3) in extreme crisis (Great Depression, rampant nationalism), a (fascist) revolt of the petit bourgeoisie will take place against both big business and organized labor (Lipset 1963; Bell 1973).

On certain points, of course, both Marxist and liberal democratic theorists are in agreement, although it is important to note that Marxists posit recurring cycles of class polarization which will be reflected in elite recruitment, while liberal democrats assert that (in the post-WWII Western industrial democracies) capitalism has been able to permanently solve the problem of depression and knows how (Keynesian economics) to damp down the business cycle. Thus Marxists posit that state elites generally try to present themselves as nonpartisan, neutral lawgivers. It is not just during the phase of mature capitalism that managerial and professional (knowledge as property) skills are recognized as desirable attributes for state elites. In this respect, Marxist thought expects relative highs in representation of managerial-professional elite backgrounds at the most stable points: the Kaiserreich and Weimar as well as Bonn (as to the Third Reich, see below).

Another point of divergence rests with the interpretation of fascism as a state system in the development of capitalism. Without going into the question of whether fascism is an inevitable, avoidable, or contingent phenomenon in this regard (see Sweezy 1942; Lipset 1963), we may note that Marxists see in fascism the counterrevolutionary continuation of capitalism—a coalition of bigbusiness conservatism and fascist movement, with a quite heterogeneous mass base, including especially the white-collar middle class and small business–smallholder middle class. Liberal democrats in general view fascism as a reactionary antimodern revolt, as mainly the product of the petit bourgeoisie (small business owners, artisans, small farmers) squeezed by the continuing rationalization of the economy, and they emphasize especially the anticapitalist and antifinance elements of Nazi propaganda (Lipset 1963: 138–148). Thus, while recognizing the influx of other elements of the middle class into the Nazi voter following after 1928, Lipset concludes that "the ideal-typical Nazi voter in 1932 was a middle-class self-employed Protestant who lived either on a farm or in a small community, and who had previously voted for a centrist or regionalist party strongly opposed to the power and influence of big business and big labor" (1963: 148). Liberal democratic theorists, in their treatment of fascism, usually only go up to 1933 and play down the coalition of the conservative nationalist DNVP with the NSDAP, which brought Hitler to power. Also, they usually fail to draw a balance between 1920s' Nazi propaganda and the reality of the 1933 to 1945 period, in which union organizations were smashed and union leaders imprisoned, driven into exile, or killed, while business organizations and business leadership remained largely intact (Bracher 1970: 218, 330–331) (with the exception of Jewish business interests); the banking system remained privatized; and no central planning of the economy or corporate social system was ever introduced. Rather, the social-fascist "Left" of the party was bloodily purged in 1934. This is important, because while the self-employed (*Selbständige*) small entrepreneur and smallholder may be presented as simply antiprogressive or antiindustrialist elements, slowly declining in economic viability, the white-collar employee (*Angestellte*) represents a growing and quite modern element of the occupational structure.

The hypotheses to be tested below represent an initial attempt to pull together both Marxist and liberal democratic considerations on class conflict and class composition of political elites and to provide two sets of competing hypotheses for the data from four German system-types over the last century. The analysis will hopefully provide some evidence of the utility of these two theoretical orientations in accounting for the social bases of political elite recruitment. Each hypothesis predicts some basic trend in the class composition of the political elite at some point(s) in the German political and economic development. Each hypothesis is summarized as follows and is identified with either Marxist or liberal democratic theory:

H1. There will be high elite-class polarization in the early stages of industrialization (liberal democratic).

H2. There will be high elite-class polarization in points of high or increasing class conflict throughout capitalist development (Marxist).

H3. There will be low elite-class polarization in mature (postwar) capitalism (liberal democratic).

H4. There will be (relatively) low elite-class polarization at the most stable points of each political (state) system (Marxist).

H5. The fascist elite represents a revolt of the petit bourgeoisie against both big business and big labor (liberal democratic).

H6. The fascist elite represents a counterrevolution of the middle class generally against the threat of socialist revolution (Marxist).

Methodology and Data Base

We shall take as our working definition of the German political elite the membership of the national parliament (Reichstag/Bundestag), covering the last century and the periods of monarchy, Weimar republic, National Socialist dictatorship, and Bundesrepublik. This institutional definition produces a universe of 6,005 individuals who held seats some time since the foundation of modern Germany. While possessing all the problems of institutional elite definitions (see Merritt 1970: 112 ff.), it has several advantages for our purposes:[1]

1. It produces a large enough grouping to allow for subgroup and within-period change analysis. Each of the four distinct eras covered contains several Reichstag/Bundestag periods and over 1,000 deputies.

1. Since this universe of deputies also includes all those who were either elected in by-elections or were named from party lists to fill vacancies caused by death, resignation, or ejection, the totals for each party in each parliament may not (in most cases do not) exactly equal the seats won in the general election. For the Bundestag period, furthermore, Berlin deputies, as nonvoting members, were excluded from this analysis.

2. It includes opposition-party (with the exception of 1933–1945) elites as well as those affiliated with governing (*staatstragende*) parties.

3. Despite some notable changes in electoral law (1919, 1949), it offers a certain continuity in terms of party elite recruitment which spans the entire period (with the National Socialist deputies only a partial exception).

4. It is widely accepted that we can identify the party faction in each Reichstag/Bundestag with the real leadership of that party (Hunt 1964; von Beyme 1971: 84 ff.; Zapf 1965: 190; Loewenberg 1967: chap. 5).

5. The main data sources for biographic abstracts of deputies are serial publications (*Reichstag-Handbuch, Deutscher Parlaments Almanach, Kürschners Volkshandbuch*) retaining a consistent information format over the last century. This gives some confidence that deputies are coded according to a relatively uniform definition of variables and particularly that meanings of variables (here especially occupational career) will change only gradually as they change within the society but will not change due to variety or shifts in information-source formats.

In examining our working hypotheses, we shall use three basic lines of analysis:

1. Most obviously, the occupational composition of Reichstag/ Bundestag membership as it evolves over time.

2. The balance of managerial-professional occupations versus occupations directly representative of the aristocratic, capitalist, and working classes.

3. The degree of occupational/class polarization within the total party system as a reflection of congruence of competing party elites with class cleavages (with the exception of the 1933–1945 period).

Class Composition in Reichstag and Bundestag

For our analysis of class cleavages among the membership of the German national parliament, we shall rely on the occupation of deputies at the time of their entrance into that body. Although two other occupational variables were coded for each deputy (first-practiced and last-practiced occupations), our hypotheses do not relate to individual mobility but rather to recruitment of a political elite, and it is the job held at the point of elevation to deputy status

TABLE 27. Occupational Structure of Selected Reichstags and
Bundestags, 1871–1972

	Kaiserreich			Weimar		
Occupation	1871 %	1893 %	1912 %	1919 %	1924II %	19: %
Worker/employee	0	6	15	30	24	37
Landowner	9	17	12	8	11	11
Business owner	6	14	7	6	7	6
Manager-administrator (private & govt.)	15	12	15	22	26	21
Professional	22	18	31	27	27	20
Landed aristocracy	18	16	7	[b]		
Govt. aristocracy	19	6	6			
Clergy	3	6	6	3	2	1
Military/police[a]	5	3	1		1	3
Not classified	3	2	0	4	2	1

[a] During the Kaiserreich, nearly all military officers in the Reichstag were of the aristocracy.
[b] For Weimar, Third Reich, and Bonn, the small percentages of deputies with title are included under the nonaristocratic occupational categories.

which is most relevant here (but see summary of this chapter). Table 27 gives, for selected national parliaments, an overview of the transformation in occupational composition over the past century. Several points are worth noting just on the basis of these values alone.[2]

Two marginal occurrences, which do not directly relate to our working hypotheses but which are important in the overall development of German parliamentary recruitment, are (1) the gradual secularization going on mainly within the Catholic Center party and the Bavarian People's party (and, later, CDU/CSU) during Weimar and continuing into the Bundesrepublik and (2) the "remilitarization" of deputy recruitment (through DNVP and later NSDAP auspices) with the ascendancy of the Nazi party in the 1930 to 1933

2. The primary elements in each occupational grouping were: for worker/employee—skilled and unskilled workers, white-collar employees, government workers not in the higher ranks of civil service, unionists, and writers with low or only vocational education; for business owner—business executives, bankers, industrialists, factory owners, entrepreneurs, business partners; for landowner—farmers, estate owners, self-employed peasants; for managerial-administrative—government higher civil servants, party

hird Reich		Bonn		
33II	1938 %	1949 %	1961 %	1972 %
	37	49	13	15
	12	8	11	4
	10	6	8	4
	10	14	35	34
	20	18	28	38
	7			
	4	5	5	5

period, followed by the lasting "demilitarization" of the postwar period.

More basically, it is clear that at the outset of the Wilhelminian Reich, under conditions of a single-member majority electoral law (quite progressive in the opinion of many scholars; cf. Molt 1963: 49–60), the aristocracy was able to dominate the early Reichstags. Although only 18% of all deputies in 1871 were landed aristocracy, and thus direct class representatives, fully 42% were of the nobility (*Adlige*), while the industrial-commercial capitalist class was only modestly represented (6%) and the working class was represented

managers, business-commercial managers, agricultural managers; for professional—writers with higher education, publishers, lawyers, judges, teachers, doctors, engineers/architects; for landed aristocracy—estate owners with titles; for government and military aristocracy—high civil servants or military officers with titles; for clergy—Catholic and evangelical clergy; for military and police—all ranks of both bodies without titles. Those not included in these groupings were primarily retired persons whose primary occupation could not be determined, housewives, and the unemployed.

only through August Bebel of the SPD. By 1893, after two decades of intensive industrialization and urbanization, representation of the industrial-commercial capitalist class peaks at about 14%, combined nonaristocratic property-owner representation also peaks at 31%, and if we add the landed aristocracy 47% of the 1893 Reichstag deputies are drawn from the propertied classes of society. By the last prewar Reichstag, class representation on the elite level fits the description given by Engels: "the capitalists and workers are balanced against each other and equally cheated for the benefit of the impoverished Prussian cabbage Junkers" (1884: 654). The aristocracy (down to 14%), capitalists (down to 19%), and labor (up to 15%) are balanced in a manner permitting the old Reich Cartel (Conservatives, German Reich party, and National Liberals) to play off the middle-class parties (by 1912 mainly Catholic Center and Progressives) against the rising electoral vehicle of the working class, the SPD. This triad of class forces is reflected in the temporary electoral coalitions of 1907 (the Bülow Bloc of all parties except the Center against the SPD) and 1912 (National Liberals and Progressives in the first balloting, Progressives and the SPD in the runoffs), which may to some extent distort the elite data for these years (more for 1907 than for 1912) as accurate reflections of the state of class cleavages at the electoral level. (This possibility for distortion is eliminated in Weimar and the Bundesrepublik by the introduction of proportional representation electoral systems.)

We can already note some support for H1 and H2, in that with early industrialization there occurs a concomitant rise in elite recruitment, first from the capitalist class and then from the working class. It is also clear that much capitalist-worker candidate competition occurred in those districts with high urban and industrial growth and non-Catholic majorities, whereas rural (mainly East Elbian Prussian) districts or areas with predominantly Catholic populations regularly returned Conservative or Center (Polish faction in Polish Catholic areas) deputies. We should also note some support for Marxist hypothesis 4 as well, in that the most stable period of the empire (under Bismarck) also exhibited the lowest total representation of "class" elements (landed aristocracy, capitalists, and workers —33% in 1871 vs. 53% by 1893 and 41% by 1912).

The election of the 1919 National Assembly (here included as a national parliament) under a new electoral law, which effectively redistricted on the basis of population for the first time since 1871, also reflects the strength of the working class following the 1918

Revolution and the disappearance of the aristocracy as a separate bloc.[3] Of all eight national parliaments elected during Weimar, the one which served longest—from 1924 through 1928, during the period of relative stability and economic recovery—is also the one exhibiting the lowest total representation of the worker/employee class (24%) and the lowest total recruitment of deputies from the classic antagonistic occupational groupings (worker/employee and landowner/business owner) (42%). The greatest class polarization among deputies occurs in the first 1932 Reichstag (the second 1932 election shows a very slight decline) during the peak of the Great Depression (see Bracher 1970: 177–178). These data would seem to support again the Marxist hypotheses 2 and 4, relating most stable and least stable points in each political system to levels of class polarization in state elites. The Weimar period, if one considers it still a period of early capitalism (although there was some further industrialization, there was, more important, considerable *concentration* of capital both before and after 1929; see Knauerhase 1972: chap. 2), *on the whole* also supports the liberal democratic hypothesis 1.

The Third Reich period appears from table 27 as a period of high class-related recruitment of deputies within the single-party dictatorship, and, while it is true that there is high representation of both wageworkers and capitalists in all three (1933II, 1936, 1938) single-slate "elections" to the Reichstag, a finer analysis of the data is necessary to test hypotheses 5 and 6. The basis is a comparison of somewhat more refined occupational groupings among all deputies of "left" parties (SPD, USPD, KPD), "bourgeois" parties (Center, Democrats, Conservatives, Middle-Class Bloc, DNVP), and the NSDAP who held seats during the period 1919 to 1938. If we disaggregate the 36% of all Nazi deputies classified as workers/employees, we find that in fact only 14% were workers or unionists, while 17% were white-collar employees in the private sector and 6% were government employees (but not higher [*gehobene*] civil servants). This is in strong contrast to leftist-party recruitment of workers/unionists (42% of KPD/SPD deputies) and white-collar employees (only 4%) and demonstrates the heavy influx of white-collar

3. Although people with titles continued to be represented by some parties (most notably DNVP and later, to a lesser extent, NSDAP), after 1918 they are considered only according to practiced-occupation status, since the political and legal privileges of the aristocracy had been de jure, though not de facto, abolished.

employees into the Nazi elite. Additionally, it should be noted that Nazi recruitment from small business owners and artisans (6%) is only fractionally higher than similar recruitment among the bourgeois parties (5%). We may recognize that, even though NSDAP recruitment of farmers (12%) is lower than such recruitment among the middle-class parties (20%), the NSDAP group is more heavily weighted with smallholders than with well-to-do farmers (cf. Bracher 1970: 152 ff.; Heberle 1963). Representation of industrialists and bigger business is not much less (5%) than among the bourgeois parties (7%). This evidence alone tends to affirm the Marxist H6 over the liberal democratic H5. We may, however, go further in identifying those occupational groupings for which NSDAP leadership recruitment lies clearly outside the boundaries established by both left and bourgeois parties. Most noticeable on the low side are the absence of women and the almost total absence of unionists among Nazi deputies. Those vocational groupings with significantly higher representation (white-collar employees, government employees, military/police officers, teachers, doctors, and engineers, a total of 41% of all NSDAP deputies) are quite modern and are not being squeezed out of existence by big business and big labor. It is further notable that all, with the exception of doctors (only 2% in any case), are middle-status occupations and that the highest-status professions (professors, lawyers, and judges) are significantly underrepresented compared to the bourgeois parties (in fact, they are not significantly higher than among the left parties).

There is an additional finding when we disaggregate the largest single grouping (white-collar employees) of Nazi deputies back to their originally coded occupations. We·find that the overwhelming bulk of these fall into two categories: (1) sales personnel (*kaufmännische Angestellte* = 10%), still a rather broad category encompassing a wide range of job roles, and (2) bank employees (*Bankangestellte* = 3%), a relatively narrow sector of the white-collar work force. Interestingly enough, the Nazi party was essentially the *only* party to recruit any number of deputies from among bank employees (not, however, from bankers and bank directors). Of the 55 deputies (out of 4,565) from 1871 through 1938 who at one time in their careers were bank employees, 47 were NSDAP deputies. Finally, the selection of bank employees as Nazi candidates first appears in sizable numbers between the two elections of 1933, when the National Socialist one-party dictatorship is being installed. The question arises as to whether this particular group of deputies in fact represents part of the broader sociological attachment of the lower mid-

dle class to national socialism during this period or whether it represents an agreed-upon infusion intending to safeguard banking
interests at the point where the NSDAP in power is deciding what
its economic policies will be.[4] In either case, however, the closer
examination of Nazi deputies indicates far more support for the
Marxist model, as opposed to the liberal democratic model, of elite
recruitment associated with the fascist state.

For the postwar Bonn republic, we see a peak in deputy recruitment of workers/employees in the 1949 Bundestag (it should be emphasized that of this only 15% are workers and 34% white-collar
employees), followed by a rapid decline, with first skilled workers
and then white-collar employees being eliminated. This process is
accompanied in the 1950s by a slight rise in recruitment of deputies
from the capitalist class (in the heyday of the Adenauer-Erhard era).
The 1961 to 1972 period (the ascendancy of the post-Godesberg SPD
under Willy Brandt) is characterized by *continued* low representation of wage earners (in 1972 only 11% of all deputies were white-
collar employees and only 4% were skilled workers) and by the notable decline in numbers of business and farm owners. These trends
would indicate affirmation of liberal democratic hypothesis 3 (end of
ideology in mature capitalism; see chap. 7) but would lend support
to Marxist hypotheses 2 and 4. It is generally agreed that the Bundesrepublik stood on quite shaky foundations in 1949 and that its development toward democratic stability on the Anglo-American pattern reached fulfillment in the late 1960s with peaceful transfer of
government leadership to the main opposition party.[5]

Balance of Managerial-Professional "Class" Recruitment

Another way of viewing the total composition of German national
parliaments is to measure the balance between deputy recruitment

4. There is a third possible synthesis between the two offered explanations
for the sudden influx of bank employees into the NSDAP faction—namely,
certain professional associations of white-collar employees, including large
numbers of bank employees, particularly the liberal Union of Office Employees and the right nationalist German National Clerks' Association,
acted to save themselves by going over to the Nazis, and they had the blessing of corporate finance circles in doing so.

5. For a summary of social and economic conditions in the 1949 Federal Republic, which was associated especially with the early strength of right-
wing and refugee parties, see Nagle 1970: chaps. 1–2.

from occupations which directly represent the classic divisions of capitalist development (aristocracy, owners, and wageworkers) and recruitment from occupations less directly associated with the relations of production (managerial-administrative and professional-technical). While this is basically a further consolidation and summarization of the data in table 27, it perhaps relates more directly to our hypotheses as they connect class polarization and system stability. If we compute differences between elite recruitment from managerial-professional and direct "class" (nobility, capitalist, worker) occupations for each parliament (see table 28), we get an over-time index of class-polarized (negative differences) versus non-polarized (positive differences) elites. It is clear that this is not a very sophisticated index; it does not, for example, take into account the size of certain occupations, mainly the clergy, the military, and housewives, although one might include the clergy as (corporate) owners, the military as simply government administrators, and housewives as (unpaid) laborers. Additionally, there is no theoretical meaning which can be imputed to the zero point, so we cannot interpret negative differences as "instability" zones and positive differences as "stability" zones but must rely on relative changes.

Still, the technocrat-class balance among German political elites does add some support to several hypotheses. The Marxist H2 and H4 are strengthened by the cyclical movement of our balance statistic, indicating the 1870s as the most stable (nonpolarized) period for the Kaiserreich, the mid-1920s for Weimar, and the period after 1961 (increasingly) for the Bonn republic. Liberal democratic hypotheses 1 and 3 receive some support if we average our balance figures for each period (7 for the Kaiserreich, −.8 for Weimar, 19 in the Bundesrepublik), but of course this misses the cyclical trends within the first two eras of modern Germany. It must be said for the liberal democratic hypotheses, and this fits in with the main assumption of liberal democratic theory, that so far in the post-WWII era there has been no downward (i.e., class-polarizing) cycle but, rather, a steady linear depolarization.

The National Socialist period appears as one of continued high class/low technocrat elite recruitment within the single-party elite. It would seem difficult to relate our balance statistic to the level of system stability for the fascist period, since the Nazi dictatorship by most judgments was quite stable politically, unless we consider the degree of overt violence and coercion necessary to establish and maintain the system. Along these lines, we may note also (1) the maintenance of the monarchy throughout the highest period of class

TABLE 28. Balance of Managerial-Professional vs. "Class"
Recruitment into the Reichstag and Bundestag, 1871–1972

Year	M + P (%)	Class (%)	Balance (%)
1871	61	33	28
1874	55	36	19
1877	53	37	16
1878	54	39	15
1881	50	43	7
1884	47	46	1
1887	48	46	2
1890	45	49	−4
1893	39	53	−14
1898	45	46	−1
1903	45	49	−4
1907[a]	51	41	10
1912[a]	53	41	12
1919	49	43	6
1920	51	44	7
1924I	45	41	4
1924II	53	43	10
1928	47	48	−1
1930	44	50	−6
1932I	41	54	−13
1932II	40	53	−13
1933I[b]	32	58	−26
1933II	28	61	−33
1936	29	62	−33
1938	30	59	−29
1949	32	63	−31
1953	42	54	−13
1957	53	41	12
1961	63	32	31
1965	68	27	41
1969	71	24	47
1972	72	23	49

[a]In 1907 and 1912, the introduction of temporary electoral coalitions (Bülow Bloc in 1907, National Liberal and Progressive in 1912) among the Reich and middle-class parties may have skewed the balance statistic by "artificially" reducing SPD representation.
[b]Only the NSDAP deputy faction of the 1933I Reichstag is included here. KPD deputies were prohibited from ever taking their seats, and other deputies of most other parties did not serve after the "Enabling Act" vote.

polarization in the 1890s; (2) the incapacity of the Weimar system to maintain itself through greater overt force in the early 1930s; and (3) the establishment and maintenance of the Bonn system under conditions of Allied occupation in 1949. In the first and third cases, the means of overt state coercion were supportive of the system, while in the Weimar case they were decidedly not.

Class Polarization and Party System

Having examined class composition of Reichstag and Bundestag largely without regard to party system, we must ask to what degree the class divisions of each national parliament are also party boundaries within the total party system. Presumably, a party system in which elite-class divisions were more or less equally represented in the major parties would contain less class polarization at the political elite level than a system where the two divisions were congruent. Treating both occupation and party as nominal scale variables, we can calculate the degree of party-system elite polarization for selected parliaments. The first interesting feature of the data in table 29 is the general stability of the degree of polarization within all three eras of multiparty competition. That is, despite the dramatic rise of the SPD between 1871 and 1912 and the sharp decline of the National Liberals and more gradual decline of the Conservatives and the German Reich party, the degree of polarization hovers around a Pearson's C of .70 for ungrouped occupations.

There is a slight drop in elite-class polarization across party lines at the outset of the Weimar system. This is mainly due to the very strong position of the SPD faction in 1919, comprising nearly 40% of all deputies, and of the SPD/USPD factions in 1920 which, despite strong policy differences, had, not surprisingly, quite similar occupational compositions in their deputy factions. This drop from 1912 to 1919 is also related to the sudden blossoming of the new bourgeois parties and to the rapid advancement within the Center labor wing of a unionist deputy faction, with a concomitant downplaying of landed interests and professional backgrounds among non-left parties vis-à-vis the last prewar Reichstag. A cynic might note that these bourgeois-party "unionists" are a case of many chiefs with few followers and are mainly window dressing to prove, in times of working-class revolutionary potential, that workers are

TABLE 29. Correlation of
Occupation and Party
Affiliation for Selected
Reichstags and
Bundestags, 1871–1972

Year	Pearson's C
1871	.72
1881	.71
1893	.71
1903	.69
1912	.69
1919	.63
1920	.63
1924II	.68
1928	.73
1932I	.68
1949	.41
1953	.33
1957	.39
1961	.39
1965	.38
1969	.37
1972	.36

now welcome and have representatives of their interests in the middle-class parties, even the reactionary nationalist DNVP.

This minor alteration is soon offset by the entrance of the KPD into the party system as a deputy faction composed at first mainly and later (1930–1932II) overwhelmingly of workers and employees. The effect of the ascendancy of the NSDAP faction in the 1930 to 1932 period is again to marginally lower the Pearson's C, as a single party accounts for an increasing share of all seats and there is correspondingly less interparty variance to be explained.

The major realignment in the party system occurs between the pre-Depression (ca. 1928) Weimar system and the postwar Bundestag of 1949. On the Left, the consolidation of electoral strength by the SPD and the virtual (completed in 1956 with the banning of the KPD) elimination of the Communist deputy faction greatly reduce the interparty class polarization in the total party system. This is undoubtedly one of the great liberal achievements of the reconstructed German democracy, unmatched in any of the other postwar reconstructed parliamentary systems in Italy, France, and Japan. Just as important, however, is the consolidation of parties on the Right, a process already in motion in 1949 and completed by 1957. In the early years of the Bundesrepublik, interbloc depolarization is marked by greater recruitment of deputies from worker/employee occupations. This of course changes very quickly, but, as long as the transformations, at least for the two major *Volksparteien* (Social Democrats and Christian Democrats), are parallel, there is no change in the level of total elite-class polarization. In fact, with the continued consolidation of the SPD and the CDU/CSU within the party system, and with the strong tendency of *all three* parties after 1961 toward deputy recruitment from managerial-professional backgrounds, there has been at least a gradual tendency toward decline to even lower levels in party elite polarization.

These data touch upon a different aspect of elite-class polarization, one much more in agreement with our liberal democratic hypotheses 1 and 3. Here the cyclical changes in polarization evident in tables 27 and 28 are for the most part lacking in the absence of major party-system reorganization. Despite the entry and "proletarianization" of the KPD in the Weimar system, which raises the Pearson's C from .63 in 1920 to .73 in 1928, the only basic shift appears with the foundation of the more integrative Bonn party system.

This of course is reflective of a basic split between Marxist and liberal democratic theories of the state. For Marxists, the development of the stable nonpolarized Bonn party system offers no real choice (not a DM's worth of difference, etc.) without a real vanguard of the working class (a strong KPD). This is the basis for Marx's criticism in the 1870s of the bourgeoisification of the SPD and the revisionist Bernstein for wanting to advance "men of science" and "adherents from the circles of the educated and propertied classes" (quotes from Bernstein) to leadership of the SPD. Marx always considered that "the emancipation of the working class must be the work of the working class itself," that one should allow these "men of science" and property, as such, "no influence in the Party leadership" (1879).

Liberal democratic theorists argue that more and more social issues are being reduced to nonideological (or ideology of "scientism"; see Lipset 1970: 267 ff.) social management or engineering levels of debate and solution. They further argue that residual class differentials persist to form the basis for rational electoral choice among competing party elites (see chap. 7) without, however, threatening the stability of the system itself. They point to the continued growth of the "new middle class" as the mass base for moderate bourgeois parties and to the economic integration of the working class as the basis for moderate workers' parties.

A Summary and Some Comments

In many respects, the above analyses only illuminate the differing basic assumptions of Marxist and liberal democratic models of the state and state elites. It is gratifying at least that both models are shown, using various organizations of the data, to have significant relevance to the recruitment of deputies in various stages of German economic- and state-system development. That is, the most disappointing outcome would have been for the data to have shown no relationship to our hypotheses, an occurrence not so rare in political science. It should not be too surprising that those measures relating polarization of elites to integration of the party system would tend to favor our liberal democratic theses (1 and 3), while those relating polarization to elite composition as a whole favor our Marxist theses (2 and 4).

With respect to an interpretation of the fascist elite recruitment, however, the data seem to support H6 over H5 and, insofar as this is the case, the Marxist interpretation of fascism as a possible (not necessarily inevitable) stage of state and state elite development under capitalism. The recent experience of Chile should serve to remind us that this is not a dead-letter issue of only historical interest.

Some notes of caution are appropriate. One cannot necessarily extrapolate from the German case to other nations, although the findings of Lipset, Bell, and Miliband tend to parallel, for other polities, the German post-WWII data. It is hoped that further historical data bases will be utilized for more systematic comparative testing of alternative models of elite recruitment (but not via cross-sectional data analyses à la Quandt).

Additionally, we have used only two variables—occupation at point of entry into parliament and, for the aristocracy, social origin—as our indicators of social class. In a more elaborated study, we will want to combine several other variables—including education, other practiced occupations, and, more systematically, social origin—into an index of positioning on our class dimension; we will want to investigate individually the composition of the political elite along these other class variables; and we will probably want to investigate the overlapping of these class variables with other cleavages (religion, region, generation).

CHAPTER 7

Elite Recruitment and the End of Ideology: Class Transformations of Bundestag Deputies

The development of the West German political system in the post-war era is of interest to Western scholars for several reasons. The Bundesrepublik has been used as an example of the emergence of a stable, pluralist democracy (Heidenheimer 1971). Kirchheimer (1966) in particular focused on the transformation of the class-mass parties of the Weimar period to "catch-all" vote-gatering mechanisms which have developed during the postwar era. Edinger (1968) and others have paid special attention to the depolarization of class/sectarian ideology and especially to the continuing evolution of the Social Democrats away from their Marxist heritage toward a mild reformist position. A commonly noted feature of this "Americanization" (Merkl 1965) of West German politics has been the gradual elimination of smaller splinter and extremist parties, as well as the growth of the Social Democrats, culminating in a position of electoral parity with the Christian Democrats with the elections of 1969 and 1972. It is now said that the SPD and the CDU/CSU represent the basic elements of an essentially two-party system, with both major parties operating under the electoral assumptions of *Volksparteien*.

On a larger theoretical plane, the West German case represents for Lipset (1963, 1970) and Bell (1960) the facets of the "end of ideology" movement expected in all advanced Western societies. Of the four major reconstructed parliamentary systems of the postwar period (Germany, France, Italy, and Japan), the depolarization of social classes and the concomitant evolution in political behavior toward the Anglo-American model appear to Lipset furthest advanced in the Federal Republic of Germany. Baylis (1973) has characterized Germany (both West Germany and East Germany) as entering upon the postindustrial era, with West Germany serving as the "pluralist" case.

From a somewhat more critical perspective, Offe (1972) and Habermas (1973) have treated this same evolution under the general problematic of legitimacy maintenance in mature capitalism (*Spät-kapitalismus*). Much attention has been given, in all these works, to public-opinion polls, election results, and economic data to support the basic end of ideology theses. On the other hand, little in the way of systematic hypothesis testing has been done at the elite level (although many illustrative data have been produced). Our purpose here is (1) to set up some general hypotheses relevant to elite recruitment as implied in the literature on depolarization of the class conflict in the postwar West and (2) to test these hypotheses against the composition of one important segment of the West German political elite, namely Bundestag deputies, as it developed from 1949 to 1972.

Elite Composition and the End of Ideology

The substance of the thesis on the decline of class-based ideology in the industrialized West is succinctly put (and cited with approval by Lipset) by Rejai, Mason, and Beller (1968: 310–311): "It means, in simplified terms, a reduction in the amount of ideological conflict, polarization, rigidity, exclusiveness, etc., in a political system." However, Lipset (1963: 439–452) and others emphasize, in their defense of this thesis, that significant but "muted" and "institutionalized" class conflict continues. From this we might expect that composition of the political elite in a maturing industrial democracy such as the Federal Republic will likewise become less and less polarized around the traditional capitalist/wage-earner cleavage, although this cleavage would not be expected to disappear entirely. We might further expect that there would be an increase in representation of elites symbolizing the new managerial, technological, or professional expertise qualities posited as the new consensus of mature capitalism. Our first hypothesis, then, is that political elite composition should show a shift from (functional) representation of capitalists and wage earners to representation of managerial, technocratic, or expert-professional types.

It is clear that the end of ideology thesis also implies similar trends in elite composition for each of the system parties, in our case the CDU/CSU, FDP, and SPD. That is, the governing (*staatstra-*

gende) parties should experience similar shifts in elite recruitment as the values of (class) conflict are replaced by those of the new consensus. This expected trend should nevertheless still leave some residual elite profile differences relatable to their historical (class) origins. Our second hypothesis is therefore that the evolutionary pattern for the political elite as a whole (first hypothesis) also holds for each of its constituent (system party) parts.

A third proposition, derivable from the literature on changes in democratic politics in mature capitalism, is that the degree of class differentiation among sets of competing political elites should also decline, though not disappear. That is, total party-system elite differentiation should reflect over time the posited class depolarization of the society at large.

Data Base and Methodology

We have chosen the Bundestag membership for a (not the only) working definition of the West German political elite. This requires some defense, since it is argued by Gorz (1973: 73 ff.), for example, that in the Western parliamentary democracies power has inexorably shifted from the legislative to the executive branch, thus making parliamentary forms mere window dressing for a centrally run state capitalism. Gorz sees no hope for reversing this process, and thus one might argue that there is little reason for studying Bundestag deputies as examples of political leaders.

On the other hand, Loewenberg (1967: chap. 2) bases the import of his research into parliamentary recruitment on the formal institutional position of the Bundestag in the Basic Law (*Grundgesetz*) of the Federal Republic, which is the primary repository of popular sovereignty and the basis for the legitimate construction of a government.

It is not necessary to adopt this position, however, in order to support an investigation of the recruitment of Bundestag deputies by the various parties as an important method of elite formation, which is also an integral and systematic part of (though by no means the whole) the larger process of elite recruitment. It is a widely accepted (see von Beyme 1971: 84; Zapf 1965: 190; Loewenberg 1967: chap. 5) fact that election to the Bundestag is a vital step in the careers of most potential national leaders, and service in the Bundestag is a general prerequisite for higher ministerial careers.

The data to be used consist of biographical abstracts of the "who's who" variety coded from successive volumes of *Kürschners Volks-handbuch*, a total of some 1,440 deputies who served from 1949 through 1972. This also includes deputies who replaced other deputies in mid-session due to resignation, incapacity, or death, and thus the individual party totals for each Bundestag do not match precisely the balance of votes for each parliamentary faction in each Bundestag session. Berlin deputies, as nonvoting members, were excluded from the analysis.

The most commonly used variables for measuring class-cleavage lines are occupation, education, and income. Since income figures for Bundestag deputies are generally not available, the analysis below rests on the occupational and educational variables. Several words of caution and a few words of optimism are in order regarding the reliability of these data. Von Beyme (1971: 52–54) cautions us about the reliability of subjectively designated occupational categories. In particular, he notes the greater tendency of SPD deputies to designate themselves as union officials or party officials in terms of occupations during Weimar than in the Bundesrepublik, as well as the inclination of Christian Democrats or Free Democrats to use more nominal descriptions of occupational classifications (business owner, farmer) rather than those which might arouse class hatred (manufacturer, landowner). Another problem is the use of certain gross categories, such as white-collar employees (*Ange-stellte*) or government employees (*Beamte*), which enclose within their ranks whole hierarchies of income and authority.

In response to the first potential difficulty, it does not make any difference for our purposes whether a deputy chooses to call himself a businessman (*Kaufmann*) rather than an industrialist (*Fabrikant*), as long as we are able to place him generally into the category of owners. Much the same can be said for party or union officials (mostly designated as simply *Geschäftsführer*), since we are still able to locate them according to their occupational skills and executive secretary/managerial authority. As far as the problem of rather crude occupational categories is concerned, we have adopted the occupational classification scheme of Loewenberg (1971), which differentiates among white-collar employees in terms of job authority and was modified in practice to do the same for government civil-service positions. Thus, for example, although both a laboratory technician and a factory director are white-collar employees, the first would be coded as a technical-scientific employee, the latter as a commercial-industrial manager. To be sure, these are still quite oversimplified occupational groupings, since both new classifications contain substantial ranges of income and authority, but at least some attempt has been made to increase the degree of distinction in social stratification. In addition, we may combine these occupational categories with education to get a still more refined measure of socioeconomic status.

Elite Transformation by Era

We began by analyzing the composition of the entire Bundestag over the period 1949 to 1972 as a test of our first hypothesis. In terms of occupational trends among deputies, most apparent is the decline in representation of office and factory workers, which were the two largest occupational groupings in the original 1949 Bundestag. Constituting together nearly half of the first Bundestag, they account for only 15% of the 1972 parliament. Because both occupations can be defined as wageworkers, without further elaboration with respect to professional status or higher education (although some do have higher education), we shall for our analysis combine these categories as group I (wage earners).

Another trend is illustrated by the two categories immediately identifiable as owners, that is, capitalists, namely farmers (none of these are farm workers; rather, they tend to be well-to-do farm owners, who produce for the market) and business owners (ranging from small business owners to, e.g., SPD deputy Philip Rosenthal). Both categories, with some minor deviations, show increasing representation during the period 1949 to 1961 and a somewhat sharper decline during the period 1961 to 1972; they account together for 14% of the 1949 Bundestag, 19% of the 1961 Bundestag, but only 8% of the 1972 Bundestag. For purposes of our analysis, they will be treated as group II (owners).

Perhaps the most notable trend in the first several Bundestags is the increased representation of the executive secretary/general manager (*Geschäftsführer*) group, from 8% in 1949 to 26% in 1961. Since 1961, the representation of this group has remained at a fairly constant level. A rather similar trend is noticeable for industrial managers. If we group these managers with the small numbers (always less than 2%) of agricultural managers under one label, group III (managers), a sharp rise in representation in the period 1949 to 1961, from a combined 14% to 35% is followed by a relatively constant representation over the next decade, remaining at 34% in the 1972 parliament.

Still a fourth trend in representation is found among occupations classifiable as professional, that is, lawyers, judges, teachers, doctors, professors, writers, journalists, and engineers. This occupational group (group IV) includes specialized or skilled-expert job roles less directly related to the daily production and distribution process than the managerial/business executive category. Common to this professional classification is an upward trend in representation among Bundestag members, which spans the entire period of the Bundesrepublik to date. While the genêral pattern of increase for certain occupations (lawyers, teachers, writers) is less steady or pronounced than for others (judges, professors, engineers), the rise in total representation for all professionals is quite steady and notable from 1949 to 1972: group IV occupations accounted for 18% of all 1949 Bundestag members, 28% by 1961, and fully 38% by 1972. By the early 1970s, this group was numerically the modal occupational category for Bundestag members, surpassing the managers by a slight margin. This information is summarized in table 30, which gives the representation for each of our four groups in each Bundestag, as well as residual occupational categories, consisting primarily of housewives and quite small numbers of the clergy, the military, social workers, and accountants.

The main distinguishing features of the data bear out our first hypothesis and can be summarized as follows:

1. A sharp drop in representation of group I (wage earners) from numerical dominance in 1949 to relatively low levels by 1961, where representation of this group has remained.

2. A moderate but steady rise in representation of group II (owners) from 1949 to 1961, followed by a steady and somewhat more pronounced drop in representation through 1972; with representation never reaching numerically dominant figures. A note of interpretive caution should be added here. These figures do not and cannot reflect the actual or total influence of the business community and its interests within the Bundestag; they are only indications of the actual seating of occupational members of this grouping. A listing of representatives of the business community for the 1961 Bundestag by the Deutsches Industrieinstitut (not necessarily to be taken as the final word either) records a total of 49 deputies, of whom only 22 are actual owners, whereas 17 are managers and 10 professionals (mostly lawyers). While farmers, bankers, artisans, and of course owners associated with the SPD are excluded from this list, it is

TABLE 30. Grouped Occupations of Bundestag Deputies, 1949–1972

Occupation	1949 %	1953 %	1957 %	1961 %	1965 %	1969 %	1972 %
Wage earner	49	40	25	13	13	13	15
Owner	14	14	16	19	14	11	8
Manager	14	21	28	35	39	38	34
Professional	18	21	25	28	29	33	38
Other	5	6	5	5	4	6	5

clear that the *interests* of the business community are associated not just with deputies who are themselves owners but mostly with managers and professionals close to business (see Braunthal 1965: 361–363).

3. A rapid rise in representation of group III (managers) from 1949 through 1965 (although a *rapid* rise in representation ends in 1961), followed by continuing high but slightly declining representation at something greater than one-third of all Bundestag members. Group III is the modal occupational group from 1957 through 1969.

4. A quite steady and somewhat less dramatic rise in representation of group IV (professionals) throughout, with this group achieving modal occupational status among Bundestag members in 1972.

Educational background of Bundestag members can be summarized as follows:

1. The rapid disappearance of those with only lower (*Volksschule*) or middle (*Realschule, Mittelschule*) levels of formal education, a trend completed by 1961 (down from 29% to 2%).

2. The rise in representation of those with some form of vocational education but without the *Abitur* (gymnasium diploma) from 1949 to 1961, followed by a gradual decline up to the 1972 Bundestag (12%).

3. The steady (with the exception of 1949–1953) rise in representation of those with the *Abitur* and higher (*Technische Hochschule, Universität*) levels of educational achievement, from a position of early numerical (60%) dominance to one of near-monopoly by 1972.

Already we may begin to select out two basic periods (1949–1961 and 1961–1972) of occupational and educational transformation of Bundestag members for further consideration in our analysis. We may note that these periods coincide on the one hand with the era of Adenauer's leadership of the CDU/CSU and the West German government, a time of electoral consolidation of the position of the Christian Democrats and their allies (FDP, German party, League of Refugees and Expelled party) over the SPD; and, on the other hand, with the era of Brandt's leadership of the SPD and his steady rise to governmental power (with the FDP as coalition ally), a period moreover of electoral stagnation and slight decline for the CDU/CSU.

Transformation by Party

We might expect that significant differences would exist among the Bundestag parties with respect to occupational and educational experiences of their factions, particularly between the middle-class parties (CDU/CSU and FDP) and the electoral choice of most workers (SPD). And, indeed, a longitudinal analysis of each faction by occupation and education does point out several distinctive features.

For the bourgeois parties, representation of group II (owners) grows to quite considerable proportions during the period of Adenauer's chancellorship, peaking at more than one-fourth of all Christian Democrats in 1961 and at fully two-fifths of all Free Democrats in 1957. During this period, the FDP was little more than a right-of-center appendage (*Anhängsel*) of the CDU/CSU, and it is clear that throughout this period the Free Democrats put up candidates for office who most clearly represented the interests of the property-owning class. While the numbers are still quite small, it may be of some interest that during this period representation of group II rises slightly even for the SPD, indicating the general trend of that era. However, the most notable feature of the SPD faction here is that the level of representation of group II never exceeds insignificant proportions. If there is any remarkable difference between the occupational composition within the bourgeois bloc and within the SPD, it is this difference.

Although the SPD faction is originally composed predominantly (nearly three-fifths) of wage earners, nearly two-fifths of whom are skilled workers, this undergoes a twofold transformation over the years. The first stage occurs from 1949 to 1953, so that the proportion of skilled workers in the SPD faction drops from nearly two-fifths to less than one-sixth. The total representation of group I also drops, but by a far smaller percentage. Within the general decrease in group I across all parties, there is a simultaneous shift from skilled workers to white-collar workers (*Angestellte*). *After* 1953, the decline in representation of group I among deputies for all parties affects white-collar employees generally more than skilled workers, who had already been reduced to minimal proportions in the first phase of group I transformation. Although there is a significant difference of 20% between the SPD and the CDU/CSU–FDP in group I as of 1949, there is little difference by 1972 although the vestigial traces of skilled-worker representation are still greater for the Social Democrats. Recalling our end of ideology theses about class depolarization, we may note that in the Bundesrepublik the wage-earner component is eliminated *first* from functional representation in the political elite, and within this group the skilled worker is eliminated from the process of elite recruitment before the white-collar employee. This is clearest within the electoral party of the working class, occurring far in advance of its becoming an equal contender for national power. Only in the second period of elite development is the direct representation of group II among the bourgeois parties also reduced.

The replacements for these two groups of occupational backgrounds seem to develop along rather similar lines for all three parties. In all party factions, the rise in representation of group III (managers) peaks in 1965, in the general area of 40%, and then begins to decline somewhat. The rise in representation of group IV (professionals) proceeds at somewhat different rates for each party, being more gradual and spread out for the CDU/CSU, more concentrated (1949–1957 and 1965–1972) for the SPD, and most pronounced and concentrated (reaching nearly 50% by 1972) for the FDP. It would seem, however, that the development of these groups also proceeds in two stages: first, the influx of managerial skills to a given plateau, which may now be slowly eroding, and, second, the influx of professional expertise, which may not yet have hit its peak but which has already become the modal group for all three parties.

In terms of educational background, the general pattern is similar for all three parties, with the percentages of those with only lower or middle educational attainments steadily dropping throughout the Adenauer period to minimal levels, where they have remained up to the present. During the Adenauer years, the numbers of those with some form of vocational apprenticeship, but without the *Abitur*, increase steadily, most notably in the SPD, where by 1961 they account for two-fifths of all deputies. This apparently represents the generation of those whose earlier chances for formal higher education were hindered by the Third Reich, the war, and the hardships of the immediate postwar years, those who were obliged to transfer their ambitions to more practical vocational apprenticeships. To a considerable extent, within the SPD ranks, this also represents the trade-unionist grouping, consisting of those skilled workers who have risen in German politics through the union movement. During the 1960s, the percentages of those with vocational training at the highest level of education decline steadily. The Bundestag, as noted earlier, has always been characterized by those with high formal education, but there have been significant differences among the three parties. The party which has most clearly represented the middle class and only the middle class—the Free Democrats—has overwhelmingly recruited, from the earliest years, men and women whose formal educational attainment has been high. The CDU/CSU, the early image of the *Volkspartei*, was at least somewhat less overwhelming in its selection of candidates with higher educational backgrounds, although it is notable that over the years the CDU/CSU has narrowed the gap with the FDP, so that by 1972 the educational profiles of both parties are very similar. The SPD, in the first several Bundestags, was the only party of the three in which those with higher education were not the majority of the party faction.[1] The general trend for the SPD is still characterized—except for the 1953 Bundestag, which seems an anomaly for all three parties in this sense—by a steady influx of deputies with high educational achievement. While there still exist some relative differences between the SPD and the bourgeois parties as of 1972, with regard to educational background of deputies, it is clear that the workers' party is predominantly led by women and men who possess higher degrees.

In terms of transformation by party factions, we may also combine occupation and education into a more general measure of socioeconomic status (SES) to see how each party has shifted its valued qualities in terms of overall social prestige. We have ranked occupational categories according to the scheme given by Claessens, Klönne, and Tschoepe (1965: 258–268), producing a five-point ordinal scale. This scale remains quite stable over the period 1949 to

1. We might note that KPD deputies in the first Bundestag were predominantly of low or vocational levels of formal schooling, again illustrating the differences between the Bonn and Weimar systems relatable to the postwar defeat and suppression of the KPD.

1972.[2] To this occupational scale we shall add the scores from a five-point educational scale, combining technical institute and university educations into a single category and the *Abitur* with and without vocational apprenticeship into a single category. This gives a nine-point SES scale ranging from those (rank 1) with university educations and high-prestige jobs (lawyer, physician, professor, judge, top management) to those (rank 9) with only elementary-school educations and low-prestige jobs (unskilled laborer). Average SES scores for each Bundestag as a whole (which also includes minor-party deputies) and for each of the three main parties are given in table 31. The percentage with highest SES rank (1) and the percentage with lower SES scores (5–9) are given for each party faction in each Bundestag in table 32.

From these data it is apparent that, for all three parties, higher deputy status has characterized each succeeding Bundestag and, with only one minor exception, each succeeding party faction (the exception being the FDP between 1969 and 1972). For the middle-class parties, the greatest rise in deputy SES occurs during the Adenauer years, with the greatest between-session increases occurring between 1953 and the Adenauer landslide of 1957 (+.64 increase for the CDU/CSU, .54 for the FDP). For the Social Democrats, the greatest single increase occurs after the elevation of Brandt to top party leadership and the passage of the Godesberg program, when average SES for SPD deputies goes from 3.77 to 3.14, an increase of .63 in four years.[3] The SES differential between the SPD and its main rival, the CDU/CSU, which increased between 1949 and 1957 (note: before Godesberg), has generally narrowed since then until it is now at its lowest point in Bundestag history. The same pattern holds for the SPD-FDP deputy SES differentials. This general trend of development is reflected in the rising percentages of party deputies who rank highest (1) on the SES scale and the decreasing percentages of those who rank in the bottom half on the SES

2. For other similar rankings of occupational categories, which would have arrived at essentially similar results, see Moore and Kleining 1960: 86–119; Inkeles and Rossi 1956: 336; Dahrendorf 1959: chap. 6; and Janowitz 1958. For evidence on the stability, both over time and cross-nationality, and the invariability of occupational prestige scales, see Hodge, Siegel, and Rossi 1966.
3. For a good commentary on the value shifts in elite recruitment by the Social Democrats after the adoption of the Godesberg program, see Schellenger 1969 and Edinger 1968: 259–266.

TABLE 31. Average SES of Bundestag and Party Factions

Bundestag	SES	SES SPD	SES CDU	SES FDP
		Faction social status		
1949	3.76	4.24	3.53	3.00
1953	3.53	3.97	3.36	2.97
1957	3.04	3.77	2.72	2.43
1961	2.62	3.14	2.37	2.13
1965	2.49	3.07	2.10	2.04
1969	2.36	2.76	2.06	1.86
1972	2.16	2.40	1.96	1.96

scale (5–9). All this generally supports our second hypothesis of similar trends for all system parties.

Transformation by Party Age Cohort

One characteristic which differentiates Bonn from Weimar, and thus a successful pluralistic democracy from the centrifugal crisis-ridden parliamentary system of the first republic, is the ability of the system-supportive parties to recruit and promote younger cadres within the party ranks. Although there was some aging of Bundestag members during the Adenauer period, this has been more than reversed during the Brandt ascendance. The transformations along occupational and educational lines for each party are to a great degree

TABLE 32. SES of Party Deputies

Bundestag	% of party faction with highest SES ranking (1)			% of party faction with lower SES rankings (5–9)		
	SPD	CDU	FDP	SPD	CDU	FDP
1949	22.4	26.0	29.5	48.6	31.5	18.2
1953	25.0	28.5	37.1	45.3	30.7	25.7
1957	29.8	40.4	38.1	32.3	18.5	11.9
1961	34.1	44.3	49.2	19.9	12.6	8.2
1965	35.2	51.7	51.1	18.9	8.8	6.6
1969	42.4	53.7	50.0	15.2	7.8	0.0
1972	39.3	55.3	50.0	11.9	7.8	4.5

TABLE 33. Occupational Background by Party Age Cohort

Occupation	Monarchy %	Weimar %	Third Reich %	Bonn %
CDU/CSU				
I	45	21	16	17
II	22	21	22	7
III	15	26	27	36
IV	10	27	27	36
Other	8	4	8	4
SPD				
I	69	40	21	16
II	1	3	2	1
III	11	28	40	33
IV	19	19	27	45
Other	0	9	10	6
FDP				
I	28	21	10	11
II	44	27	26	11
III	13	21	29	15
IV	9	25	29	59
Other	6	6	3	4

I = Worker.
II = Property Owner.
III = Manager.
IV = Professional.

mirrored in the changes in generational profiles for each party age cohort. If we designate age cohorts in terms of the political era in which a deputy reaches maturity (age 21), we can summarize the generational development of the leadership of each party and, presumably, the qualities it most prizes in its elite recruitment processes. Table 33 gives a breakdown of occupations for all 1,440 deputies from 1949 to 1972 according to the period in which each deputy grew up.

Representation of group I, which accounts for about half (45%) of the generation of CDU/CSU deputies maturing under the Kaiserreich (pre-1918), drops to modest levels for each of the three succeeding generations. Only the earliest generation of Christian Democrats could be said to contain significant percentages of wage earners in the political leadership of this classic *Volkspartei*. With respect to the SPD, this decrease in representation of group I is more gradual from generation to generation, reflecting in part the continuing evolutionary pattern of the SPD away from its working-class origins, and one would suspect also that this reflects the more limited opening up of educational opportunities for those of working-class origin. While the process is more gradual for the SPD, it arrives by the fourth generation (those maturing after the fall of the Third Reich) at the same end point: the latest generation of Social Democratic deputies is recruited from wage earners in about the same degree as for the CDU/CSU (or the FDP for that matter).

With respect to group II, the representation level remains fairly constant for the CDU/CSU (somewhat above 20%) until the latest generation (the one which began to enter the Bundestag in large numbers in the 1960s), when it falls off sharply. It is not clear whether this represents a response of the CDU/CSU to the electoral success of the Social Democrats or an increasing disinterest or abstinence of owners from direct candidature in the face of a CDU/SPD and then an SPD/FDP left-liberal coalition. Likewise, the Free Democrats, as the party which has shown the sharpest social profiles at various points, have decreased their recruitment of deputies from the owner class among the youngest postwar generation.

In the transition from groups I and II to groups III and IV, it would appear that the Social Democrats drew very heavily on managerial occupations from that age cohort which matured during the Third Reich, quite significantly more than was the case for either of the middle-class parties. This was followed, however, by a shift in the postwar age cohort to an even greater emphasis (45%) on the professions as a source of candidates. This shift in emphasis coincides with an even more dramatic break in the tradition of the Free Democrats, who shift from recruitment of owners and managers (nearly 55% in the Third Reich generation) to predominant recruitment of professionals (nearly 60%) from the postwar age cohort. The Christian Democrats, while increasing the influx of both managers and professionals into their faction from the third to the fourth Bundestag age cohort, at the expense of the owner category, have not chosen to build their leadership on the bases of professionalism to nearly the same degree as have the parties of the governing left-liberal coalition. In some sense we might view the transformation in elite recruitment of the FDP as a transition from its earlier alliance or satellite status vis-à-vis the Christian Democrats to a status befitting its new coalition partnership. If the FDP surpassed the CDU/CSU in the recruitment of deputies from property owners in the Adenauer years, in the 1970s it is even more pronounced than the SPD in its recruitment of professionals.

What is striking with respect to generational shifts in educational background of deputies is that, within the overall rise from generation to generation in proportions of those with higher education, there is, from the third to the fourth age cohorts, a sharp rise in the proportions of those with a university education, as opposed to those merely holding an *Abitur* with or without vocational apprenticeship or those having attended a technical institute. Here again the most recent trend to professionalism as the desired occupational experience for Bundestag deputies is reflected in the rise from 54% to 69% of those with university educations from the third to the fourth age cohorts for the CDU/CSU, from 34% to 53% for the SPD, and from 45% to 75% for the FDP. The earlier trend toward technical educations for deputies, which peaked during the third generation at levels between 15 and 20% of all deputies from the third age cohort, falls to between 7 and 12% for the youngest generation of deputies. If the present trend continues, the Bundestag membership will soon be drawn almost entirely from the highly educated and, moreover, the university educated.

It would thus appear that the trends expected by our second hypothesis are most clearly visible for each party in the influx of younger deputies. That is, the value changes reflected in elite composition are strongly related to generational turnover.

Tenure Differentials

The valued qualities for elite recruitment may be viewed in another form, namely, the tenure which deputies of varying occupational and educational backgrounds have held in the Bundestag. Longer tenure is taken as an indicator of greater valuation of a particular deputy in the eyes of the party leadership. Conversely, those deputies whose tenure runs for only one or two terms may be considered, on the aggregate, more dispensable. It is certainly true that electoral contingencies and chance factors (personal situations, deaths, local patriarchs) may for individual cases either prolong the tenure of a party "maverick" or cut short the tenure of a deputy considered very valuable by the party leadership. However, for the aggregation of all deputies who have served with each party, I shall assume that these factors bear little weight and that significant differences in tenure patterns across occupational and educational groupings are indications of preferential/nonpreferential valuation by the party leadership.[4]

The basic distinction to be made here in length of tenure is between those who served only one term (four years, except for the sixth Bundestag), those who served two terms, and those who served three or more terms (more than a decade). Since current Bundestag deputies first elected in 1969 or 1972 have not yet had the possibility of serving three terms, these deputies will be excluded from the analysis, and only those current deputies who have served three or more terms will be included. The figures in table 34 indicate that, for all three parties, deputies from the wage-earner grouping are disproportionately represented among deputies serving only one or two terms. For the Social Democrats, in fact, they constitute the great bulk of all one-term (75%) and two-term (47%) deputies. Those deputies with group I occupations who have served in the Bundestag have in general not had as long a tenure as those from any other group. Even to the extent, then, that wage earners are present within each faction, they have tended to be short-termers with presumably less impact in their party caucus.

Deputies with group II occupations have generally been found in representative proportions among all tenure categories, although the Social Democrats seem to have disproportionately prized their few token owners. On the other hand, deputies from managerial backgrounds seem to have had the best chances for achieving long tenure. This differential is clearest for the SPD, since over 75% of its group III deputies have seen long Bundestag service, compared to

4. For more evidence on the weighing of factors in candidate selection for the Bundestag by the major parties, see von Beyme 1971: 82–100 and Kaack 1974: 565 ff. It does not affect the analysis here whether we accept the judgment that elite recruitment (nomination and electoral support) to the Bundestag rests in the hands of top party leaders or is, at least compared with Weimar, decentralized and includes regional leadership groupings (cf. Kaufmann, Kohl, and Molt 1961; Loewenberg 1967: 69–70; Kitzinger 1960: chap. 2; Claessens, Klönne, and Tschoepe 1965: 73–80), since in any case it rests with a small group of party leaders and does not operate through some form of open primary system (see von Beyme 1971 for some rather optimistic reform expectations from the introduction of primary elections into the candidate selection process).

TABLE 34. Occupational Background by Tenure for
SPD, CDU/CSU, and FDP Deputies

Terms served	Occupational grouping				
	I %	II %	III %	IV %	All %
SPD					
1	46	(13)	11	10	24
2	19	(0)	12	21	16
3+	35	(88)	78	70	60
CDU/CSU					
1	35	18	15	26	23
2	35	25	15	12	22
3+	29	56	71	62	55
FDP					
1	56	42	36	33	41
2	36	26	18	30	29
3+	8	32	46	37	30

only 11% one-term deputies. Deputies from professional occupations have also been advantaged in length of tenure, more so for the SPD and the CDU/CSU than for the FDP and somewhat less so than the managers. This is, of course, affected by the relatively more recent trend to professionals by all three parties, with significantly fewer opportunities for professionals to have yet served three or more terms. Of those deputies who could not be included in these tables for this reason, one-third of the CDU/CSU and approximately half of the SPD and the FDP deputies were modern professionals by occupation. It is quite probable that, if present recruitment trends continue, tenure patterns for this group will show a more marked length of service advantage.

With respect to educational background and tenure in the Bundestag, there is again the tendency for those with higher education to have served longer. This is most clearly illustrated for the Social Democrats, who have presumably made special efforts to recruit men and women of higher education and who apparently value these people highly. Also of interest, however, is the relatively favored treatment of those with vocational education, especially with the SPD and only somewhat less so with the Christian Democrats. This is in large measure accounted for by the group of trade-unionist deputies, who also enjoy higher tenure patterns, both for deputies who are members of unions and those who are union officials. Only 8% of trade-union officials are one-term deputies, while over 75% have served three or more terms. Pretty much the same pattern holds for deputies who are union members. And around 50% of all deputies who are union members and officials (43 and 54% respectively) had vocational-education backgrounds, as against only 4% of nonunion deputies. This higher tenure for trade unionists is true for those affiliated with the Christian Democrats only to a slightly lesser degree than for those affiliated with the Social Democrats. However, it is interesting to note that, even for this nominal representation of the working class through that group of deputies affiliated with the union movement, the educational characteristics have changed considerably over the years, especially for those deputies who are trade-union members but not officials. While trade-union *officials* in the Bundestag currently have an educational profile not so different from those of 1949 (although they are now represented in greater numbers), union *members* in the 1972 Bundestag present a very altered aggregation in terms of education from those of 1949 and 1961. This is primarily due to the increasing numbers of trade unionists who are also professionals, whose unions (Teachers Union; Union of Commerce, Bank, and Insurance Employees; Union of Civil Service and Transportation Employees) include a large number of teachers, professors, scientists, engineers, and specialists in banking, insurance, and public service. Thus the educational profile of deputies with trade-union membership has followed, with some lag, the general trend for all deputies connected with the unions, with nearly two-fifths coming from the professional grouping and another quarter from the managerial grouping as of 1972, compared with a total of slightly more than one-fifth from groups III and IV for such deputies in 1949. If the present transformation continues, we may expect that (with some time lag), for this category of deputies also, recruitment will draw predominantly from the highly educated and from those with managerial and professional occupations, again supporting our second general hypothesis. If we again combine occupational status and educational attainment, we can correlate on a more general level the SES of deputies with length of tenure in the Bundestag. For the SPD, the correlation (gamma) is .35, for the CDU/CSU .24, and for the FDP .14, indicating that high SES is a more important factor in terms of tenure for Social Democrats than for the two middle-class parties. This may be a reflection of a more economical use of high-status candidates by the SPD, in list or district placement, operating in a system of interparty candidate status competition, as suggested by Kornberg, Clarke, and Watson (1973) in their Canadian studies.[5] What is clear is that, while Bundestag tenure is positively associated with deputy SES for all three parties, it is correlated in increasing degrees as one moves from the party of strict middle-class representation through the classic *Volkspartei* to the party of the working-class voter.

Transformation by Party System

It is clear from the above analysis that there has been a rather complete transformation in the educational-occupational characteristics of Bundestag members by political era for each of the three (to date) durable parties. What remains to be tested is the degree to which this transformation has made the party elites, as represented here through their Bundestag factions, more congruent with each other (hypothesis three). If we take as one measure of visible interparty differentiation the variance in recruitment patterns for Bundestag members, we may characterize the degree of class polarization in the *party system* by the degree of differentiation in educational and occupational experiences among the Bundestag party factions in each parliament. Taking both education and occupation here as nominal scale categories, we may calculate for all three parties (using Pearson's C) a measure of the development of party-system

5. Kornberg, Clarke, and Watson (1973) report a monotonic relationship between ordering of candidate SES and ordering in the election results. Thus parliamentary elites in Canada are seen as the embodiment of high social status, both by other elites who influence the nomination process and by voters who decide among candidates. An important note here is their finding that protest parties do not follow the normal rules of the game in nominating highest-status candidates and that for these system-protest parties such a strategy is perfectly rational as an electoral tactic. That is, system-supportive parties nominate according to the dominant status values, while protest parties quite rationally deviate from this criterion. This would, not surprisingly, seem to mark one boundary between "usual" and "dissident" politics in terms of elite composition.

choice over the course of the Bundesrepublik. This has been calculated in two ways, first using occupational and educational
categories as originally coded (ungrouped) and then using the combined (grouped) categories developed in this chapter (see table 35).
While it is expected that, with fewer categories, the grouped data
contingency coefficients will tend to be smaller in magnitude, any
gross discrepancies in trends indicated by the two methods would
point out effects not consistent with the proposed occupational
groupings and would thus indicate a need for revision in these categories. Fortunately, this does not appear to be the case, thus giving
some reassurance to the use of our occupational and educational
groupings as a means of conceptualizing without obscuring important developments.

The first comment to be made about the results in table 35 is that
from the beginning of the Bundesrepublik the level of party elite
differentiation was not very high. It is clear that, compared with the
Weimar system, which had a significant KPD faction of deputies,
elite differentiation started out at a moderately low level.

The second comment is that the degree of variation over the last
quarter century is relatively small, with a range in Pearson's C of .23
to .33 for occupational groups and .21 to .28 for educational groups.
That is, despite the very broad transformations in the aggregate educational and occupational composition of Bundestag deputies, the
degree of interparty elite differentiation which characterizes the
party system has remained at a fairly constant low level.

Even so, we may still note a drop in interparty differentiation from
1949 to 1953 in both occupational measures, and at least in the
grouped educational measure, followed by slight increases in interparty elite differentiation through 1961 in the case of occupation
and through 1965 in the case of education. After 1961, a gradual decline in occupational differentiation sets in (after 1965 for education), which has continued up to the 1972 Bundestag. These slight
trends are relatively minor compared to the quite amazing constancy of party-system elite differentiation throughout the occupational and educational transformations we have noted.

If we look at interparty elite differentiation by pairs of parties (listing only the Pearson's C for the grouped educational and occupational variables for purposes of less tedious presentation), we can see
that at a gross level the Free Democrats have always been closest in
occupational-educational profile to the Christian Democrats and
were most differentiated from them occupationally in 1957, when
the FDP, even more clearly than the CDU/CSU, styled itself as the

TABLE 35. Party-System Differentiation of Deputies by Occupation and Education, 1949–1972

Bundestag	Occupation		Education	
	Ungrouped	Grouped	Ungrouped	Grouped
1949	.41	.29	.27	.23
1953	.33	.23	.29	.21
1957	.39	.29	.32	.24
1961	.39	.33	.30	.25
1965	.38	.32	.32	.28
1969	.37	.30	.29	.25
1972	.36	.25	.29	.23

Note: Figures are Pearson's Contingency Coefficients.

party of business and farm owners. Conversely, the greatest differentiation among party pairs has been in the case of the Social Democrats and the Free Democrats, again peaking in 1957. Of some interest is the gradual lessening of SPD/FDP differentiation after 1957, especially the rather distinct drop from 1969—when the two parties formed the first Brandt-Scheel coalition government—to 1972—after the defection of the nationalist Mende-Zoglmann-Starke faction to the Christian Democrats. This may indicate some effects of the SPD/FDP coalition on elite recruitment values in the FDP and may also point out something about prospects and party planning for a longer-term social-liberal coalition government. On the other hand, it is still true that the Free Democrats, largely due to their continued nominal representation of group II (owner) occupations in their faction, are closer to the CDU/CSU than to the SPD in occupational-educational experiences of party deputies. The trend toward less differentiation between FDP and SPD deputies is also matched by a similar trend toward homogeneity between the SPD and the CDU/CSU, indicating that the decrease in system elite differentiation during the sixties, as noted in table 35, is largely a function of a general though quite gradual decrease in differentiation between representatives of the labor bloc and the bourgeois bloc.

At best, we might say that our data give weak support to our third hypothesis during the 1960s, after the SPD had accepted its new Godesberg program of abandoning the last remnants of its Marxist tradition, while emphasizing the stability of the degree of class differentiation among competing party elites.

Summary of Findings

We may extract from the above analyses some general findings regarding the development in valuation of occupational and educational characteristics for recruitment of Bundestag deputies over the period 1949 to 1972:

1. There has been a rise in valuation of managerial experience and skills as a basis for political influence, especially during the Adenauer era and the years of CDU/CSU dominance, 1949 to 1965.

2. There has been a more gradual rise in valuation of professional skills over the entire timespan of the republic, more accelerated during the period of SPD ascendancy, 1965 to 1972.

3. There was an early decline in valuation of basic wage-earner status (first skilled worker, then unadorned white-collar employee), which has continued low throughout the rest of the Bundestag development.

4. There was a slight rise in valuation of ownership skills and experience during the 1950s, followed by a sharper decline in valuation during the 1960s.

5. There has been a steady rise in valuation of higher education throughout, as well as an increasing valuation of occupational and educational combinations with the highest SES rankings.

6. These valuation changes are most clearly represented in the age cohort generation which came to maturity (age 21) after 1945.

7. Differentials in Bundestag tenure, or length of service, are consistent with and reinforce the changing valuations of occupational, educational, and socioeconomic status. One significant exception is that group of deputies who are officials in trade unions. Deputies affiliated with the trade-union movement as members constitute a partial exception, although their occupational-educational profile has, with some time lag, followed the general pattern of all deputies.

8. All three main Bundestag parties have participated in these basic trends, with only minor exceptions (lack of owner representation in SPD ranks even in the 1950s) or time lags for individual parties.

9. Throughout the course of these basic transformations, which have altered the background characteristics of Bundestag deputies, party-system elite differentiation has remained relatively constant, although some long-run decrease in occupational-educational faction differentiation may be indicated by the results for the 1961 to 1972 period.

What picture does this present, then, of the development of the

German political elite under the Bundesrepublik? While it is necessary not to assume that other segments of the political elite (or, for
that matter, of other elite groupings in education, business, communications, the military, and so forth) have followed a similar pattern of development, others (Zapf 1965: chap. 10; von Beyme 1971:
194 ff.) have singled out the parliamentary elite as the most open to
diversity of origins and experiences (i.e., the most pluralistic) and
have noted its symbolic role as the institutional embodiment of system norms. With this brief defense, we may draw several more ar-
gumentative interpretations as a successful case of pluralist democratic development in mature capitalism.

First, whereas the development of German political parties and of
the party system has been characterized by many Western observers
as a development from the class-mass parties of Weimar to catch-all
vote-gathering mechanisms or *Volksparteien*, from the vantage
point of elite analysis the trend has been in the opposite direction.
With the defeat of the KPD and its suppression in 1956, the only
party faction made up predominantly of workers with low or secondary education disappeared from the Bundestag. In terms of occupational and educational representativeness, the 1949 Bundestag
was far closer to the general distribution of occupations and educations than any Bundestag since, and, when Lorenz curves with associated Gini indexes are constructed, the disproportionate representation of higher social strata increases with each parliamentary
session. If, for example, we use the occupational stratification
categories developed by Moore and Kleining (1960) from their sur-
veys, and if we use the population percentages closest in time to
each federal election from 1949 to 1972, we get the series of Gini
coefficients given in table 36, rising from .48 in 1949 to .74 in 1969
and 1972. Thus, while it may be true that at the electoral level political parties have been transforming themselves into vote-catching
mechanisms, in terms of elite recruitment they have been transforming their valuations to meet the qualities of the upper middle
class.

Second, within the movement toward a parliamentary elite of the
upper middle class, there has been a change in elite composition
which reflects changes in the composition of the upper middle and,
to a lesser extent, the middle strata of the middle class. Within these
classes, the general trend over the last two decades has been a decline in the numbers of self-employed, as both farm and small business owners. This is matched by the overall trend in representation
of employers. There have, on the other hand, been increases in the

TABLE 36. Representation of Occupational Strata in the Bundestag
Compared to the General Population, 1949–1972

Stratum	% in Bundestag						
	1949	1953	1957	1961	1965	1969	1972
Upper, upper middle	26	36	47	55	59	60	59
Middle middle	13	14	17	20	19	20	21
Lower middle	43	38	27	18	16	15	15
Upper lower	16	12	9	7	6	5	5
Lower lower							
Gini index	.48	.54	.62	.70	.72	.74	.74

percentages of those in managerial and professional positions. Thus,
while the valuation of occupational experience for Bundestag recruitment is not sensitive to composition of the occupational structure as a whole, it is sensitive to changes in composition at the
upper end of the stratification ladder. The integration function
through the nomination of candidates, which Kirchheimer (1966)
saw as the single most important activity of the catch-all party, thus
applies only at the top of the stratification ladder, in terms of inte-
grating elements of the upper middle class into the political elite.

Third, the change in symbolism embodied in parliamentary composition is consistent not only with the end of ideology interpretation but also with the Marxist notion of representation in a
capitalist democracy. From the first approach, this evolution appears as a decline in the symbols of class conflict, in terms of the
reduction of both group I (wage earners) and group II (owners) occupational categories to nominal figures in all parties. Still, there remains a residue of political elite differentiation, providing for a rem-
nant of class politics and a basis for some rational distinctions
among competing leadership groups. Or, as in Lenski's (1966: chap.
11) view of modern society, the basis of influence shifts from property to authority (management) to knowledge (professional expertise).

All of this is quite consistent with the Marxist interpretation of
the state as the guarantor of the rights of property. Marx noted in
several of his studies (especially *Eighteenth Brumaire of Louis
Bonaparte*) that a capitalist ruling class did not need to govern in
person but, in crisis, could turn to fascism for its rescue from parliamentary democracy. He also noted that the social order is most

secure which can draw the upwardly mobile into the governing class, and to this end he severely criticized the bourgeoisification of the SPD leadership of the 1870s. Marx's point was that the safest and most secure political form of the capitalist order was the liberal democratic state, in which the direct rule of the property-owning class would be unnecessary (cf. Miliband 1969: chap. 3). The Social Democrats of the Bonn republic, in their Bundestag faction, symbolize the norm of upward mobility into the upper middle classes of management and professional expertise, though not business ownership, and they no longer functionally represent the values of blue- and white-collar job experience. The bourgeoisification of the SPD leadership, which has often been noted as a long-term trend within social democracy, seems to have reached its ultimate peak after a quarter century of a prosperous and stable postwar parliamentary system (see Hunt 1964). It is clear that the present SPD-led government in no way threatens the rights of property and proposes no program of changes in the social order. All three parties of the Bonn system, from some early representation of occupations symbolic of proletarian/capitalist class conflict, have given way to elite recruitment from occupations less (managerial) and less (professional) directly associated with capitalism, yet in social prestige positively identified with the reward structure of the present order.

Thus, much of the debate as to whether the political elite of the Federal Republic represents a power elite (Jaeggi) or a democratic pluralism of contending, anxious leadership groups (Dahrendorf, Zapf) misses the point if we take note of Marx's contention that the main function of the capitalist state is the maintenance of the underpinnings of the current social order. Given a set of elites, *none* of which intend to press for basic social changes, the question of cartelist/pluralist characterizations of elite interactions diminishes considerably in importance, at least from the vantage point of commitment to basic changes in the social order.

CHAPTER 8

Post-Cárdenas Mexico: Evolution of a Filtered Class Recruitment System

Evaluation of the Contemporary Mexican System

The development and institutionalization of the Mexican one-party system have attracted the attention of numerous Western scholars in the last thirty years. Practically alone among Latin American political cultures, the PRI-dominated Mexican system has stabilized politics to the point where Irving L. Horowitz could say that Mexican politics has become uneventful, if not a nonevent (in González Casanova 1970: x). In the 1950s especially, Mexico provided for several scholars (Scott, Cline, Needler, Padgett) the example of a "one-party democracy," that is, a political system in which one party dominated and yet permitted (of course only by its own choice) nominal competition from a number of minor parties or political groupings. Especially apparent from their descriptions was the growing conservatism of the PRI leadership after the burst of reformism under Cárdenas' presidency (1934–1940). The capitalist road of development launched most forcefully under Alemán and Ruiz Cortines (cf. Brandenberg 1964) seemed to eradicate the possibility of a socialist order as the end result of a mixed-heritage Mexican Revolution (cf. esp. Womack 1969; Cockcroft 1968): this had seemed a real possibility during the period of land reform, growing unionist militancy, and populist-oriented educational politics of the 1930s, at least to many Western observers. The expropriation of American-owned oil holdings by the Cárdenas government in 1938, a rare and bold move by an underdeveloped nation in those days (see esp. Cornelius 1973), had heightened Western scholarly sensitivity to the revolutionary possibilities inherent in the Mexican system at that time.

This feeling is quite absent in the post-Cárdenas literature on Mexican political development. Despite the welfare reformism of President López Mateos (1958–1964), post-1940 political and economic development in Mexico generally warrants the conclusion of Horowitz that the middle-class, not the agrarian or working-class, vision of the Revolution has triumphed. The PRI regime continues to pay lip service to, and perhaps cannot openly repudiate, the radical/socialist elements of the 1910 to 1920 experience (see esp. Gruber 1971: 481–482). Yet, although one may hear a socialist rhetoric, especially in foreign policy, it is clear that the political system aims only at coopting or physically eliminating the leadership of potential antisystem (socialist) movements (Johnson 1971; Anderson and Cockcroft 1969; Cockcroft 1972). Indeed, so sharp have been the class cleavages of the urbanization and industrialization process that recently a liberal-based criticism of the conservatism, corruption, and inattention to popular needs has been voiced (González Casanova 1970; Johnson 1971). Hansen's summary is perhaps most cutting:

> Two generalizations with regard to the course of economic development in Mexico seem valid. The first is that no other Latin American political system has provided more rewards for its new industrial and commercial agricultural elites. . . . the Mexican government is as much a "businessman's government" as any in the United States during the decades of the Republican ascendancy (1860–1932).
> The second generalization is that, excepting the impact of land distribution, in no other major Latin American country has less been done directly by the government for the bottom quarter of society. Trends in prices, wages, and occupational opportunities in Mexico have probably left most of the families within this stratum with a standard of living at or below that which they enjoyed in 1940. Even for those families within the next quarter of the population, real wages remained below 1940 levels until the early 1960s. (1971: 87)

The following analysis utilizes a Marxist concept of social class and class struggle to test the relationship between the widely perceived post-Cárdenas trend toward conservatism in the Mexican political system and changes in the social bases of political office-holding recruitment. Our findings hopefully provide insight into the relationship between political institutionalization, political stability, and elite composition *under* capitalism. At the same time, they offer an admittedly partial defense of the applicability of a strict class approach in a region where such an approach is usually regarded by Western scholars as only marginally productive (cf. esp. Wiarda 1973; Fagen and Tuohy 1972). And, ironically, we shall be using elite-level analysis, which has traditionally, even if unwarrantedly, been seen as an anti-Marxist approach to understanding political systems (cf. Lipset and Solari 1967: vii–viii).

From a class-struggle perspective, the conservative reaction to the radical populist reforms under Cárdenas and the reversal of policy thereafter have put Mexico squarely on the path of capitalist development. The Mexican Revolution from the start was predominantly (cf. Gruber 1971: 468–469; Eisenstadt 1966) a middle-class revolt against an aging Porfirian oligarchy, but in the course of a ten-year civil war large segments of the popular masses were mobilized, and a minority radical populist, and sometimes socialist, vision of the Revolution emerged to compete with the original bourgeois revolt against the *ancien régime*. The Cárdenas burst (1935–1940) of radical reform represented the one breakthrough of this minority strain, a temporary dominance of the populist (cf. Cornelius 1973), rather than the middle-class, translation of the revolutionary demands for bread, land, and "no reelection." The presidencies of Alemán and Ruiz Cortines effectively reestablished the bourgeois definitions of these demands as material prosperity for a growing middle class and commercially effective utilization of land. The "no reelection" stipulation, however, has been retained and still provides for high personnel turnover while, as we shall see, preserving effective class control over political power (cf. Hansen 1971: 176–179 on the stabilizing effects of "no reelection" and land distribution).

Internal Structures of the Capitalist State

Our theoretical point of departure shall be the Marxist view of the state and of state elite recruitment, in particular the "internal structures" approach developed by Offe (1972, 1973) and extended more recently by Gold, Lo, and Wright (1975). Offe develops the concept of "selective mechanisms" within the state apparatus which are intended to serve three crucial functions:

(1) *negative selection*: the selective mechanisms systematically exclude anti-capitalist interests from state activity; (2) *positive selection*: from the range of remaining alternatives, the policy which is in the interests of capital as a whole is selected over policies serving the parochial interests of specific capitalist groups; (3) *disguising selection*: the institutions of the state must somehow maintain the appearance of class-neutrality while at the same time effectively excluding anti-capitalist alternatives. (in Gold, Lo, and Wright 1975, no. 6: 37–38)

In their review of Marxist analyses of the state, Gold, Lo, and Wright are somewhat critical of Marxist sociological attempts (cf. Miliband 1969; Bottomore 1966) to view elite recruitment as a purely instrumental function of the economically dominant class. However, I believe that the social bases of political elite recruitment can be usefully analyzed as attempted fulfillment of the three selective mechanisms described above. The Mexican PRI (and its associated satellite parties), with its clearly self-conscious role as both system stabilizer and promoter of a developing capitalist economy (cf. esp. Anderson and Cockcroft 1969; Cornelius 1973), would seem in fact to be an excellent candidate for such analysis.

Our working hypotheses in examining the social composition of the Mexican political elite in the post-Cárdenas era will be these:

1. In terms of *negative* recruitment selectivity, we would expect a progressively more careful screening of those elements which were either proletarian or radical petit bourgeois from positions of effective political power. This would include those elements from the growing urban working class as well as those associated with the radical populism of the Cárdenas years.

2. In terms of *positive* selectivity, we would expect an increase in recruitment from that class associated with the success and survival of the system as a whole but not with any one capitalist grouping. In most modern capitalist systems, as has been empirically demonstrated many times over (Miliband 1969; Bottomore 1966), members of this class are from the modern professional or managerial-technocratic stratum; their social positions and well-being depend on the system, and they are best positioned to judge the interests of the whole system. Recruitment from this stratum may also serve as a partial fulfillment of the *disguising* selectivity function, although this would seem to be more true in the affluent Western democracies than in Mexico, where a posited class neutrality among the new *técnicos* is not very plausible.

TABLE 37. Primary Occupations of the Mexican Political Elite by Office and Presidential Administration

	1940–1946				1946–1952			
Occupation	dep %	sen %	gov %	cab %	dep %	sen %	gov %	c %
Worker/ employee	11	8	9	4	12	6	9	
Owner	5	3	2	0	5	3	2	
Military	15	24	45	22	8	9	20	
Professional	65	61	43	70	70	75	67	8
N	88	38	65	23	100	32	59	3

3. In terms of *disguising* selectivity, we would expect, especially with the successful aggregate industrialization and urbanization over the last thirty-five years, increased cooptation from the growing urban work force and very limited direct officeholding by industrialists and landowners. Recruitment from the lower social strata would be channeled more and more exclusively into noneffective, or *symbolic*, political offices.

We shall argue that these selective mechanisms have become progressively stronger as the PRI system has become institutionalized and as the country has been firmly placed on a capitalist road of industrial development. This evolution, in the field of elite recruitment, has produced a filtering system in which lower social strata have been progressively shut out of *effective* political officeholding while being used for show in *symbolic* officeholding. In fact, we shall argue that, as class cleavages have grown within Mexican society, the regime has felt it necessary to upgrade cooptive elite recruitment from a growing industrial work force, but it has segregated this recruitment into symbolic offices (mainly deputy, but also senator) while reserving with ever greater exclusivity effective elite positions (governorship, cabinet post) for individuals drawn from the upper social strata.

Social Bases of Elite Recruitment, 1940 to 1970

The following analysis takes in four levels of political officeholding (deputy, senator, governor, cabinet member) of the national political elite and includes all individuals who have held office at one or more

1952–1958		
sen %	gov %	cab %
14	6	0
0	2	0
29	18	18
57	74	73
42	49	22

of these levels at some time since 1940.[1] This definition covers also those deputies and senators from the nominal opposition parties, since it is apparent (cf. Hansen 1971: 113) that, at least presently, the PRI in fact chooses the members of the "loyal opposition." We can safely consider, on the basis of scholarly consensus, the offices of deputy, senator, governor, and cabinet minister as an ascending hierarchy and can further make a basic division between those offices (governor, cabinet member) which *as offices* command effective political power (cf. Alisky 1965 and Brandenberg 1964 on the growing authority of governors), as opposed to those offices (deputy, senator) which, while perhaps important steppingstones in a political career, are in themselves symbolic elite institutions (cf. Mabry 1974 on recent trends).

The best available evidence on class composition of each elite level comes from consideration of primary occupation and highest

1. Taking note of Welsh's methodological criticisms of studies in Latin American leadership, we will explicitly argue, with Peter Smith (1974), that all four positions included in this study are in fact national elite offices, though we would not argue that they include all political elites (they clearly do not include many top PRI leaders). Also, we would assert that, on the basis of some other studies and our own data (which are the same as Smith's), the findings reached here would also apply to the nongovernmental political hierarchy (cf. Welsh n.d.). One methodological problem which does arise is the differing amount of missing data for occupation, education, and birth year for each office membership. Missing data are more frequent for lower office levels and for earlier years covered, and it is possible that a bias in the social composition of missing data might affect our profile of the Chamber of Deputies as it existed in 1940 to 1946, though probably not enough to significantly alter our basic conclusions.

TABLE 37. Primary Occupations of the Mexican Political Elite by Office and Presidential Administration (continued)

	1958–1964				1964–1970			
Occupation	dep %	sen %	gov %	cab %	dep %	sen %	gov %	c %
Worker/ employee	18	8	2	10	24	13	2	
Owner	4	4	2	0	4	5	6	
Military	8	20	17	10	4	13	6	
Professional	69	62	79	76	67	65	86	8
N	236	49	48	21	362	56	52	2

Note: In columns where percentages do not total 100, the remaining officeholders were in almost all cases clergy.

educational attainment of officeholders. Actually, except for officeholders from military backgrounds, the educational variable would be somewhat redundant, since occupational and educational stratifications are closely linked, and our main purpose in using educational attainment is to better understand the class-composition changes in the Mexican elite related to the "demilitarization" (cf. Lieuwen 1968) of the Mexican political elite. The basic organization of occupational categories follows a class definition separating wageworkers, capitalists (here large landowners and industrialists), and the liberal professions of the upper social strata; for the Mexican case, the important military category is added as an extra class component. The basic class composition of military officeholders is initially unclear, as a historically important source of elite recruitment in Mexico, and the social origins and status of military officeholders could be quite varied. Examination of all four levels from 1940 through 1970 initially reveals three distinctive trends which confirm our basic thesis about the middle-class-dominated cooptation and control system.[2]

The most obvious pattern of change, visible in table 37, is the

2. The occupational groupings used here are as follows: for worker/employee—factory-worker unionists, agricultural workers, small farmers, white-collar workers/employees (public or private sector), artisans; for owner—landowners and industrialists; for military—military/police; for professional—lawyers, doctors, engineers, teachers, professors, media specialists. Clergy, who might have been included as professionals, have been excluded; they account for the small percentages in those cases where the columns do not add up to 100%. Technically speaking, of course, arti-

1970–1976		
sen %	gov %	cab %
11	3	0
4	6	3
13	0	10
68	88	87
53	34	31

gradual elimination of the military as a source of elite recruitment. This process, actually begun in the 1930s (see Lieuwen 1968), is accelerated under Alemán, whose administration took drastic steps to undo the Cárdenas reform programs in favor of big business, both domestic and American, in an effort to produce an industrial capitalism in Mexico. The Alemán regime, known also for its blatant corruption, had generated some stiff resistance by the early 1950s, and the demilitarization of elite recruitment was somewhat reversed under Ruiz Cortines. Since 1958, however, the military has gradually been downgraded as a source of political officeholders at all levels.

Over this same time period, the liberal professions, a minute segment of the population at large, have held the bulk of offices at all levels of the national political system. However, it is this occupational grouping, not the capitalists directly, as might well have been the case in less stable Latin American politics, which has filled the vacuum left by the elimination of significant political recruitment from the military ranks.

Of considerable interest is the steady absence of direct officehold-

---

sans and some small farmers are self-employed and might be considered as small entrepreneurs; however, our purpose is to get a measure of elite recruitment from among the lower social strata, in which the artisans and *ejidatarios* must be counted. It would be interesting to have more than illustrative data on family social origin as well as occupation, since it is likely that some professionals, especially teachers, came from humbler origins. However, no evidence indicates that this is a significant factor, and some evidence (Fagen and Tuohy 1972) would indicate that it is in fact minuscule.

ing by industrialists and landowners, despite the unambiguous judgment that since 1940 government policy has favored entrepreneurial interests over others. To some observers (e.g., Hansen 1971: 97–98) this personnel differentiation between economic and political power might seem incompatible with a class interpretation of the Mexican political system. And, if we were to take a simplistic Marxist position that the bourgeoisie must govern in person in a capitalist society, then the lack of capitalist representation in high office would be telling. But, from the Marxist-based theory of the state utilized here, this absence of capitalists in high office is seen, in conjunction with the dominance of the liberal professions, as a confirmation of the positive selectivity thesis, which relegates the role of providing a suitable environment for capitalist development not to individual capitalists themselves but to the modern professional-managerial-technocratic strata (see also chap. 7). In addition, the low visibility of industrialists in political office is a fulfillment of the disguising selectivity thesis, which posits, in an effective recruitment process, avoidance of too great visibility for capitalists as the governing class. The preference is, rather, for increasing representation from the liberal professions. This trend toward greater dominance by the liberal professions in officeholding has been most pronounced at the levels of governor and cabinet member, so that by the Echeverría inauguration in 1970 nine-tenths of all governors and ministers, versus seven-tenths of all deputies and senators, were drawn from the liberal professions. This fits our theses on positive as well as disguising selective mechanisms.

The above differential is important to our analysis, for the third observable trend in Mexican elite recruitment has been a bifurcated rise in representation of the lower social strata among the symbolic lower levels of the national system as well as an almost complete elimination of these same strata at the effective higher levels. While this evolution has had some discontinuities, the general pattern is remarkably consistent with the thesis that, as the Mexican system as a whole has moved to the Right, down the capitalist road of development, effective political power has been increasingly monopolized by the upper social strata, while a notably increased segment of symbolic posts has, for purposes of regime legitimation and visible links to the popular masses, gone to individuals coopted from the wageworking classes, especially industrial workers and unionists from the growing urban work force.

The effect of these three trends on the class composition of the Mexican elite is further highlighted by a cross tabulation of the edu-

Table 38. Educational Attainment of Elite Occupational Groupings by Office Level

	Occupation		
Education	Worker-employee %	Military %	Owner-professional %
Cabinet			
Primary	100	18	1
Secondary	0	65	7
College	0	18	92
N	3	17	122
Governor			
Primary	64	34	2
Secondary	27	45	7
College	9	21	91
N	11	29	148
Senator			
Primary	58	32	2
Secondary	26	56	7
College	16	12	91
N	19	25	198
Deputy			
Primary	55	16	3
Secondary	31	54	11
College	14	30	86
N	125	37	704

cational attainment of officeholders for each elite level with primary occupation (see table 38). Here we see evidence of the lower-middle-class positioning of the great majority of the military in Mexican politics. The educational profile of the military at all levels indicates its intermediate position between the upper-strata professionals and the working class. This confirms on a systematic basis the general characterizations of the leaders of the revolutionary armies drawn from examples by Lieuwen (1968) and Womack (1969) and indicates the key role of demilitarization in the monopolization of effective political officeholding by the professional middle class. Thus, the removal of the military from the mainstream of elite recruitment, especially to the important post of governor, is in large measure relatable to the elimination of a petit-bourgeois radicalism, nationalism, and animosity to big business, which at times (the early Calles regime and later, of course, the Cárdenas era) erupted as a viable element or interpretation of Mexican revolutionary tradition.

Generational Cleavages in Elite Recruitment

The post-Cárdenas transformation of the social basis of elite recruitment has been, on the evidence of the above data, gradual and achieved in large part by the differentiated recruitment processes across successive political age cohorts or generations of officeholders. We have divided our elite population into three age groupings: those born between 1880 and 1899, who came to maturity during the overthrow of the Porfirian *ancien régime* and the revolutionary struggle; those born from 1900 through 1919, whose young-adult years fall after the era of civil war, during the period of interwar attempts at stabilization, frustrated reform, and finally the reform breakthrough of Cárdenas; and those born after 1920, who came to maturity in the latest era of conservative-regime institutionalization. Table 39 indicates how closely the passing of the oldest, revolutionary era generation is related to the demilitarization of Mexican politics and—at the higher, effective levels of officeholding—to the consolidation of a strictly professional middle-class recruitment process. While wageworker as well as military backgrounds have been generationally phased out at gubernatorial and cabinet levels, the demilitarization is coupled with some increased recruitment from the ranks of lower social strata for the deputy and senator positions. There seems to be some drop in this trend, however, after the interwar generation, so that representation of lower social strata among the youngest age cohort is below that of the interwar cohort, although still considerably above the level of the oldest generation for senate members. Since it will be some time before the youngest generational profile will be completed, and since future officeholders from this cohort may have attributes different from those officeholders elevated to the national elite up to now, we may speculate on the meaning of this latest generational shift in background. One explanation is that this youngest generation of elites may be the portent of an even more exclusively middle-class recruitment system, extended even to the lower levels of the national system. Another is

TABLE 39. Generational Differences in Occupational Background by Office Level

Occupation	Generation 1880–99 %	1900–19 %	1920– %
Cabinet			
Worker/employee	9	1	0
Owner	0	3	0
Military	28	8	3
Professional	61	87	97
N	43	72	32
Governor			
Worker/employee	12	3	5
Owner	1	5	0
Military	49	8	0
Professional	35	84	90
N	77	79	19
Senator			
Worker/employee	4	15	11
Owner	1	5	3
Military	41	5	6
Professional	51	70	71
N	70	113	36
Deputy			
Worker/employee	18	25	15
Owner	2	5	4
Military	29	4	0
Professional	41	62	77
N	90	428	277

Note: In columns where percentages do not total 100, the remaining officeholders were in almost all cases clergy.

that members of lower social strata, in Mexico as in other societies, rise more slowly in their political careers and may not, as of 1970, have yet achieved their eventual share of deputy/senator positions. There is some reason to expect that the youngest age cohort representation of wageworkers among symbolic elites will over time rise to the level of the 1900 to 1919 generation, if not beyond.

Summary intercorrelations among occupational, educational, and generational characteristics of the Mexican political elite since 1940 are given in table 40. For these correlations, the small numbers of officeholders from the propertied class have been combined with those from the liberal professions to give an index of the upper-class strength; the military has been considered as a lower-middle-class social grouping; and wageworkers have been assigned the lowest status ranking. Officeholders from the clergy have been excluded as before.

Considered as either ordinal or nominal variables, we find our occupational triad highly correlated with our educational triad at all four levels of elite recruitment. This alone indicates the constancy of the educational linkage with occupational stratification and strengthens our belief that the revolutionary military component is accurately conceived as a middle grouping in the total social stratification of elites.

At the higher office levels, where demilitarization was accompanied by deproletarization, as was needed to eliminate the small percentages of elites from lower-class backgrounds, higher educational attainment and higher occupational status are both moderately associated with generational turnover, more so at the gubernatorial level, where the military presence in the 1940s was greater and the degree of transformation thus also greater. Again there is little difference between levels of association whether education and occupation are considered as ordinal or as nominal scale variables.[3]

This contrasts with the very low correlation between generation and both education and occupation, considered as ordinal scale variables, at the senator and deputy levels; the displacement of the military contingent at these levels by individuals from both lower and higher occupational strata is indicated by the greater correlation level (.38 as opposed to .18; .39 as opposed to .19) between generation and occupation considered simply as nominal categories. This

3. It is immediately clear that in a strict sense we should not be comparing values of Somer's D with a Pearson's Contingency Coefficient; with descriptive statistics, these measures are comparable only with themselves. However, in a rough sense both are measures of accounting for variance, and it is only in this sense that we take the similarity/dissimilarity between nominal scale and ordinal scale measures of strength to be meaningful. Obviously, the results would have been somewhat different had we used gamma for our ordinal data correlations, but with only three rankings on each variable Somer's D is the more appropriate (conservative estimate) statistic.

TABLE 40. Nominal and Ordinal Scale Correlations of Occupation, Education, and Generation by Office Level since 1940

	Pearson's C			Somer's D		
	occ	edu	gen	occ	edu	gen
Cabinet						
occ		.67	.35		.70	.30
edu	.67		.30	.70		.24
gen	.35	.30		.30	.24	
Governor						
occ		.59	.49		.68	.48
edu	.59		.32	.68		.28
gen	.49	.32		.48	.28	
Senator						
occ		.61	.39		.69	.19
edu	.61		.09	.69		.06
gen	.39	.09		.19	.06	
Deputy						
occ		.57	.38		.61	.18
edu	.57		.12	.61		.08
gen	.38	.12		.18	.08	

pattern is less clear for the nominal scale generation/education correlations, primarily because of increased educational attainment of younger unionists and white-collar employees picked for deputy/ senator seats.

Elite Recruitment Trends and Mexican Political Development

Overall, even using the broad occupational, educational, and generational groupings above, the correlations summarize and strengthen our thesis of a growing division in the social bases of elite recruitment between effective and symbolic offices, an increased fulfillment of disguising selectivity. These findings are consistent with recent critical interpretations of Mexican political development as a whole. Anderson and Cockcroft (1969) have, in their consideration of Mexico as a developmental model, stressed the manipulation of the revolutionary tradition through a system of cooptation of ambitious leaders from lower-strata groupings (cf. also Peter Smith 1974) and repression (cf. Johnson 1971) of those who refuse to be coopted. Gruber's (1971: 481–482) conclusions on the cultivation of the myth of the "ongoing Revolution" within the PRI system of "control and manipulation" are along similar lines. They particularly point out the symbolic uses of nationalist and revolutionary slogans by the regime as a stabilizing counterbalance to the actual drift of policy in favor of business and professional interests. This process of cooptation and control is mirrored in the bifurcation of recruitment values as seen in our elite data.

Interestingly enough, although our analysis is in line with radical and class-oriented critiques of the Mexican system, it is also in accord with trends noted in more narrow studies of Mexican political leadership. For example, the demilitarization and deproletarization trends at the higher office levels are the converse of the rise of the cabinet *técnico* observed by Cochrane (1968) in the Díaz Ordaz presidency and by Camp (1971, 1972) as a general trend dating from the end of the Cárdenas years. These processes are also touched on, in their converse, by Alisky (1965) in his remarks on the transition among governors from military men to well-educated public-administration "expediters." The generational differences in social background at higher national elite levels have also been mentioned by Camp (1973), with respect to the particularly successful National University class of 1925 to 1929, and have more generally been handled by Peter Smith (1974) with respect to the newly promoted officeholders of the 1946 to 1970 period taken as a whole. Smith has also noted the overwhelming proportion (78%) of the national political elite (again taken as a single grouping for the entire period of 1946–1970) drawn from the liberal professions, compared to the tiny fraction (3%) of the economically active male population in these same professions (cf. also Gruber 1971: 476; Camp 1974: 457, 477, 478). By breaking down the national elite both by levels and by smaller time periods, we are able to add a developmental framework within the post-Cárdenas period which shows substantial differentiation between office levels.

However, most of the empirical studies of Mexican elite backgrounds have concentrated on questions of governmental efficiency and expertise (the *técnico* issue) and have viewed recent trends positively or have noted the limitations on professionalism in government imposed by the "no reelection" rule. Our findings speak not only to the evolution of a more refined and manipulative recruitment filter by social class (which Smith hints at, 1974: 21–22, 31) but also give support to a Marxist class analysis of Mexican political development.

Potential for Conflict: Popular Legitimacy vs. Class Control

Several years ago, González Casanova (1970), in his analysis of and prescriptions for the Mexican system, argued that, from the viewpoint of Western political sociology (chap. 10), what Mexico needed was a full-blown capitalist democracy. He also asserted, using a grotesque of legalist Marxism (chap. 11), that socialists should also support the fullest development of capitalism in Mexico, including the range of parliamentary institutions and civil liberties which characterize Western democracies. Apart from the logic or illogic of González Casanova's argumentations from liberal and pseudo-Marxist stances, what are the likely implications of his prescriptions for elite recruitment?

We have seen that in the post-Cárdenas era the process of demilitarization in elite recruitment has eliminated the radical petit-bourgeois threat to the domination of government by an upper-class elite. However, a genuine multiparty system, with fairly held competitive elections, carries with it the implication of an effective national Congress, which would in turn mean that the offices of deputy and senator would become more significant *as offices,* capable of autonomous political influence. To the extent that these offices, in a "normal" capitalist democracy, become effective positions of power, we might expect that upper-class domination over these offices would have to be even tighter than it is now, more comparable to the situation in the U.S. Congress or the West German Bundestag (cf. Miliband 1969; Bottomore 1966). Of course, this would require the complete abandonment of any but the most token representation of lower-class elements in the Chamber of Deputies and the Senate, an abandonment of one important disguising selective mechanism, an explicit repudiation of the popular revolutionary links which the conservative PRI evolution has not attempted thus far and, in fact, has seemingly avoided by providing increased visible working-class placement in lower-level symbolic offices.

Another possibility is that, with the lower-middle-class military removed from power for some time now, the cleavage between a totally upper-class effective leadership and a working-class segment of the symbolic leadership may at some crisis point become the springboard for a class confrontation within the PRI umbrella organization. The strike movement at the National University in 1968, the 1971 riots, and increasing rural unrest (cf. esp. Johnson 1971: chaps. 6–7; also Gruber 1971: 482) provide examples of the potential radicalization of previously coopted lower-level unionists and party officials. Of course, the PRI system has shown great flexibility in its neutralization of potential dissident leaders. It has also been a source of disappointment to those critical observers who are aware of how much poverty is borne silently in the midst of conspicuous upper-class consumption (Cornelius 1974) and how often negative judgments of actual political outcomes coexist with positive affective orientations to the system itself (Fagen and Tuohy 1972). Yet, there are signs of an increasing pool of "uncooptables" (Cockcroft 1972), as well as visible strains on both working-class tolerance of economic inequality and the ability/disposition of the PRI leadership to promote the revolutionary myth of greater social justice. It may be that the cooptive system has reached its outer limits of buying off dissidence without threatening the material privileges of the higher social strata. It is indeed hard to imagine how, in the face of the tremendous class disparities described by both supporters (Brandenberg 1964; González Casanova 1970) and critics (Anderson and Cockcroft 1969; Cockcroft 1972; Fagen and Tuohy 1972) of the capitalist road of development in Mexico, there could fail to be violent confrontations and unrest which would either radicalize or discredit the PRI's remaining links to the working classes. Either situation would have the effect of progressively revealing the class character of effective political power in Mexico, denying an important element of legitimacy to the PRI regime, and undermining the purpose of the dual-track elite recruitment outlined in this analysis.

CHAPTER 9

A Generational Interpretation
of the Soviet Elite: 1

The comparative analyses of part 2 have already suggested age
cohort or generational composition of the Soviet political elite as a
theoretically interesting focus for further study. The next two chapters continue the study of elite recruitment for the entire duration of
the Soviet system (1917–1971), using a generational perspective to
organize the data and making specific assumptions derivable from a
generational theory built up from a variety of empirical studies. The
present research is methodologically not pure deductive empiricism, in the sense of deriving a set of propositions on the basis of a
preexisting theory and then applying them to a data set for verifica-
tion. Neither is it purely inductive empiricism, in the sense of taking a body of data and inductively arriving at propositions, or a more
general theory, in the course of analysis. While Fleron (1969) has advocated the inductive empirical method in studying communist
systems as being generally the most appropriate with respect to the
still limited possibilities of types and accuracy of data which can be
collected about Soviet politics, we would argue in this case for an
admixture, on the basis of intuition proper to the process of discov-
ery, of both deductive and inductive components. This does not
mean letting the data "speak for itself," in the sense of raw empiricism, which as Searing and Edinger (1967) have pointed out has
sometimes characterized the use of background information in predicting elite attitudes and/or behavior. Rather, since there exists a
body of (non-Soviet) empirical research which has developed a set of
theories about political behavior and political generation, we shall
argue, on the basis of the data to be examined here, that there is a
justification for the future application and development of the generational model in hypothesis generation and testing in the area of
Soviet elite research.

The analysis concerns only one aspect of Soviet elite behavior, namely, the pattern of elite recruitment into the Central Committee of the CPSU over the period 1917 to 1971. Since most of the research on the Soviet system has been elite research and since background information on the Soviet political elite, particularly on members of the Central Committee, is one of the few areas in which we have empirical data (even if the data are quite sparse for certain periods and are often questionable relative to available data on Western political elites), the analysis of elite cooptation into the Committee has been a frequent theme for political scientists (see, among others, Donaldson and Waller 1970; Hough 1967; Lewytzkyj 1967; Gehlen 1966; Gehlen and McBridge 1968; Fleron 1969; McHale and Paranzino 1971; Donaldson 1972). There are a number of general theoretical approaches to elite circulation in Soviet politics, and it is necessary to show, prior to and through the present analysis, how the generational approach either adds to, supersedes, or contradicts these theories in explaining the phenomenon in question. To the extent that the actual analysis provides a basis for further explication and elaboration of the generational model in Soviet elite studies, it will have fulfilled its intended purpose. We can set forth the general scheme of this chapter as follows:

1. Description of the basic components of the generational model as developed through empirical studies in other polities with regard to a wide range of attitude and behavior types.

2. A priori defense of the intuitive applicability of this model, with its central assumptions, to the Soviet political elite for the period in question, despite the paucity of Soviet analyses which verify this applicability and the lack of data in many areas which could empirically affirm many of these assumptions for the Soviet elite.

3. Consideration of the first two alternative models, which have also been used in Soviet studies to explain elite recruitment, plus an analysis of their utility and a description of the difference between these theories and the generational approach.

4. An analysis of Central Committee turnover organized from the concept of political generation, concentrating on the process of generational renewal and comparing the results with the findings of other explanatory approaches to the question of elite advancement into the Committee.

5. A summary of contrasts between interpretations of Central Committee composition and recruitment according to the generational approach and those of other models.

6. Finally, some speculative propositions on the future patterns of generational turnover and their policy consequences.

A Generational Approach to Political Change

The basic model to be used is an age cohort theory of sociopolitical change developed by Lambert (1971), Ryder (1965), Cutler (1971), and Mannheim (1952) in their writings on the relationships between changes in population composition along the lines of political generations and changes in the political system and its components. Lambert asserts that, in the maturation process of individuals, there is a "most probable" time when political events are most "impactful" on the developing political consciousness of the individual and that during this period the basic political orientation is stabilized. This period is given by Lambert (1971) and Keniston (1970) as the age range from 17 to 25, although other authors have differed slightly in their own working definitions of this timespan. Merkl (1970: 99–111) uses ages 15 to 20, Cutler uses the ages around 20. There is no doubt that cultural variation from society to society and even within a society (between groups or longitudinally) may alter somewhat the age range most appropriate for this definition, and the intent is not to attach a too great specificity to any given definition. Rather, the purpose is to segregate a relatively small timespan from the life cycle of the individual and to impute certain important events to that period.

Substantively, the generational model asserts that (modally), between the ages of 17 and 25, the basic formation of political consciousness, or *Weltanschauung*, takes place and that, after this period, the changes in broad political outlook are relatively smaller and represent marginal revisions, or attempts to adapt, within the general framework already established.

There is a considerable, if very disparate, body of empirical evidence to support this contention. Gusfield (1957) has used the generational model in studying the difficulties in leadership turnover and rejuvenation in the Women's Christian Temperance Union; Rintala (1958, 1962) has focused on generational changes within left- and right-wing segments of Finnish politics; and Cutler (1970) has analyzed American attitudes to foreign-policy issues, using age cohort analysis; Lipset and Ladd (1971) have noted the strong generational differences in attitudes among American political scientists. In perhaps the most valuable piece of work on intergenerational change in a comparative setting, Inglehart (1971) has found significant generational shifts from what he terms "acquisitive" value orientations to "post-bourgeois" orientations in six West European nations. More important, he has defended these findings against competing life-cycle interpretations and has found that intergenerational cleavages remain when other variables, such as education and socioeconomic status, are controlled. Finally, there is strong evidence in Inglehart's work that the rate of generational change is directly related to the intensity of change taking place in the social environment during early maturation of each generation (in Inglehart's case, specifically the economic rate of growth). Lambert (1971: 24), in his theoretical discussion of American "youth" of the 1960s, emphasizes the intensive qualitative differences between that generation's perceptions of "history-as experienced" and all previous ones; the generational model clearly distinguishes between the life-cycle interpretation of youthful rebellion and the intergenerational cleavages in sociocultural consciousness which develop "if what is experientially significant during this critical period (17–25) differs from generation to generation."

Several points should be noted here about the generational approach to understanding social change. First and most distinctly, the generational model does not posit that all members of a given generation are *equally* affected by salient events occurring during their politically formative years. As a macrosociological approach to understanding and measuring change, the generational approach focuses on aggregate shifts in values and behavior between generations and does not presume to predict at the individual level. It is only too evident that, while a major social or political event may have the effect of shifting the aggregate position on a certain value in one direction for a maturing political generation, there may at the same time be some polarization within that aggregate shift. It is a question of measuring central tendency shifts versus individual shifts, and the two should not be confused when we talk about the central concepts of the generational approach.

Second, just as the generational approach does not assume an equal degree of change for individuals between political generations, neither does it assume that there is any *particular* degree of homogeneity of values within any given generation. This would be ridiculous on the face of it and is entirely unnecessary here as a requisite for the construction of a politically meaningful concept. Just as one need not claim homogeneity of values or attitudes for blue-collar workers, Catholics, or the college educated in order to utilize the variables of class, religion, or education, so it is not necessary for the development of the concept of political generation. In the Soviet case, the use of other background variables in analyzing the composition of the Central Committee involves at least as much of an inferential leap as will the use of political generation.

Finally, Welsh (in Beck et al. 1973) has pointed out that there is a tendency for those engaged in Soviet research to reify their analytic concepts by presuming that they are perceived as such within the Soviet political arena. This is a valid point, and the repeated use of the concept of political generation or the description of each Soviet elite generation used in this chapter is, of course, itself not evidence that something comparable to what we term a "political generation" actually exists as a recognized variable in the behavior of Soviet elites.

However, the tendency toward reification of an abstract theoretical concept is no more inherent in the use of our generational variable than in the use of numerous other constructs current in Soviet elite analysis, perhaps less so, since there is evidence, for example, from Brezhnev's speeches at the 23d and 24th Party Congresses, that political generation is, at least for some Soviet leaders, a recognizable and meaningful social division.[1]

A Priori Applicability to the Soviet Political Elite

Before embarking on the analysis itself, it would seem appropriate to spell out the intuitive grounds for applying the generational model to the particular case of the Soviet Central Committee. This rationale is intended only to justify the attempt and to strengthen the logic of generational inference developed from other empirical studies.

The first factor enhancing the plausibility of the generational

1. See here especially the constructs used by Fleron (coopted/recruited) and Fischer (dual executive/technician/hybrid executive/official) in their studies of the Soviet leadership (Fleron 1969; Fischer 1968). Brezhnev, in his speech to the 23d Congress, noted: "Some Party and YCL organizations at times fail to consider the fact that the present generation of boys and girls has not passed through the harsh school of revolutionary struggle and tempering that fell to the lot of the older generation" (1972: 81–82).

model as an explanatory approach in Soviet politics generally is the dramatic upheaval of modern Russian history. The significance of generational cleavages has been proportional to the degree of experiential differences by successive age cohorts in their early maturity (ages 17–25 to be assumed as the equivalent of this term for our purposes). It is not difficult to make a case for the assertion that Russian history in this century has been a succession of momentous events—economic, social, political, and military—from whose impact few Russian citizens have remained isolated. Only in the post-Stalin years has there been a period of relative calm and stability, and this, too, provides Soviet youth with a stark experiential contrast to the preceding late Stalinism period of 1946 to 1952. Thus the salient events in which successive Russian political generations have matured have been in sharp contrast to those of other political generations. On the basis of empirical studies in other nations, this should support the plausibility of strong generational cleavages in Soviet politics.

Second, while we have asserted above that it is not necessary to argue either for equal impact of events on individuals in any given political generation or for any particular degree of homogeneity within a political generation, it can be maintained that, relative to the Western societies in which most of the attitudinal work on generational change has been done, the Soviet political system has a more developed mechanism for controlling the elite recruitment process and for homogenizing political orientations of its cadres.[2] One need not posit that the degree of this control or the degree of unity of opinion within the political elite has been constant, for it clearly has not, and the intergenerational differences will play a significant role in our interpretation of Central Committee recruitment. Rather, this argument serves only as a further element in the relative merits of the present application to a grouping which can be seen, over its history in power, as more politically homogeneous than the society at large from which it is recruited, more homogeneous than political elites in most Western systems.

Third, I will argue, as do Lipset and Ladd in their analysis of the

2. This argument would be relevant as well to the application of the generational model to any specialized organization or movement which has similar power over leadership recruitment. Thus, for example, Rintala's studies of the Finnish Right and Left or Gusfield's study of the Women's Christian Temperance Union could similarly expect greater within-generation homogeneity (Rintala 1958, 1962; Gusfield 1957).

views of American political scientists, that the political orientations of members of the Soviet political elite are far more developed and are held at a higher level of consciousness than could be assumed for any mass-level survey of citizens in any society. In their generationally oriented study of the politics of American political scientists, Lipset and Ladd state:

> We should note that opinions on questions as diverse as Vietnam, race, and the legalization of marijuana almost certainly could not be organized into a single liberal-conservative dimension for the general population. That these opinions did consistently represent a single dimension in the factor analysis can be attributed to the fact that we are dealing here with a community of professional intellectuals whose very "business" requires them to maintain a basic consistency of ideas. It is to be expected that professors' opinions are more highly structured and interrelated than those of most groups in the society. (1971: 137–138)

This rationale holds as well for the Soviet political elite, a community of professional politicians, even if the motivating factors are very different. It might be added that, since we are dealing with the highest levels of the Soviet political system, this assertion, combined with our second argument, is strengthened further.

These positions enhance the potential for analyzing the Soviet elite from a generational perspective and ease the qualifying conditions for behavioral and policy inferences based on political age cohort. The question remains as to how one actually goes about partitioning Russian history to obtain a precise, quantifiable unit of observation called a political generation. There are two fundamental hurdles to be cleared involving the questions "How long is a generation?" and "How shall individuals be assigned to generational categories?" With regard to the first problem, we shall note, from Cutler (1971: 7–9), that there is no consensus on the (even approximate) length of an average generation, although the most usual range given is 15 to 30 years. But this is a biological definition of generation, and there has been a tendency in studying social change for the time period referred to as a political generation to shrink. Therefore, the historical partition points of our schema will correspond to what may be termed basic turning points in modern Russian history. We shall be relying on scholarly opinion in much of this, and there is no doubt that the set of partitions suggested below is debatable and/or refinable.[3]

With respect to the second question, that of placement of elite members into a particular political generation, we shall use age cohort membership, in this case the year in which each person turned 21, even though some of the politically formative years may lie outside the political generation in which the age of 21 was attained. Each generation spans a sufficient time period so that, in each case, an elite member's early maturity will fall mainly within the time period in which the age of 21 was reached.

In developing our scale of political generations, we are building on the use of "generation" by other scholars in their analyses of the Soviet political elite. Lewytzkyj (1970: 32–38), for example, has described elite conflict and the aging of the 1966 Central Committee in generational terms, although he interprets the major formative events of the generation in power as occurring later in life than most generational theorists would. Using decade of birth and five-year timespans of entry into the party as his basic variables, he depicts a situation of generational entrenchment by what he calls the "War generation," acting out of "bureaucratic instinct for self-preservation." Although he notes the qualitatively better education of younger party cadres and posits the need for their skills in an increasingly complex economy, his main emphasis remains one of power maintenance for a generation grown comfortable with itself and avoiding the advancement of younger members to top levels.

Donaldson and Waller (1970: 11–13, 33–36), in a much more theoretically based comparison of the Soviet and Chinese 1956 Central Committees, also utilize the concept of elite generations and generational conflict, but here the idea of a political generation is not related to any formative experience but rather to skills, and generational conflict is viewed in terms of the skills turnover required by a modernizing economy in which the political elite is directing the modernization (see the connection to the rational-technical model below). The conclusions of these authors focus on the relatively higher Soviet rate of *personnel* turnover and the correspondingly more advanced changeover from a "generation" of "revo-

---

3. An alternative method devised by Klecka (1971) for seeking age partitions would have a statistical routine segment the independent variable on the basis of greatest explanation of variance in a dependent variable. This is not appropriate here, since there is no single dependent variable. Additionally, this method may arrive at quantitatively optimal partitions but may be theoretically void.

lutionary modernizers" to one of "managerial modernizers." Without being critical of this study, it is necessary to clearly separate the concept of generation based on skills, career pattern, or other characteristics from one based on a defined period of early political maturing related to age cohort members. It will become evident that the two may overlap in places, but there is a great difference in interpretation of political values between the two approaches. To illustrate, it is a question of associating a sixty-year-old member of the 1971 Central Committee, who matured during the 1930s and who has an engineering degree, with a forty-seven-year-old member who matured during World War II and who has the same (on paper) engineering degree, or of associating the first member with another sixty-year-old member who went to the Party School.

Using the age cohort standard comparable to the one advocated here, Hough (1967) has delineated in some detail one particular Soviet elite generation (labeled the World War II generation) and has advanced a number of propositions as its political value orientations. Hough's description of this particular political generation is incorporated into the total scale of Soviet elite generations, covering all political generations represented on the Central Committee from 1917 through 1971.

The pre-1905 political generation (see table 41) includes those who reached adulthood before the first dress rehearsal for the fall of the czarist system. For these people, early maturity occurred in a period of repressive and still strong czarist rule, of Russification and early rapid, concentrated, but erratic industrial growth, with the early theoretical disputes among revolutionary dissidents regarding the application of Marxism in Russia. This generation might be expected to correspond roughly with the category of "revolutionary modernizers" developed by John Kautsky (1968: 165), described as cosmopolitan intellectuals, specialists in persuasion, the earliest founders and organizers of the party. Maturing in an era prior to the first signs of czarist weakness, these are the "revolutionary intellectuals" which Huntington (1968: 290) sees as a concomitant of (particularly) the early stages of a modernizing society.

The next generation of the Soviet political elite matured (1905–1920) in a period of repressive yet degenerating czarist rule, the failure of liberal parliamentarianism, further early industrialization, defeat in war, and the final revolutionary overthrow of the old order (the 1917 Revolution and War Communism). The experience of 1905 showed that the old order was vulnerable, and the industrialization and repression, plus the failure of the Duma to rationalize the autocracy, brought more young people into the ranks of the party. The Revolution and civil war attracted a new political generation dedicated to building a new society but first pragmatically engaged in securing the defeat of the old order and managing the Revolution as it won the struggle for state power.[4] This was also a period of relatively free debate within the Bolshevik party, when the leadership of Lenin was not imposed by force and factionalism was relatively open and frank.

The third political age cohort came to maturity after the achievement of state power had been secured, during argumentation (the industrialization debate) over the course of the Revolution in power (in a single country, encircled by a hostile capitalist environment) and the settling of that debate with the victory of the Stalinist faction. These are the members who, as political aspirants, are to represent the new consensus of the first two Five-Year Plans, who will be the first technically trained "managerial modernizers," who fought for and rose with the rapid industrialization drives, the forced collectivization of agriculture, and, in general, the establishment of the basic structures of Stalinist society prior to World War II. They represent the value principles and organizational principles of the new industrialization paradigm outlined by Hardt and Modig (1968: 308–315), in which key human and material resources are placed first at the disposal of the heavy-industry and defense sectors of the economy, with the residual going into consumer goods and agriculture.

During these years (1921–1939), the drive for enforced party unity reached its (irrational) peak: the openness of the party to a broader membership and to debate disappeared behind a tightening process of membership screening and a façade of unanimous votes and toadying to official party leadership. Marxist-Leninist ideology was subordinated to the service of state policy, which now coordinated all aspects of Soviet society toward the goal of rapid industrialization.

4. Donaldson and Waller (1970: 11–13) generally recognize only two skills generations—revolutionary modernizers and managerial modernizers—although they do note Lowenthal's "party apparatchiki with administrative skills." These people, while constituting part of the pre-1905 generation, might also be expected to constitute the upwardly mobile cadres of the political generation which matured from 1905 to 1920. Waller (in Beck et al. 1973: 186–188) has also emphasized the influx of this second generation of "organization" members into the Chinese Central Committee and the lack of growth of a managerial modernizer type in the Chinese political elite.

The war generation, maturing during the bitter struggle of the Great Patriotic War, entered a party which "was no longer engaged in warfare against the peasants or against its own members. On the contrary, it was leading the country in the defense of the motherland against a foreign invader. At this time the party de-emphasized Marxist-Leninist ideology, and even restored fairly close relations with the Orthodox Church. Many hoped that it would make peace with the Russian people after the war and that the population could begin to enjoy the fruits of the industrialization drive" (Hough 1967: 25).

Hough posits, for this generation, an indifference to ideological questions, emphasis on patriotism, a nostalgia for more leeway in day-to-day decision making, a greater responsiveness to consumer demands, an armylike respect for the need to maintain discipline, but a revulsion over the irrationalities of the postwar Stalinist period, and an unconcern with the "ancient history" of the Great Purge.

The political elite generation maturing under the last seven years of Stalin's rule (1946–1952) experienced the irrationality and growing paranoia of the aging dictator, the reimposition of strict ideological controls in all sectors of Soviet society, and the resumption of the goal of rapid industrialization. Domestically, the society was rebuilding to its prewar levels of output, while externally the Soviet Union was emerging as the major rival of the United States in the Cold War, no longer as the sole communist state but as the putative leader of a significant bloc of communist states. While the war generation may have been disaffected by the rigid dogmatism of the late Stalinist period and may even have had misgivings about the abandonment of the wartime cooperation with the United States, the young potential elite members of this neo-Stalinist generation, we may hypothesize, bore the rationale of the Cold War origins, of Berlin confrontations, of Czechoslovakia, of the Yugoslav split and the East European purges of the 1948 to 1952 period, and of Korea as basic political orientations.

The post-Stalinist political generation (1953–1973) is presented here as a single era despite the several changes at the top leadership level and despite notable differences between the Khrushchev and the Brezhnev-Kosygin styles of politics. This era is characterized by a gradual and general relaxation of tension and repression domestically, by a limited yet clear process of political destalinization, by increasing verbal and more slowly increasing actual attention to consumer goods, and by a rather jerky but continual development of peaceful coexistence with the West, at the same time that the Soviet Union is achieving superpower parity with the United States. We may hypothesize for this elite generation a more outgoing and less defensive orientation toward the West, intermingled with impatience in regard to the development of a higher standard of living. We may also posit a greater willingness to question the basic structures of Stalinist society as well as the cult of Stalin and the purge mechanism denounced during the Khrushchev period of ascendancy. It is a period in which issue debate is relatively freer, if still clearly requiring sanction from top levels, and in which the penalties for political failure are more limited.

Table 41 gives the basic outline of successive political generations used for this study. Thus, for some examples, Brezhnev, born 1906, is reckoned as a member of the 1921 to 1939 political generation, since he turned 21 in 1927; V. A. Demchenko, born 1920, would belong to the war generation (1940–1945); K. F. Katushev, born 1927, would be figured in with the 1946 to 1952 late Stalinist political generation. It should be noted that, while four of the six defined generations cover periods of 16 to 24 years, two generations (the World War II and postwar late Stalinism eras) are considerably shorter and reflect the interruption of the war effort, followed in the immediate postwar years by the reimposition of strict controls and the reaffirmation of the basic structures and priorities of Stalinist society, established with so much effort and coercion during the first two Five-Year Plans.

Alternative Approaches to Soviet Elite Mobility

There are, of course, a multitude of "models" and "theories" of Soviet elite recruitment, and it would be impossible to adequately treat each of them separately in this chapter. Therefore, the following will entail some compression and grouping of approaches in order to briefly outline the points of competition, agreement, or irrelevance of several major types of approaches to the problem of explaining Soviet elite recruitment.

Philip Stewart and his associates (1972: 1269–1272), for purposes of their own multilevel testing, have divided the literature on elite mobility in Soviet politics into two broad categories: the patron-client model and the rational-technical model. Within the first general model they include the totalitarian and the Kremlinological

TABLE 41. Summary of Cohort-Defined Soviet Elite Generations

Political generation	Birth years	Era of early maturity[a]
1. Revolutionary modernizers	1860–1883	1881–1904 Repressive czarism
2. Revolutionary managers	1884–1899	1905–1920 Degenerating czarism
3. Managerial modernizers	1900–1918	1921–1939 Establishment of Stalinism
4. War generation pragmatists	1919–1924	1940–1945 Disruption of Stalinist structures
5. Cold War neo-Stalinists	1925–1931	1946–1952 Reaffirmation of Stalinism
6. Post-Stalinists	1932–1952	1953–1973 Limited relaxation of Stalinist structures

[a] Period in which age 21 was attained.

theories of the Soviet political system. While there is certainly a great deal of overlapping and disagreement within these groupings of theories, it may be useful to retain this basic partition for our purposes. In general, it may be said that the totalitarian model, as represented by Brzezinski and Huntington (1963) or by Fainsod (1963), says more about the vehicle (purge process) of elite mobility than about the characteristics, either skills or policy orientations, of elite members. The basic assertion by the totalitarian school is the systematic need for a monolithic party with a single personal leader at the top. Kremlinological theories may or may not accept this assertion, but they do posit the existence of fierce factionalism within the ranks of the political elite, based on the contradiction between a (posited) ideological insistence on party unity and the lack of legitimizing institutions or processes for elite promotion or demotion.[5] The relationship of patron-client may be deduced, according to the varieties of Kremlinology, from a series of personal or organi-

5. There is basic disagreement within the ranks of Kremlinologists as to the effect on the system of prolonged collective leadership. Rush (1965), an advocate of the cyclical theory of Soviet politics, and Wesson (1972, 1972a) imply system degeneration as a result, and Tatu (1970) also leans in this direction. However, others such as Linden (1966) and Lowenthal (1968) do not see this as inherent, and Lowenthal in fact seems to view the present collective leadership as quite successful and skillful.

zational tangencies in the careers of elite members. It is important here to note that neither totalitarian nor Kremlinological analyses relate elite composition to general social or economic structures or to trends in Soviet society, nor do they, in general, give any predictions for long-term policy outcomes. Several practitioners, noting that the victors in several succession struggles have appropriated the policies, or considerable elements thereof, of their defeated opponents, thereby suggest the tenuousness of extrapolating short-term elite turnover with policy or policy change. The limitation of both totalitarian and Kremlinological theories, as has been pointed out for quite some time now, is that they do not relate elite composition or elite change to the substance of Soviet politics or Soviet society.

The rational-technical model, likewise, is not a homogeneous school of thought but, rather, includes scholars with interest group (Skilling 1971), structural-functional (Gehlen and McBridge 1968), skills-meritocratic (Gehlen 1966), and systems (Fleron 1969) approaches to Soviet politics. While there are severe differences in emphasis and interpretation within this school, a central tendency is nevertheless clear: the assumption that the industrialization process in the Soviet Union carries with it the need, expressed in a variety of ways by each approach, for the political elite to include people with certain characteristics. These characteristics may be identified as group affiliation (for certain key groupings within the political, economic, and social structures), functional roles within an industrializing system, proven or putative technical and administrative skills, or specialized information. It is posited, in most cases implicitly, that the industrialization process changes these needs over time and that in a planned economy these characteristics must be found within the political elite itself.

The patronage model focuses on personal hierarchical relationships inferred from information locating individuals within the same geographical or institutional area at some point or points in time. The generational model broadens this to include the possibility of meaningful and also nonhierarchical ties between elite individuals on the basis of shared historical experiences, concentrating on those of early maturity and asserting a basic stability of orientation through later years. The generational model does not deny the premise of personal conflict but, rather, seeks to associate individuals with a common political orientation, within which it is perfectly likely that there will still exist personal or clique rivalry.

The goal of rapid industrialization, and the overriding priority placed on it within the Soviet system, is recognized by the rational-technical model as a stable given; the generational model, on the other hand, sees it as a generation-specific priority perfectly capable of being overridden or at least demoted at some point in time. The assumption of the generational model is that the Stalinist industrialization paradigm is most deeply held by those elite members who matured during the years of the industrialization debate and the harsh establishment of the Stalinist values and structures during the first two Five-Year Plans (as well as by the small group of Stalin's immediate associates who enforced this development at the time). Further, the assumption is that, for other Soviet political generations who matured both before and after this period, this priority may not be held as highly, and this will affect the recruitment of new members into the Central Committee. There is, in human priorities, nothing inherently rational about continued industrialization ad infinitum, nor is there a single economic goal to which technical and administrative efforts must be tied. Thus, while the rational-technical model may indeed be appropriate as an invariate assumption for the period in which there is elite consensus on the value of industrial expansion, it should be viewed as a variable in a longitudinal study covering several generations of Soviet development.

The generational approach relates changes in the Soviet economy and society to changes in the composition of the political elite, such as skills, social background, nationality, career pattern, or organizational affiliation, but within the context of posited value priorities which characterize the most salient events of early maturity for successive age cohorts. Elite turnover in the Committee is related to generational consensus/cleavage over current issues within the dominant elite generation and to the ease with which generational rejuvenation is achieved under the given circumstances of each era in Soviet political development. Thus, what may be a situation of consensus within an elite generation during one period may be one of dissension in the next period. Likewise, the differing characteristics which represent the salient cleavage between the two elite generations may be nonsalient as a cleavage for successive elite cadres.

What, then, does a generational approach to elite composition and turnover in the Soviet Central Committee expect to find? First, in an elite body characterized by group cooptation from above as opposed to election from below, generation theory would predict greater generational renewal in a situation where there is no strong consensus on current salient issues among the older and still dominant elite generation. Where there is strong consensus among the

TABLE 42. Central Committee Membership by Political Generation 1917–1971

Political generation	Apr. 1917 %	Aug. 1917 %	1918 %	1919 %	1920 %	1921 %	1923 %	192 %
Revolutionary modernizer	63	76	60	68	68	56	40	35
Revolutionary manager	25	24	40	26	32	40	55	56
Managerial modernizer								
War generation								
Neo-Stalinist								
Post-Stalinist								
Date of birth unknown	13	0	0	5	0	4	5	10

dominant elite generation, we would expect to find a low rate of generational turnover.

As a corollary to the above hypothesis, we would expect the possibility of greater generational turnover in the face of a consensus elite generation only when the power of promotion to and demotion from the elite body is lost by the elite as a group. This could occur in several ways: through the establishment of a personal dictatorship over the collective elite, through the development of some effective process of elite selection from below, or through external (i.e., foreign) intervention in the selection of the political elite.

Second, generation theory says little about *personnel* turnover rates per se, but we would expect that, in periods of growing or strong consensus within the dominant elite generation (with no loss of collective power over cooptation), personnel turnover would decline or be low in correlation with generational turnover. In periods of waning consensus or dissension among the dominant elite generation, personnel and generational turnover would be increasingly or more closely associated. And, as a corollary here, we would expect the *possibility* of highest association between personnel and generational turnover in periods where the collective political elite has lost its power over membership selection.

27	1930 %	1934 %	1939 %	1952 %	1956 %	1961 %	1966 %	1971 %
	30	20	18	4	2	1	1	0
	56	61	26	17	14	7	6	3
		3	35	55	76	85	83	72
				1	1	4	7	13
						2	3	8
						1	1	0
	14	17	21	23	8	2	1	4

A Generational Analysis of Central Committee Membership

Table 42 presents the generational composition for Soviet Central Committees from 1917 to 1971. In the period of War Communism, from 1917 through 1920, the generation of revolutionary intellectuals or revolutionary modernizers constitutes the great majority of the Committee's full membership, with no clear trend toward generational renewal, perhaps understandable under the pressures of the civil war, the relatively short time period involved, and the youthfulness of the "older" generation of the Bolshevik elite. This corresponds to the period in which the paramount goal for the party is to secure the revolution in state power. If we characterize this as a period of primary goal consensus (even if imposed by the exigencies of war) within the revolutionary modernizer generation, the first proposition is strengthened, in that generational turnover is low for the period 1917 to 1920.

Beginning in 1921, with the 10th Party Congress, the inauguration of the NEP, and the strictures on factionalism in the party, there is a clear and steady influx of second-generation elites (revolutionary managers) into the Committee. This corresponds to the period of intraparty struggle over the course of the Revolution and over the Lenin succession question. At the beginning of this period, there is no elite consensus among the revolutionary modernizers, and during this period (by 1923 at least 55% of the Committee was composed of second-generation elites) the balance of generational representation shifts in a steady evolutionary manner. The ascendance of this second generation of elites through 1934 coincides with the defeat of the Left, Trotskyite, United, and Right Opposition factions within the party elite and represents the development of a new consensus about the course of the Revolution.[6] But (as table 43 demonstrates) this second elite generation of revolutionary managers, which rose politically with the Stalinist faction of the first elite generation, was of low educational attainment and could have directed the industrialization drive only as political commissars, loyal to the Revolution, the party, and Stalin but technically incompetent to map out and judge industrial development. The political commissar system had been Trotsky's method in the building of the Red Army and had been used economically in the form of "Red managers" in the factories, but it was not Stalin's choice for the period after 1934. Despite the new consensus, shared by the Stalinist victors over the "cosmopolitan" elements of the revolutionary modernizers, and by the new second generation of elites, the purge period of the thirties saw the rapid installation of a third elite generation in the Central Committee, as well as the decimation, not primarily of the Stalinist faction of the earliest revolutionaries, but of the second, transitional, elite generation. The Central Committee installed at the 19th Party Congress saw the reduction in representation of the first elite generation from 20% to 18% (not including the considerable portion for which date of birth is unavailable), an insignificant change, but the drastic reduction of, over only a five-year period, the second generation from 61% to only 26% of the new Committee. As of 1939, the modal elite generation in the Committee is the third, or managerial modernizer, generation, and this has remained the most represented generation for the last thirty-seven years, comprising over three-fourths of the Central Committee for the entire post-Stalinist era. Indeed, for the last two decades, no other political elite

6. We would differ with those interpretations of generational change which see the process as merely a transition from the revolutionary modernizers to the managerial modernizers, since, both from a skills definition and from an age cohort definition of political generation, there is clearly an intermediate grouping.

TABLE 43. Educational Background of Central Committee Members by Political Generation, 1917–1934

Education	1917 %	1921 %	1925 %	1930 %	1934 %
Revolutionary modernizer					
Low, secondary	25	55	43	50	67
Technical	0	0	14	10	17
Professional, university	75	46	43	40	17
N	4	11	14	10	6
Revolutionary manager					
Low, secondary		100	75	79	74
Technical		0	0	0	5
Professional, university		0	25	21	21
N		3	12	14	19

generation has had more than token representation among the full membership of the Central Committee, and this has meant a sharp aging of the Soviet leadership, as various scholars have noted. If we represent Soviet elite history from 1921 through the 16th Party Congress in 1930 (the defeat of the Right Opposition), or even the Congress of Victors in 1934, as a period of first-generation elite struggle to achieve a new consensus, then our first proposition is borne out by the Great Purge carried out by Stalin, involving the decimation not of the Stalinists among the revolutionary modernizers but of the second-generation revolutionary managers. The long-term entrenchment in power of the second elite generation, still a young group as of 1934, which would have been expected after the political defeat of the various oppositional groupings during the NEP and the first years of the Five-Year Plan, was cut short by the accumulation of power by a personal dictator able to use the power of the Bureau of State Security to purge the revolutionary managers from above.

While there is evidence that Stalin, near the end of his life, was about to escalate the Doctors' Plot into yet another wholesale purge, since his death the power of cooptation has remained largely with the collective political elite itself, with no one person able to exercise the kind of elite changes which Stalin, at his peak, was capable of. Thus, the original strong consensus of rapid industrialization reflected by the third generation of the Soviet elite, differentiated from the generational experience of younger party cadres, has become a generational entrenchment of power and a strong unwillingness to pass power on to younger, middle-level elites. The strong elite consensus of the generation of managerial modernizers, entrenched in the Central Committee for almost thirty-seven years now, again provides evidence affirming the first proposition of the generational approach.

The question arises as to how closely these age cohort generations actually correspond with the various descriptive names given them and how much they overlap with the skills-defined generations used by other scholars. What are the salient differences from generation to generation in Soviet elite history, and how well do they reflect the experiential cleavages of successively maturing Russian youth?

The first generation of Bolshevik leaders, in its period of numerical dominance in the Central Committee, was indeed, for the vanguard of the proletariat, a highly educated group from middle- and upper-class origins. There is no representation of technically educated types and very little peasant representation among this group until 1920.

The second elite generation, in its ascendancy, carried into the Committee members predominantly from the toiling classes of workers and peasants (see table 44), compared to the heavy representation of middle-class, intelligentsia, and aristocratic origins among the members of the first elite generation in its prime years of dominance, during the period of the Revolution and War Communism. As this generation gains in representation, the cosmopolitan, highly but not technically educated members of the splintered first generation are weeded out of the party leadership, as can be seen from the decline of middle-, upper-class, and well-educated elements of the pre-1905 political generation from 1921 to 1934.[7]

The upheaval of the Great Purge brings (see table 45) a new, technically educated elite generation into the Central Committee in sizable numbers, drawn also predominantly from the toiling classes, although with greater representation from the peasantry than was true of the previous elite generation in its peak years of representation. Over the period of third-generation dominance, the less educated among the second generation are weeded out, although there is never a significant number of technically educated members among

7. Of those with known dates of birth, the survivors of the revolutionary modernizer generation in the Central Committee at the Congress of Victors were Stalin, Manuilsky, Badaev, Chuvyrin, Krupskaya, Liubimov, Petrovsky, Krzhizanovsky, Piatnitsky, Bubnov, Voroshilov, Litvinov, Yenukidze, and Kalinin.

TABLE 44. Social Origin of Central Committee Members by Political Generation, 1917–1934

Social origin	1917 %	1921 %	1925 %	1930 %	1934 %
Revolutionary modernizer					
Peasant	0	42	25	29	33
Worker	25	33	31	35	33
Middle class, intelligentsia, nobility	75	25	44	35	33
N	4	12	16	17	12
Revolutionary manager					
Peasant		40	41	27	32
Worker	100	40	50	43	44
Middle class, intelligentsia, nobility		20	9	30	24
N	1	5	22	30	34

the second elite generation throughout its history in the Central Committee. In addition, throughout the post–World War II period, there is a gradual and moderate rise in the representation of elites of peasant origin in both the second- and third-generation members, corresponding with the gradual reconciliation of the regime with the peasantry, undertaken by Khrushchev and continued by Brezhnev and Kosygin. The origins of the managerial modernizer generation lie within the third age cohort generation.

The entire post-1939 period has been one of marginal changes in the social and educational backgrounds of elite recruitment into the Central Committee, and even these marginal changes have taken place within the composition of the managerial modernizer elite generation. The Soviet economy has grown tremendously since the initial industrialization drive of the first two Five-Year Plans, becoming increasingly more complex and differentiated. Many scholars have commented on the need for persons in high office with more contemporary, better formal educations, with presumably more innovative ideas for continuing economic modernization. Fischer, in his study of Soviet top executives, comments:

> Almost two-thirds of the 306 executives listed in this study were born in the ten years before the Revolution, 1907–1916.

TABLE 45. Educational Background of Central Committee Members for Selected Political Generations, 1939–1966

Education	1939 %	1952 %	1956 %	1961 %	1966 %
Revolutionary manager					
Low, secondary	57	37	33	27	20
Technical	21	16	11	9	10
Professional, university	21	47	56	64	70
N	14	19	18	11	10
Managerial modernizer					
Low, secondary	25	19	12	9	8
Technical	42	50	61	61	62
Professional, university	33	32	27	30	30
N	24	54	85	145	160
War generation					
Low, secondary				0	8
Technical			100	57	69
Professional, university				43	23
N			1	7	13
Neo-Stalinist					
Low, secondary				0	0
Technical				67	80
Professional, university				33	20
N				3	5

Most of them came of age in the late 1920's and early 1930's. In Soviet history, this is a period in which men with organizational and technical skills were greatly needed, and these men had little chance to get formal training of a solid kind. Inevitably, this often meant a spotty education or no advanced schooling at all. Many of today's top executives had their initial training in narrowly specialized and highly applied skills in a given branch of the economy. (1968: 94)

Lewytzkyj (1967: 39) speaks of an "educational gap" between this generation of managerial modernizers and younger, better-educated party cadres. Thus, while the third elite generation certainly represents a necessary first step, according to the rational-technical model of Soviet elite mobility, it is apparent that there are now available party cadres with higher educational and skills backgrounds, more relevant to the operation of the present Soviet economy, who are not being advanced to Central Committee level, as would be predicted by a rational-technical model.

Advocates of the patron-client model have suggested that, in periods of collective rule, there is a deadlock among the various contending factions and aspirants for sole leadership which hampers leadership renewal and leads to the entrenchment in power of the oligarchs. Wesson, for example, views collective rule versus personal dictatorship as the relevant issue for *both* personnel and generational turnover:

> Senescence thus looms for the oligarchic leadership, which seems to lack capacity for renewal of personnel or institutional change. The present system must soon require revitalization and overhaul. A new dictatorship might rejuvenate and enliven to some extent, and this cannot be viewed as unlikely. The Soviet system contains impediments to dictatorship but may require it; it has usually, of course, had a dictatorship to cap the political edifice. (1972: 213)

Rush also considers an oligarchic leadership within the top Soviet leadership to be inherently unstable and a threat to the system:

> The prolonged absence of a dictator need not mean the collapse of the Soviet system, but it might entail loss by the state of some of its great power in circumstances where it was unable to exercise them effectively. (1965: 79)

Rush clearly presents the phase of oligarchic rule (within the Politburo) as relatively short, likely to be undermined by a leader or faction which gains control of the Secretariat and uses that body as leverage to gain control over the Politburo as well. He assumes that the oligarchy must try to maintain personnel stability in order not to upset the factional balance in the Politburo, but this does not, in his view, preclude the expansion of the Central Committee. In fact, the Committee is likely to grow by leaps and bounds, but this presumption says nothing about the composition or the nature of this expansion.

Tatu describes the continued power of the oligarchy (which he calls the "political generation of 1938") in the post-Khrushchev period, but he sees a process of democratization as more probable than a return to personal dictatorship, in terms of redressing the loss of decision-making power which the collective leadership entails. He depicts a combination of a single political generation operating as a collective leadership within the Politburo as the main impediment to the rejuvenation of the political elite, but he is at some loss to explain the nature of this group solidarity:

> This is due either to the rulers' natural inclinations or to the fact that the patronage extended by members of the ruling group to their respective clients cancels out. (1970: 539)

The problem lies with the necessary distinction between personnel and generational turnover. The second major proposition advanced here relates the two on the basis of consensus/dissension within the dominant elite generation. To test this proposition, we can measure the level of association between personnel turnover and generational turnover in the Central Committee, conceived as two grouped ordinal variables, for different periods of Soviet history. For pairs of Central Committees, personnel are classified as either "not returned" from the earlier to the later Committee, "continued" from one to the other, or "newly promoted" into the later Committee but not members of the earlier one. Appropriate statistics for measuring strength of association between two ordinal variables in this case would be Somer's D or Kendal's tau-c.[8] (In fact, the actual figures in table 46 for tau-c differ by insignificant amounts from those for Somer's D.) The generational model predicts low association levels for the period of War Communism, declining for the postpurge period of growing dominance of the generation of managerial modernizers, high levels of association for the early NEP period, declining toward the 1934 Congress, and the possibility of very high levels of association for the Great Purge era. The data generally support these expectations. For the 1917 to 1920 period (Seventh Conference Central Committee through the 9th Party Congress), there is almost no association (D = .03) between personnel and generational turnover, although personnel turnover was quite substantial during this period (see table 47 below). For the early NEP (up to the 14th Party Congress in 1925) the level of association jumps to .34, declines in the 1925 to 1930 period to a very weak .06,

8. Measures which calculate reduction of error between two nominal scales or deviation from expected values were deemed inappropriate here, since there is directionality involved in the hypothesis. Among ordinal scale measures, gamma was not preferred because it measures curvilinear as well as monotonic correlations. Cf. Garson (1971: 160–162) and Blalock (1972: 300–303, 421–425).

TABLE 46. Correlation of Personnel and Generational Turnover in the Central Committee, 1917–1971

Time period	Strength of association		Generational model expectation
	Somer's D	Tau-c	
1917–1920	.03	.03	Low
1920–1925	.34	.32	High
1925–1930	.06	.08	Declining
1930–1934	.27	.24	Declining
1934–1939	.34	.32	Possibly quite high
1939–1952	(.42)[a]	(.39)[a]	Declining
1952–1956	.19	.17	Declining
1956–1961	.18	.17	Declining
1961–1966	.11	.09	Declining
1966–1971	.27	.24	Declining

[a] Figures for 1939–1952 are not really comparable, due to the much longer time interval.

and rises to .27 for the 1930 to 1934 period. While the proposition would have expected a higher correlation for the late twenties and a lower correlation with the incipient entrenchment of the second-generation elite up to the Congress of Victors, the retention of several politically defeated Right Opposition leaders (e.g., Tomsky, Rykov, and A. P. Smirnov of the first generation of Bolshevik leaders) on the Committee at the 16th Party Congress and their formal removal from the Committee later reduce the coefficient for the earlier period and raise it for the latter. For the Great Purge era, the level of association is again relatively high, but not as high as might have been expected. This is due to the fact that, while generational turnover is heavy between second-generation members being purged and third-generation newcomers to the Committee, there is a proportionately larger core of first-generation (including Stalin, Voroshilov, and Kalinin) holdovers from the Congress of Victors. If we had used a statistic which (for nominal scale data) measures all deviation from expected values (Cramer's V = .47 or a Contingency Coefficient = .55), this period would show peak values for all periods of Soviet rule. As it is, the peak value for D (.42) is achieved for the 1939 to 1952 period, but this should clearly be discounted due to the incomparability of the timespan with other periods. For the 1952 to 1956, 1956 to 1961, and 1961 to 1966 periods, the levels of association (.19, .18, .11) are low and declining, but they rise moderately for

TABLE 47. Age and Tenure of Central Committee Members, 1917–1971

Age group[a]	Aug. 1917 %	1921 %	1925 %	1930 %	19⫶ %
Under 36	48	25	23	13	6
36–45	48	63	54	54	56
46–55	4	12	23	26	28
Over 55	0	0	0	7	10
Tenure[b]					
Newly elected	67	44	22	21	27
1–9 years	33	56	78	67	37
10 or more years	0	0	0	12	36

[a] Normalized to 100% for those with known birth years. Up to 25% are of unkno⫶ birth date for certain Central Committees.
[b] Years as full member only.

the 1966 to 1971 period (D = .27). It would appear that, after thirty-seven years as the dominant generation, personnel turnover is becoming somewhat more closely associated with generational renewal, although the managerial modernizer age cohort still holds nearly three of every four seats in the Committee. For actuarial reasons, as well as the increasing discrepancy between the conditions of early maturity and contemporary ones, the dominance of the third elite generation in Soviet history is slowly waning.

The average age in the Central Committee rises from 39 in 1921 to 45 in 1934, from 45 in 1939 to 58 by 1971. In 1934, the modal age group in the Committee was 36 to 45 years old, still predominantly in the "ideological" elite category as defined by Quandt (1970) from his cross-national comparison of national elites. The average age in the current Committee is nearly a decade above the average age of those termed "non-ideological" by Quandt. And yet, in personnel terms, the percentages of newcomers elected to full Committee status have been impressive, with fully 37% of the 1971 Committee composed of first-timers (see table 47). The major reason for the high percentages of newcomers in the post-1939 period of Party Congresses is the numerical growth of the Committee. In the last decade, despite relatively high personnel turnover, the tenure of Committee members has risen to all-time highs.

1952 %	1956 %	1961 %	1966 %	1971 %
3	0	2	1	1
25	15	15	6	6
53	65	53	43	28
19	20	30	50	65
70	40	62	26	37
0	41	32	44	16
30	19	6	30	47

It was also true that, by 1934, despite the generational transition and the high annual rise of newcomers added during the early 1920s, fully 36% of the last prepurge Committee members had at least a decade of experience on the Committee. This incipient second-generation elite entrenchment, with declining rates of newcomer influx, was forcefully changed during the purge period.

During Khrushchev's ascendancy, another low in terms of length of service was reached in 1961, when only 6% of that Central Committee had served a decade or more at that level of the political elite. And yet, at the height of Khrushchev's power, he could only marginally rejuvenate the Soviet political elite. Ultimately, the failure of many of Khrushchev's reform proposals might be attributed to his inability to significantly alter the generational orientation of the political elite, despite the numerous (62%) newcomers promoted to the 1961 Committee. Since 1961, Committee tenure has risen for a large percentage of the Soviet political elite, so that by 1971 nearly half (47%) had served for 10 or more years. This is a tenure pattern more comparable to the U.S. House of Representatives, which in 1971 had 54% of its members with 10 or more years of service (cf. chap. 5). The House of Representatives, however, has maintained an average age of 50 to 52 years for several decades now, with only 10 to 15% newcomers after each election, because the modal turnover pattern is for a relatively young member to replace a relatively aged one. It is not, therefore, for lack of personnel turnover or influx of newcomers into the Central Committee that the average age has continued to rise to the borders of (collective) incipient gerontocracy. This was clearly not the case during the early NEP years of collective leadership, when high personnel turnover corresponded to at least moderate rates of generational renewal. The difference is that the dominant (revolutionary modernizers) elite generation was split during the NEP, while the third elite generation has presented an enduring united front against younger generations of leaders.

Summary

The above analysis seeks to put into a generational perspective the work done through both the patron-client and the rational-technical models, at least with respect to recruitment of elites into the Soviet Central Committee. The aging of the Soviet elite is the aging of the last political elite generation which achieved a consensus among itself on the basic framework of Soviet society. The rational-technical assumptions applied to analyses of educational and career backgrounds are generation-specific and fit only because of the long dominance of a single political generation within the Soviet elite. Otherwise, there is no valid explanation for the refusal to allow younger people with better formal educational achievement and a more contemporary grasp on technical problems to reach Committee status. The rationale assumed for the influx of a new generation of managerial modernizers does not treat the issue of which (of many) priorities technical training may be applied to. The generational model posits such value positions on an age cohort basis.

The patron-client model has difficulty in recognizing, among other things, the intragenerational trust which may account for the ability of the Soviet elite, in the post-Stalin period, to minimize its internal policy differences and to maintain a generally united front against the political aspirations of younger cadres. The bond of generational solidarity among the third-generation managerial modernizers and their apparent distrust of those younger, but by no means inexperienced, persons in intermediate ranks in the party must lead to the conclusion that there are significant differences in value orientation between the last consensus position of the Soviet elite (namely, the construction of Stalinist structures in the economy and society) and the positions of those in the World War II, neo-Stalinist, and post-Stalinist elite generations. This bond must be strong enough to predominantly restrict client mobility into the Committee to increasingly older members of the managerial modernizer generation.

What are the prospects for generational renewal in the Soviet elite? The present situation, as mentioned earlier, cannot last much longer. On the other hand, the war generation and the neo-Stalinists of the postwar period represent relatively short eras and presumably conflicting values in many areas. Neither is particularly youthful at this point (those in the war generation are now between 52 and 57, those in the neo-Stalinist between 45 and 51, compared to the arrival of the managerial modernizers in 1939 (all under 40). It is possible that internal exigencies and the popular demand for more than marginal changes within the basic structures of Stalinist society will lead to a sudden influx of post-Stalinist cadres, embodying (in coalition with the war generation) a new consensus position on the future course of Soviet society, largely bypassing the neo-Stalinist generation and its (posited) Cold War and ideologically dogmatic positions. Or it is possible that those most die-hard among the managerial modernizers will opt to prolong their dominance in social values through continuing low representation of the war and post-Stalinist generations, hoping to form a coalition with a markedly increased contingent of neo-Stalinists. These generational shifts may *not*, however, correspond to any great changes in the composition of the Central Committee along educational, social-background, or career-pattern lines. Nor will they necessarily reflect a change in the collective nature of the Soviet leadership. But the generational model would predict that they will represent either, in the first case mentioned above, a decisive policy shift and an overhaul of major institutions of Soviet society, especially in the economy, or, in the second case, the continued temporizing and hesitancy in adaptation, or even ideological regression and institutional reaffirmation with correspondingly higher levels of repression. As Hardt and Modig have noted:

> Institutions universally tend to outlive the original purpose for their creation, and the persistence of the administrative status quo in the Soviet Union is perhaps even stronger than it is in other societies. . . . Challenges have been permitted, even those

directed toward the collective form of agriculture. But challenges are not changes; new central planning methods have yet to be adopted, collectivization continues in agriculture, and foreign trade is still a monopoly. The basic institutional structure of Stalinism in economic development remains basically unchanged, if not unmodified. (1968: 317–318)

The ease or difficulty of political adaptation to further development of Soviet society will depend in great measure on which pattern of elite generational succession will prevail.

CHAPTER 10

A Generational Interpretation
of the Soviet Elite: 2

Having dealt with the patron-client (or totalitarian/Kremlinological) interpretations of the Soviet political elite, we shall contrast our generational approach with two prevalent Marxist interpretations of the Soviet elite system, namely, the "bureaucratic stratum" thesis of Trotsky and the "new-class" thesis of Djilas.[1]

The Degeneration of the Workers' State

A first Marxist critique of the Soviet elite comes from the Trotskyites, beginning with Trotsky himself (1957: 248–252), who alleges that, while the Soviet Union remains a workers' state with no private ownership over the means of production, a bureaucratic stratum representing a denial of workers' democracy has raised itself above the proletariat and is now the commanding stratum in Soviet society. Trotsky and such like-minded observers as Deutscher and Mandel, however, have refused to recognize this leading stratum as a social class, and this is partly responsible for Deutscher's optimism (1968: 159–174) regarding the future for a democratic socialism after Stalin's death. Trotsky, in particular, notes that in the absence of stocks and bonds—formal legal titles of ownership—the privileges of the bureaucratic stratum cannot be passed on to one's children, and thus this political clique has no secure means of

1. It is, of course, a matter of serious contention whether either the Trotskyite or the Djilas theses constitute a "Marxist" interpretation of the Soviet system, but an analysis of this question is quite beyond the scope of this chapter. For a good running commentary on both sides of the issue, see Lane (1971: chap. 6) for criticism, and see especially Sweezy and Bettelheim (1971) for a defense of the Marxist foundations of both critiques.

providing for its long-run succession as a cohesive political group-ing. Therefore, the bureaucratic stratum is not seen as an econom-ically exploitive class which must be overthrown by a new social revolution, which Djilas calls for. Mandel, the contemporary Trotskyite economist, suggests that the bureaucratic deformation of the October Revolution is "only the product of an accident of the historical process characterizing the transition between feudalism and capitalism" (1972: 16). Mandel, like Trotsky and Deutscher, re-gards this leading stratum as a parasitic outgrowth of the proletariat, a deformation caused by the historical circumstances of the civil-war period of 1918 to 1921 (War Communism). From this perspec-tive, there is no functional rationale by which this elite stratum can perpetuate itself in power, since it fills no necessary function of a social class:

> Because it is not a new class . . . the bureaucracy has no politi-cal, social, or economic means at its disposal to make the de-fense of its own special material interests coincide with the de-velopment of the mode of production from which it draws its privileges. (Mandel 1972: 16–17)

Yet Mandel goes on to argue that there is still the possibility that the Revolution, already betrayed (Trotsky 1957: 252), may still be over-thrown and a new class established as an explicit bourgeoisie, but not without "crushing the resistance of the Soviet proletariat" (p. 39), which it has apparently not yet done. He is convinced that the Soviet political elite does not constitute a historically necessary force for rapid economic growth, for the industrialization and mod-ernization of the process of production. Rather, he views it as a hin-drance, without which a democratic centralized planning directed by the "associated producers" could do better.

The New-Class Thesis

Another Marxist critique of the Soviet political system charges that the Soviet political elite represents the interests of a new propertied class, a new collective bourgeoisie, which has not only betrayed the Revolution, as Trotsky admits, but has also effectively overthrown it. The Stalinist transformation of the economy is seen as the crea-tive mechanism for the rise of this new class, the political bureauc-racy, although the roots of its birth lie in the type of professional revolutionaries required by Lenin for the early Bolshevik party (Djilas 1961: 321 ff.). Djilas asserts that this new class is "better organized and more highly class-conscious than any class in recorded history" (p. 337), although he adds quickly that it deludes itself into believing it is not a new exploitive ownership class.

Nevertheless, for this new class, state property is treated as a collective possession, so that the means of production no longer belong to the workers but to an exploitive economic class, which monopolizes the political sphere and, through it, manages (though not juridically owning the means of production) the economy to suit its own interests. The privileges of this new ruling class are derived from this monopoly over administration of the economy. Djilas is somewhat fuzzy as to just who constitutes this new class, however. At some points it seems to stem from the party hierarchy, but at other points it appears to be centered more in the governmental (more specifically, ministerial) apparatus of the state system. With the passing of time, Djilas contends, the role of the party grows weaker and that of the state bureaucracy stronger (p. 321). Stojanovic (1973: 46 ff.), in his extension of Djilas' new-class thesis into a theory of "statism," speaks of the coalescence of the state's apparatus with the Communist party and defines the "personal share" of the exploitation of the working class by each member of this new statist class as proportional to his/her position in the state hierarchy. This confusion need not be fatal to the theory of statism, or the new-class thesis, however, since it can be said that more "orthodox" Marxists have similar difficulties in precisely defining the boundary between social classes in Western societies, and this need not undermine the basic premises of Marxist analysis. There is also some disagreement within this school of thought regarding the historical necessity of the new class in the industrialization of Russia. Djilas (pp. 320, 323, 329) affirms this necessity, but Stojanovic (pp. 51–56) generally denies it, positing that the extension of social self-government based on worker control had certain, if somewhat fewer, prospects for realization in the early years of Soviet development.

Marxist Critiques of the Soviet Political Elite

What is interesting, for our purposes here, about these two now classic critiques of Soviet society and the Soviet political system is how heavily, for Marxist interpretations of politics, they, like most non-Marxist approaches, rest on a typing of the political elite and how they seek to characterize the nature of the political system from the top down, so to speak. Moreover, because one expects from Marxist analyses more emphasis on the generation of social elites from large-scale social and economic developments, it is sometimes unclear just how the privileged political elite described by proponents of both schools is able to perpetuate itself in terms of elite socialization and political succession within its own ranks. David Lane (1971: 178–183) has pointed out these (and other) difficulties with such models of the Soviet system. For the Trotskyite degenerate workers' state thesis, it is difficult to understand how such personal characteristics as "riffraff" or "gangsters" (Trotsky 1940: 24, 25) could be passed on to successive cadres within the party, since it is not denied that the party does still have its social roots in the toiling classes. The moral misdirection of the top leadership cannot be explained sociologically as a long-run phenomenon. This may explain Deutscher's optimism in the early post-Stalin period, but it is difficult for contemporary Trotskyite writers to explain (see especially the exchange on this and other issues in Sweezy and Bettelheim 1971). For the new-class position, Lane is also dubious regarding its asserted ability to reproduce itself:

> The dynamics of the society would indicate that factors outside the dictates of the ruling class account for mobility: for example, achievement based on educational qualification rather than family ties, though family background affects educational chances. . . . The boundaries of the "new class" are characterized by such flexibility in Djilas's theory that it is impossible to conceive of it developing a consciousness of its class position which, by definition, in Marxist theory, is an essential trait of a ruling class. (1971: 181)

The problem for which this chapter offers an alternative solution, therefore, is that of political succession for the top political elite of the Soviet system, for which the Trotskyite and new-class theories lack entirely satisfying explanations. We shall be concerned with a long-run view of elite turnover, covering the entire history of the Soviet state. Given that both Marxist critiques of the Soviet system rely on a characterization of the top leadership as a cohesive and self-conscious ruling group, we shall be examining one possible explanation (generational cleavage) for the development and persistence of this group solidarity, as well as some perspectives for its future, which bear directly on the viability of both the Trotskyite and the Djilas approaches.

Alternative Definitions of Soviet Elite Generations

What is suggested here is that, in the historical circumstances of the revolution in power, in a backward agrarian society surrounded by an extremely hostile capitalist environment with diminishing chances of help from an international proletarian revolution, the party embarked upon a path of domestic economic development which constituted the Stalinist political-industrial revolution of the 1920s and 1930s. With this Stalinist revolution, a new generation of Soviet leadership rose quickly to the top levels of the political system, and it is this political age cohort which both the Trotskyite and the Djilas theses describe, although the bases for this group's solidarity are explained primarily in different (nongenerational) terms.

Trotsky in part saw the formation of the bureaucratic stratum as related to a conscious process of generational shifts in the composition of the party, although he dates this from the Lenin Levy after Lenin's death in 1924. The young bureaucrats, Trotsky says, were "perfectly suited" for operating the Stalinist machine, since they had little attachment to the making of the revolution but were "perfectly suited to exploit it" (1957: 315). The reconstitution of the party membership, in the mid-twenties, was intended "to dissolve the revolutionary vanguard in raw human material, without experience, without independence, and yet with the old habit of submission to authority. . . . Under the guise of a struggle with the Opposition, there occurred a sweeping replacement of revolutionists with *chinovniks* (professional governmental functionaries)" (p. 318).

Our operationalization of Soviet elite generations rests on an age cohort model of social change, which posits a "critical" period in the formation of a person's political consciousness between the ages of 17 and 25 and which considers this period as most revealing of the basic value orientations of a political generation.

The Soviet leadership has also been defined generationally in terms of its technical and managerial skills (Fischer 1968; Fleron 1969; Unger 1969; and esp. Donaldson and Waller 1970) and is currently seen as a skills-defined leading stratum (the managerial modernizers) coming to power in the course of the rapid industrialization set in motion by the first Five-Year Plans of the 1928 to 1938 period. According to this skills-based approach, the managerial modernizers are differentiated from the earlier political generations of revolutionary modernizers, characterized by higher education in fields outside engineering and the physical sciences, and from their immediate predecessors, the revolutionary managers, pictured as those who entered the party with low education and worked their way up through the party hierarchy in the course of the Revolution and the civil-war period (see Welsh 1969). It is assumed that, beyond the initial influx of managerial modernizer types into the top Soviet elite in the 1930s (see esp. Unger 1969 for the magnitude and sharpness of the break), all elite members with higher education in technologically oriented fields are still members of this political generation regardless of age or other characteristics.

A third approach to the problem of Soviet political succession in terms of generations, suggested by Lewytzkyj (1967, 1970a) and Hough (1967), is that of party cadre generations, according to the year in which each elite member joins the party, which is seen as the basic formative period of that member's political career and the best indicator of his/her expected career pattern within the party. Both Hough and Lewytzkyj concentrate on possible generational differences between those elite members who joined the party during World War II (the war generation) and their immediate party cadre seniors. This approach, in contrast to a skills definition, does not view all the Stalinist and post-Stalinist elites with higher technical education as one single grouping but, rather, posits differences resulting from the party environment at the time of early induction (by self-selection) into the world of professional party politics:

> Perhaps the crucial fact about the World War II generation is not their postwar careers, but precisely their entrance into the party (and often into party work) during World War II. While we tend to think of the post-purge years as an unbroken period of repression and overcentralization, we must not forget that the war years did not fit such a pattern. (Hough 1967: 25)

Table 48 presents a comparison of Soviet political generations as defined through age cohort, skills, and party cohort approaches to the question of elite generations. The skills definitions of elite succession in the Soviet system present three political generations based on educational background of each elite member. For the party cohort definition, we have chosen the same break points in the partition of the development of the Bolshevik party as for the age cohort approach, but here the elite members are placed according to

TABLE 48. Three Approaches to a Definition of Soviet Elite Generations

Age cohort[a] (year of birth)	Skills (education)	Party cohort (year joined party)
1. Revolutionary modernizers (birth years 1860–1883)	1. Revolutionary modernizers (high nontechnical education)	1. Before 1905
2. Revolutionary managers (birth years 1884–1899)	2. Apparatchiki with administrative skills (low formal education)	2. 1905–1920
3. Managerial modernizers (birth years 1900–1918)	3. Managerial modernizers (high education in technical areas)	3. 1921–1939
4. War generation pragmatists (birth years 1919–1924)		4. 1940–1945
5. Cold War neo-Stalinists (birth years 1925–1931)		5. 1946–1952
6. Post-Stalinists (birth years 1932–1952)		6. 1953–1973

[a] Years of early maturity for each age cohort correspond in each case to the timespan of the corresponding party cohort generation, but it remains an empirical question whether elite members in fact joined the party during early maturity for each age cohort.

year of joining the party, not year in which they reached their majority (21).[2]

For our definition of the Soviet political elite, we shall take the Soviet Central Committee, which represents throughout Soviet history the best shorthand institutional definition of those people who, by virtue of positions of power held elsewhere, are entitled to seats on the Committee (Donaldson and Waller 1970: 2–3). This gives us a total universe of 1,114 individuals who served on the Committee from 1917 through 1971. If we consider these definitions as simple nominal scale variables, we can calculate the degree of overlap

2. One problem, in quantitative terms, is that there are so few members of the Soviet Central Committee born after 1931 that to subdivide this period into smaller segments would produce zero cells for most subsegments. This is not a substantive argument against differentiation within this larger age cohort, however, and our main justification rests on what is perceived as a basic continuity of social and political trends throughout these years.

among them in terms of "reduction of error" correlation methods (in this case the Contingency Coefficient C) for all members of the Soviet elite who have ever sat on the Committee, either as full or as candidate members (see table 49a).[3] The results indicate a rather high association between age cohort and party cohort definitions, as well as moderately strong overlap between these two approaches and a skills definition of elite generations. If we restrict our universe to only *full* members of the Committee over the span of Soviet history, for which information is more complete, the levels of association are only marginally raised (see table 49b). However, it is clear that for our data to relate to the sequential succession of elites, and in order to pose a generational alternative to the Trotskyite and Djilas-Stojanovic interpretations of the Soviet elite, we must assume that these three operationalizations of political generation represent a temporal sequence of turnover and, therefore, represent ordinal-level variables, with a clear directionality attached to them. If we intercorrelate them as such (now using gamma as our index of overlap), we find that (see table 50, a and b) there is a very high association between age cohort and party cohort approaches (gamma = .96 for the complete Committee membership, .98 for full members only). And, for the association of skills generations to age and party cohorts, we find that levels of association are somewhat lower for the entire universe than for the data base restricted to full members only.

We have shown here that, to a great extent, our age cohort definition of elite generations is very closely related to a party cohort definition, moderately so to a skills operationalization of the same concept. To the extent that all three approaches are convergent, we might expect higher salience of generational cleavages arising out of different experiences according to the three understandings of political generation. An interesting empirical question for cross-national research is the degree of overlap or correlation in different political systems of all three approaches to the definition of political generation. One would expect that the higher the degree of overlap (level of correlation), the greater the potential for generational conflict. This would then have implications for the ease or difficulty of political elite succession in the course of economic and social developments.

As we have seen in the analysis of the previous chapter, the pat-

3. For a discussion of the use of "reduction of error" statistics for nominal scale polytomies and ordinal scale statistics of association when directionality is involved, see Garson (1971: 160–162) and Blalock (1972: 300–303, 421–425).

TABLE 49. Intercorrelation of Age Cohort, Skills, and Party Cohort Definitions of Soviet Elite Generations, Taken As Nominal Scales

	a. All members of Central Committees (1917–1966)				b. Full members of Central Committees only (1917–1966)		
	Age cohort	Skills	Party cohort		Age cohort	Skills	Party cohort
Age cohort		.48	.81	Age cohort		.51	.81
Skills	.48		.44	Skills	.51		.47
Party cohort	.81	.44		Party cohort	.81	.47	

Note: Figures are Pearson's Contingency Coefficients.

tern of generational succession in the Soviet elite is marked by an early period (through the NEP years) of gradual replacement of the original Bolshevik generation of revolutionary modernizers (cosmopolitans with high education) by a second generation of party functionaries with administrative skills but low educational attainment. The Great Purge interrupts the nascent entrenchment of this second elite generation and brings a new plurality into the Central Committee, representing the third, managerial modernizer generation. In the absence of any new purges from above, this third generation has retained the overwhelming bulk of Committee seats ever since. The postwar history of the Soviet elite has been one of considerable *personnel* turnover, but with very low correlation to

TABLE 50. Intercorrelation of Age Cohort, Skills, and Party Cohort Definitions of Soviet Elite Generations, Taken As Ordinal Scales

	a. All members of Central Committees (1917–1966)				b. Full members of Central Committees only (1917–1966)		
	Age cohort	Skills	Party cohort		Age cohort	Skills	Party cohort
Age cohort		.36	.96	Age cohort		.47	.98
Skills	.36		.34	Skills	.47		.42
Party cohort	.96	.34		Party cohort	.98	.42	

Note: Figures are gammas.

generational renewal. It would seem that the post-1939 Soviet system has been able to provide elite circulation at a rather high level, but with the stricture that, in cooptation to top leadership, positions are to be refilled predominantly by candidates from the same age cohort.

It may be argued that our definition of the managerial modernizer generation has been too inclusive or too broad, that any political age cohort covering all those born in the first two decades of the century would be expected to provide the bulk of elite membership during most of the postwar period. This contention is belied by a comparison of age cohort turnover in the Soviet system with that in the United States, West Germany, and Mexico for the same postwar period (see table 51).[4] It is clear that only in the Soviet case has the generation born in the first two decades of the century (the interwar generation for all four nations) dominated the political elite in both the early (72% of the Central Committee in 1952) and the late (77% of the Committee in 1971) postwar years. For the two pluralist democracies, representing presidential and parliamentary systems, the same age cohort never held so great a share of a comparably sized political elite body. And, for both the U.S. House and the German Bundestag, the political age cohorts born after 1920 were already, as of the late 1960s, close to majority status in these national elites (45% of the U.S. House, 55% of the German Bundestag). The Mexican comparison is important because it indicates that, even in a dominant one-party system, generational succession can still take place in an evolutionary manner. Here too, even more so than for the U.S. and West German cases, the transition to post-1920 age cohorts by 1970 had far exceeded the Soviet pattern (64% of the Mexican Chamber of Deputies, 48% of the Mexican Senate).

In addition, if one measures the diffusion of elite generational representation for pre–World War I, interwar, and postwar political age cohorts in all four nations, using Rae's index of fractionalization (see Rae 1967: 56), it is clear from table 52 that again the Soviet case is exceptional. Only in the Soviet case has elite representation been so concentrated in a single political generation—that of the managerial modernizers. Taken for each Central Committee or averaged over the five postwar Committees, the level of elite generational diffu-

4. For a more detailed cross-national analysis of elite turnover in these four distinctive political systems for the post–World War II period, see Nagle 1973, which relates the ease or difficulty of generational succession both to system-type and to the salience of cleavages between political elite generations.

TABLE 51. Generational Turnover in Four National Elites

Birth years

	Senate		House	
	1949	1969	1949	1969
United States	%	%	%	%
Pre-1900	75	13	50	3
1900–1919	25	58	50	52
1920 and after	0	28	1	45

	Bundestag	
	1949	1969
West Germany	%	%
Pre-1900	50	1
1900–1919	48	44
1920 and after	2	55

	Senate		Deputies	
	1952	1970	1952	1970
Mexico	%	%	%	%
Pre-1900	62	8	18	2
1900–1919	38	44	73	34
1920 and after	0	48	9	64

	Central Committee	
	1952	1971
Soviet Union	%	%
Pre-1900	27	3
1900–1919	72	77
1920 and after	1	20

sion has been and remains significantly below any elite body of our other three cases.

It cannot be said, therefore, that our definition of Soviet political generations has in advance predetermined the result that a single generation has remained dominant throughout so much of Soviet history. Rather, the four-nation comparison is a further indication that political generation is a strong explanatory variable in the cooptation of new members to the Soviet political elite, at least for the period since 1939.

Bureaucratic Stratum, Social Class, or Political Generation: Summary

These findings suggest that in large part the bureaucratic stratum and new-class descriptions of the Soviet system are in fact descriptions of a particular elite generation, which has shown (from both cross-national comparisons and from earlier Soviet history) a quite remarkable endurance and solidarity vis-à-vis younger elite cadres. The self-consciousness of this managerial modernizer generation in its refusal to give way to younger, better-educated, and yet by now quite experienced candidates for top leadership relates directly to the problem of political succession, which neither the Trotsky nor the Djilas theses are able to adequately handle. The criticisms raised by Lane and others as to how the degenerate norms of the bureaucratic stratum or the class consciousness of the new class are to be transmitted to new generations are at least partially substantiated by the above analysis. That is, at the national elite level, there is good evidence that there are indeed severe problems in socializing new elite cadres into the value positions of the managerial modernizer generation, and the result has been an increasingly apparent reluctance to rejuvenate the elite.

The reverse side of the above argument is that the Soviet system, characterized by the Soviet political elite, may be depicted through the values of a particular political generation, steeled in the bitter experiences of the formation of Stalinist society. Lacking any evidence regarding how a new class would be able to effectively pass on a sense of class loyalty and class consciousness, one must question Djilas' characterization of the Soviet elite as the embodiment of a new social class. There may be less disagreement between a generational interpretation and Trotsky's bureaucratic stratum model of the Soviet system, especially since Trotskyite observers like Deutscher also doubted the ability of the Stalinist political leadership to maintain Stalinist structures over long periods of time. However, if this elite stratum is mainly unified by its generational commonalities and its sense of identity arising from common struggles during early maturity, then it is no longer identified specifically with either the party or the state bureaucratic structures, although it

TABLE 52. Fractionalization of Elite
Membership by Political Generation (Rae's F$_e$)

United States	Senate	House
1949	.37	.50
1953	.45	.53
1957	.52	.56
1961	.47	.55
1965	.54	.54
1969	.57	.53
Average	.49	.53

West Germany	Bundestag
1949	.52
1953	.50
1957	.51
1961	.52
1965	.51
1969	.51
Average	.51

Soviet Union	Central Committee
1952	.41
1956	.28
1961	.23
1966	.26
1971	.37
Average	.31

Mexico	Senate	Deputies
1946	.50	.46
1952	.47	.43
1958	.44	.43
1964	.51	.50
1970	.57	.47
Average	.50	.46

may be historically identified with their establishment and growth during the period of Stalinist consolidation within the Soviet state. If Soviet scholars continue to identify the nature of the Soviet system through a classification of its political leadership, then one must also expect that, when the managerial modernizer generation passes from the scene, the description of the Soviet elite will probably also require revision, perhaps major revision, since its perspectives are likely to be quite different from those of the present elite.

In short, it may be too soon to classify the Soviet system as "statism" in the sense of the rise of a new exploitive social class, as Stojanovic and Djilas claim. And, while it may be accurate to describe the present Soviet elite as a bureaucratic stratum lacking the functions of a social class but monopolizing the political process of the Soviet state, it may be more useful, in terms of future expectations for systematic change, to watch for points of generational transition within the top leadership.

Part 4. Closing Thoughts

CHAPTER 11

Ideology and the Relevance
of Elite Representativeness

Before summarizing the main findings of the foregoing chapters, we shall attempt to place this entire study in some perspective with regard to the debate within political science concerning the importance of elite "representativeness." This discussion raises again, in much more detail, the issues outlined in chapter 1, and hopefully clarifies (1) the ideological underpinnings of political science as a discipline; (2) the "politics" of the academic enterprise; and (3) the development of the political debate within academic research in the specific area of political elite studies over the last thirty years.[1] Following Connolly (1974: 32 and chap. 5), we shall argue that academic inquiry on the representativeness of elite composition and especially on its substantive importance is a subset of the larger political struggle. Representativeness is one of those "essentially contested concepts" (Connolly 1974: chap. 1), a value-laden and valuable prize for pluralists, radicals, and Marxists alike, one which each school would like to infuse with its own interpretation. Our discourse here, then, could not hope to impartially establish for academics what the substantive significance of elite composition actually is: it can only hope to illustrate the postwar connection between academic inquiry on this topic and the larger lines of politics. It can further show that the answer regarding the substantive importance of elite composition affects the quantitative rigor in the em-

---

1. Our definition of ideological perspective is close to that expressed by Connolly (1974: 45): "The perspective, comparable to Toulmin's 'idea of natural order' in significant respects, involves a set of fundamental *assumptions* or *expectations* about the 'normal' operation of society and politics and relatively integrated set of *concepts* within which interpretations of society are constructed." We shall, however, make basic distinctions along a pluralist/radical/Marxist trichotomy of perspectives, rather than along the consensus/conflict dichotomy which Connolly uses.

pirical testing of representativeness. Specifically, we conclude that the pluralist downplaying of the *importance* of elite composition has tended to inhibit quantitative precision in empirical measurement.

The predominance of the pluralist view of substantive importance within Western social science, the attack on this view from the antiwar radical/liberals, and the revival of a still modest body of Marxist-oriented literature from within the Western academic community on the importance of elite composition follow the general pattern of postwar stabilization, social calm, and construction of Cold War friend/enemy alliances, succeeded by the rising social and political discord of the sixties and early seventies. Our position is that the scholarly community builds a consensus of substantive import on an ideological basis, that this is a political question, and that it can be altered or challenged only under changed political conditions. The pluralist academic consensus was provided in the latter forties and early fifties both through overt coercion and through a revival of economic growth and widened prosperity in the industrial West. This consensus began to break down in the wake of a deterioration of economic performance, the setbacks to Western imperialism, and the erosion of liberal democracies' ability to deal with a wide range of social issues (crime, corruption, drugs, job and educational opportunities, health care distribution). The prospects for reestablishing a consensus on substance or relevance in elite composition research will depend on the evolution in the political environment in which the social researcher lives, works, and takes a stand. Based on the observed handling of this particular issue over the last thirty years, our thesis is that the present uneasy coexistence among competing ideologies in the field tends to undermine the pluralist claim to scientific neutrality, and thus to Truth, while not being so much a problem for Marxists, who quite openly view political teaching and research as part of political socialization—the production of social norms which either support or oppose the present system.

Social Bases of Elite Recruitment in Pluralist Theory

It is not necessary here to outline the entire revisionist model of Western democracy as it developed during and after WWII. Both the major protagonists (cf. Schumpeter 1942; Sartori 1962; Aron 1950;

Lipset 1963) and the numerous critics (cf. Bottomore 1966; Bachrach 1967; Miliband 1969; Leggett 1973) have done a thorough job of spelling out the major components of pluralism and the changes which it represents vis-à-vis the idealist (or classic) theory of Mill or Greene (see esp. MacPherson 1973).

What concerns us here is the resolution, in advance of basic empirical research, of the seeming contradiction in the revisionist democratic theory between (1) the explicit reliance on government by elites who are not representative of the society at large, with no prospect for even gradual change, who agree not to compete in ways which would fundamentally alter the social order, and (2) the claim that, in this "elites rule," representation of the interests of the lower strata is equitable. An admittedly select survey of the considerable tonnage of democratic pluralist literature leaves little doubt on these points.[2]

The early formalizers of pluralist theory are generally clear about the nonrepresentative nature of the governing elites. Schumpeter was quite explicit in his desire for elites of "sufficiently high quality" (1942: 290), who were not too accessible to outsiders and who were able to assimilate any additional elements to their norms (p. 291). Lasswell, Lerner, and Rothwell, in their early work at the Hoover Institution on comparative elites, note quite matter-of-factly: "It is typical for the parliaments of Western powers to underrepresent certain elements in the population, such as manual workers, clerks, farmers, women, and young people" (reprinted in Bachrach 1971: 18). Matthews, in his pathbreaking comparative study of social backgrounds of decision makers, shows that the American myth of equal opportunity for political officeholding has little standing in fact and, ironically to him, though not to Marxists, less standing than in other, more "class-divided" societies like Britain and Germany (1954: 57). There are a few, terribly twisted pieces of the massive literature on Western political elites which try to picture them as socially heterogeneous and representative (cf. interestingly Lasswell, Lerner, and Rothwell 1952: 14; also Hitchener and Levine 1967: 75–78).

Likewise, it was clear to the revisionists of democratic theory that elite pluralism, while it called for competition for elective offices at

2. Literature of comparative scope is cited in preference to purely American or one-nation studies, and non-American scholars (e.g., Aron, Sartori, Schumpeter, Dahrendorf, Bottomore, Miliband) are included in order to expand the scope of the discussion beyond the U.S. and, particularly, to steer it away from the seemingly endless "community power" debate.

regular intervals, should be circumscribed so as not to threaten the basic capitalist order. Schumpeter simply asserts that the range of political decision making should be relatively narrow (1942: 291–292); Aron is straightforward in calling for the suppression of groups and individuals who want basic structural changes in the society (1950: 140) (cf. esp. Bottomore 1966: 112–127 for good lucid commentary; also Bachrach 1967: chap. 4 for a radical democrat's critique of elite consensus).

On the other hand, pluralist advocates desperately want to lay claim to supporting a neutral, not a class-biased or class-based, mechanism for political governance. It is a good bet that, within a few pages, sometimes leading, sometimes lagging the admission that Western political elites are monotonously drawn from the upper social strata (with the clear exception of Western Communist parties where permitted and electorally significant), a pluralist author will nevertheless assert that there is no ruling class in these societies (cf. Matthews 1954: 32; Aron 1950: 11; Lasswell, Lerner, and Rothwell 1952: 22; Janowitz and Marvick 1955; Riesman, Glazer, and Denney 1950: 217–224). Even in Schumpeter's quite stark defense of elites rule, there is the defense of the nonclass nature of the elite-electorate relationship (cf. esp. pp. 284–285, 297–298).

Revisionist democratic theory, heavily advertised from the start as more "realistic" than the idealist or classical model, required the *recognition* of the first element—the upper-class dominance in elite composition; in the struggle of Western capitalism against communism, it required the *legitimation* of the second—the claim that there is no ruling class in Western democracies. The only solution is the conclusion, in advance of empirical study, that social composition of the political elite does not matter in terms of interest representation and elite behavior, at least not for Western democracies.

This foregone conclusion has been reaffirmed over the years by defenders of the faith, who have had occasion to examine the social bases of elite recruitment. The rationales for reaffirmation, however, have varied remarkably, and it is to these themes that we now turn.

Apologia for a Class Elite: Variations on an Answered Question

Since the academic founders of the new pluralist theory mainly succeeded in establishing that, for proponents of capitalist democracy, the answer to the question "Is there a ruling class in X?" (a Western democracy) must be a resounding "No!" there have emerged not one but a number of commonly given reasons or rationales for this answer. They are presented here in order of ascending subtlety.[3]

1. Despite the near-monopoly on officeholding by members of the upper social strata, there is no ruling class because the interests of the lower classes are adequately represented by "sympathetic agents" (Matthews 1954: 33) of the higher classes.

Sometimes this rationale is given in reverse, to simply destroy the notion that class composition and interest representation could be related:

> Another warning is in order. It is misleading to assume that a group must literally be represented among the political decision-makers to have influence or political power. . . . In America at least lower-status groups have political power far in excess of their number in Congress, the Cabinet, and so on. And there seems to be some evidence that those at the very apex of the social hierarchy are also represented not literally but by sympathetic agents such as lawyers and professional politicians. (Matthews 1954: 32–33)

In this way, there is no explicit defense of "adequate" representation of lower-class interests, but when (usually later) the system is judged to produce basically fair representation of interests, not a class-biased one, the final connecting link is laid in place: ". . . the virtual absence of working class members (in leadership positions) in the United States does not mean that they are being exploited" (p. 59). Thus, a concerned liberal like Matthews, at the conclusion of his, in many respects quite good, comparative background study, suggests and hopes that "every effort might be made to reduce existing blocks to political achievement and to broaden the base of recruitment" (p. 61), but there is no hint that the interests of blacks, workers, women, and other lower-strata groups are not now adequately represented. Rather, the reason given for reform proposals is that "less native talent would be wasted and recruitment very probably would be more efficient than it is now" (p. 61).

3. One sometimes offered rationale is not reviewed here. Matthews (1954: 32), among others, asserts that there is no ruling class simply because there is no formal (or proved) conspiracy to recruit officeholders overwhelmingly from the higher classes. Since this is not in common-sense usage taken as a requirement for class rule, this rationale only strikes at the flimsiest of straw men and is not worth consideration.

A bolder and more aggressive line is adopted by Rasmussen in his introductory comparative text. He cites the fact that neither Marx nor Lenin were from the working class (of course, he also doubts that they had the "true" interests of the working class at heart), whereas FDR, squire of Hyde Park, was a known class traitor to the business world: "Specific instances of advocates of social justice being drawn from the more fortunate groups in society could be compounded. 'True' representation is unnecessary" (1969: 165). Rasmussen also paints a pessimistic picture of class betrayal by working-class union leaders who sell out workers' demands as they are assimilated into elite status themselves. Here the message is that leaders with common class backgrounds may have very different views: they are not a "monolithic group." Finally, "if leaders drawn from lower-class occupations are not seduced away from advocating their class's interests, the fact that they had the interest, drive, ability or whatever to become leaders would still mean that they would differ from their followers in some significant way even though the two groups were matched exactly on a long list of attributes. Leaders can never represent their followers in the sense of mirroring them" (p. 166).

This argument suffers from a logical non sequitur known as the individualistic fallacy. While it is undeniably true that several communist and other revolutionary leaders were and are of middle-class origins (as early as 1848, Marx noted the key, though not controlling, role of bourgeois renegades in the theoretical leadership of the Revolution; cf. Marx 1848: 343), one can hardly extrapolate from these individual cases or small groups, as critic Dankwart Rustow (1966) has pointed out, to envisage an elite drawn predominantly from the upper strata going over (collectively) to the workers' side or substantially altering the social order in which that elite occupies the top spot. And it should not be surprising if, especially in the context of American unionism, those few leaders of lower origins are rather heavily resocialized to the dominant elite outlook. In other contexts, such as the French and Italian Communist parties, some evidence exists to suggest that this is not an inevitable occurrence (Putnam 1973) but depends on the existence of nonbourgeois alternatives reaching some viable critical mass in leadership orientations.

2. Class background is not able to predict policy attitudes of elite individuals, and therefore the social bases of elite recruitment are not related to policy-issue outcomes.

This is essentially an extension of the first rationale to the field of attitudes toward specific issues or issue areas, but it avoids the individualistic fallacy of the first rationale and must be taken more seriously. This argument rests on the very few pieces of literature which attempt to deal in a systematic way with this question. Most studies of American elite behavior fail to research this thesis altogether, although one must admit that, at the national elite level, there is so little representation of lower social strata as to block any meaningful tests. By default, policy differences among U.S. political elites must be relatable to other than class differences. However, Matthews does cite the 1924 Rice study of farmer-worker voting cohesion in state legislatures and admits that "farmers and workers voted with the members of their occupational groups a good deal more than with members of their respective parties" (1954: 39). This is evidently disturbing to the pluralist thesis of no relationship, but Matthews is able to discount the Rice findings as not conclusive:

> . . . the farmers may not have voted together so often because of their occupation as because farmers tend to be elected to state legislatures from similar constituencies. The studies made so far indicate only correlation, not cause and effect. (p. 41)

A second study in this area is that of Searing and Edinger (1967), who tried to predict policy attitudes (latent and manifest) of German and French elites through background characteristics. They basically conclude that some background indicators are better than others in predicting attitudes and that the French elite was markedly less cohesive in attitudes than the German elite. The better predictor variables were social class, occupation, party and voluntary organization affiliations, region of birth, university education, and military service. More interesting, perhaps, is the fact that no mention was made of the breakdown of class and attitude by party, which would show a sizable antisystem bloc of leaders in France associated foremost with the Communist party and the working-class deputies for that party, as well as the complete lack of such a bloc (the German KPD at that point being both illegal and powerless) in West Germany.[4] Interpretations of the Searing and Edinger study vary with one's position on pluralism. Thus, Putnam, citing Searing and Edinger as well as Matthews, argues that both give strong evidence for the pluralist "no relationship" thesis:

4. Cf. Searing and Edinger 1967: 442 ff. The closest they manage to come to identifying the major cleavages in French political elites is their oblique reference to a system alienation/approbation cleavage in which "alienated elites are generally oriented . . . to a diffuse internationalism" (p. 442, n. 32).

At the urging of sociologists and under the aegis [*sic*] of Marxist and neo-Marxist social theories, countless scholars have counted the social background characteristics of political leaders. But there have been persistent complaints that these studies assume the unproved: that social background conditions behavior. Recently, these murmurs of discontent have been amplified by evidence that many aspects of the belief systems of political leaders are virtually unrelated to their social origins. (1973: 238)

See also Parry (1969: 102) and Merritt (1970: 123) for somewhat more modest interpretations of Searing and Edinger. On the other hand, Hughes and Dowse, two British political sociologists who maintain a critical attitude toward the pluralist model, report:

Most significantly, they found that by clustering social background data they were able to make predictions about manifest attitudes which varied between 66 per cent and 80 per cent in accuracy of assignment. Hence, although the conclusions are "admittedly tentative" it does seem that elites do have at least some attitudes in common. (1972: 152)

One clear exception to this rule is Quandt (1970: 195, 198), who interprets Edinger and Searing as a clear finding for a good fit between background and attitude but who, as a pluralist, does not go into the implications of this for the pluralist claim to government "neutrality" or equitable interest representation.

Putnam, in his recent survey of Italian and British MPs, finds that social class is "quite strongly related to respondent's images of social harmony or discord" (1973: 218), as well as to political egalitarianism, but finds that party affiliation in Britain (data for Italy were insufficient) is very highly related to a five-point left-right ideological positioning (pp. 130–133). On this basis, Putnam posits, but cannot test, a four-variable model ("quite tentative") in which social class is deemed to have no direct link to elite attitude. However, his conclusion sounds much more assertive:

If one wants to predict a politician's position on economic planning or European integration, his social background may well be irrelevant. But if, on the other hand, one wants to predict his orientation toward social conflict or his commitment to political equality, his social background may be considerably more important. The day of blanket assumptions that social background characteristics are politically relevant has passed. (pp. 238–239)

The evidence for this second thesis must thus be taken seriously, but it by no means warrants the conclusion which pluralists require. Neither Edinger and Searing nor Putnam can in the crunch say that social class is not in fact an important variable (more powerful than any other) in the attitudes of elites. Edinger and Searing's work in fact substantiates the relationship but tries to downplay it as far as possible by pointing to national differences. Putnam's conscientious work also inadvertently strengthens the Marxist case, insofar as orientation toward conflict and commitment to political equality (which for the Communist party of Italy and the left Laborites includes economic equality) are attitudes with clear (as Putnam admits on pp. 129 ff. and 213 ff.) ties to party positioning along the ideological continuum.

The main point, however, is that differences among elite individuals of similar class origin do not prove that a class relationship between elite recruitment and interest representation does not exist. No one can seriously doubt that the political leaderships of the Italian and French Communist parties, the only two parties in these studies with predominantly working-class MPs, have very sharp differences of attitude with respect to social and economic policy of the present governments (cf. Aron 1950: 126 ff.). If one then ascribes this only to party affiliation or party ideology, not to class relationships, one must then ask why the other parties aren't also recruiting deputies more proportionately from the working population.

3. All political elites are unrepresentative/all political elites are middle-class.

If it can be shown that, even in socialist systems, the condition of elite composition is invariate and one must simply accept this fact, then the search for a more socially representative elite takes on a utopian, nonrealist onus. If all elites are unrepresentative and/or middle-class, the argument goes, then the equitability of interest representation will have to rest on other (variable) factors. Merritt, for example, states both cases rather succinctly:

> By itself, representativeness or non-representativeness is doubtless of little importance. Most populations are led by elites who are in some way or another unrepresentative of the masses: Elite members are generally older than a random sample of the

entire population, better educated, higher in terms of socio-economic status, male rather than female, and come from the larger towns. (1970: 121)

Matthews makes much the same argument (1954: 57) and also claims, using Schueller's 1951 Soviet elite study, that the Soviet elite is as unrepresentative in social composition as are Western democratic elites (p. 55). Rasmussen takes this line one step further and asserts that, "like democratic political leaders in many countries, the Communist, Fascist and Nazi leaders tended to come from a middle class background" (1969: 161). A few pages later, unable to fathom the possibility of a classless society, he finds the mathematics of elite representativeness quite too much:

> First, what attributes of the population are the regents to reflect? Economic class alone is hardly sufficient, unless one adopts the Marxist position that economic relations are the foundation upon which the entire superstructure of society depends. One's political values and policy desires are influenced as well by his religion, his race, the region of the country in which he lives, to mention only a few factors. How many of the virtually endless personal attributes need to be represented? . . . If the number of attributes to be represented is large, the procedure [sic] becomes almost hopelessly complex and inoperable. (p. 165)

Of note is the tacit admission that background factors do in fact relate to political values but, contrary to modern sociological knowledge, the class factor no more than any number of other variables. And, since we could not imagine an elite representative along all these variables, there is no reason why it should be representative along the class (i.e., Marxist) variable.

The trick to this claim is to draw a line between perfect representativeness and everything else, a test which, to be sure, will find both communist and Western elites on the same side, with a zero frequency on the other side. A modest seeker of quantitative rigor is tempted to ask: what is the degree of nonrepresentativeness? A general rule of thumb (by induction) is that, when pluralist scholars are studying American (less so other Western) democracy, they emphasize that workers (Brennan), blacks (Brooke), and women (Grasso) are not entirely shut out of top positions (cf. Matthews 1954: 32; Rasmussen 1969: 169, 170; Brzezinski and Huntington

1963: 133–134).[5] When pluralist scholars are studying Soviet society, they emphasize that complete equality does not exist (Schueller 1951: 140–141 esp.; Mickiewicz 1973: 16–22, esp. p. 22; Jancar 1974: 118–148, esp. pp. 147–148). Much of the judgment on the non-representativeness of the Soviet elite comes from a single source—the twisted Hoover Institution study of the early 1950s (the institution's Nazi elite study is also widely recognized as badly botched)—which is cited over and over (Matthews 1954; Merritt 1970: 120; Merkl 1970: 133; Rasmussen 1969: 159–161) when far better analysis has long since become available (see Nagle 1973 for both sources and data).

The ideological constraints of pluralist theory in the field of elite composition have led to less, rather than greater, quantitative rigor and sophistication in this instance. For example, if one takes a time-series look at nationality representation in the Soviet Central Committee, using a simple Schutz Coefficient, one finds (see table 53) that, prior to the Stalinist Great Purge era, the nationality representation had been becoming more equal, with still disproportionate representation of Jews, Georgians, and Baltic minorities. During the height of Stalin's one-man rule, the inequality increased sharply, with overrepresentation of Great Russians, Georgians, and Jews in 1939 and Great Russians, Georgians, and Baltic peoples in 1952. Since Stalin's death, the trend has clearly been toward greater equity in nationality representation.

More important, if we look at the occupational composition of the U.S. House from 1948 through 1968, the German Bundestag from 1949 through 1972, and the Soviet Central Committee from 1925 through 1971, we can see three quite different patterns (see table 54). The American political elite (figures for some other bodies are also given) has generally remained highly unrepresentative throughout and shows no trend toward greater equality. The Bundestag membership, as the German political system has evolved into a more stable pluralist democracy, has become increasingly unrepresentative, though not yet reaching the American level. The Soviet elite, which

---

5. Brzezinski and Huntington do a neat bit of footwork on the social compositions of U.S. versus Soviet political leadership. They announce that both the log cabin image of American political leadership and the proletarian image of Soviet political leadership are myths (1963: 130), but the evidence they present shows only that American leadership is drawn from the middle class while Soviet leadership is drawn from the working class, i.e., only the American log cabin propaganda is a myth.

TABLE 53. Representativeness of the Soviet Central Committee along Nationality Lines, 1921–1971

Year of Party Congress	Schutz Coefficient for Committee membership
1921	.28
1934	.19
1939	.35
1952	.39
1956	.15
1961	.09
1971	.08

has always underrepresented mainly peasant occupations, has shown a steady pattern of greater representativeness since the 1920s and is now significantly more representative than the American or German elites.[6]

Apart from the degree of representativeness, it can quite easily be shown that not all political elites are drawn from the middle class. The Schueller study, concentrating on the five-member Politburo of the civil-war years, has been used to give the impression of a middle-class intelligentsia as a new political leadership. But, while this is true enough for the early years of the Revolution, it has long since ceased to be accurate. Already, in the mid-twenties, the overwhelming majority of Central Committee (though not yet Politburo) members were of working-class or peasant origins and were from working-class occupations. Today most Committee members (and Politburo members as well) are of lower-class origins, and over half have primary occupations in the blue- or white-collar sectors barely visible within the U.S. political elite. Another good comparison is offered by the two paths which West and East Germany have taken in terms of elite recruitment. Here recent studies of the East German leadership (cf. Ludz 1972; Baylis 1973), when compared with West German data, indicate how greatly the political and mili-

6. Although there are certainly cross-national differences in occupational categories, there is also quite high correlation of occupational stratification ladders across systems (Lane 1971: chap. 12). And, while we cannot ascribe a functional equivalence to the Bundestag, the Soviet Central Committee, and the House of Representatives, this should not inhibit us from comparing the social basis of recruitment for national elite bodies of roughly similar stature and exclusiveness.

TABLE 54. Time-Series Schutz Coefficients for Occupational Representativeness of German, Soviet, and U.S. Elites

German Bundestag		Soviet Committee		U.S. House		Other U.S. elites[a]	
Year	Schutz	Year	Schutz	Year	Schutz	Body	Schutz
1949	.32	1925	.79	1948	.77	Senate, 1948	.79
						State leg.,	
1953	.34	1939	.60	1956	.73	1925–35	.66
1957	.39	1952	.51	1960	.73		
						State gov.,	
1961	.50	1966	.41	1964	.71	1930–40	.70
						President,	
						VP, cabinet,	
1965	.53	1971	.40	1968	.71	1877–1934	.80
1969	.55						
1972	.55						

[a] Calculated from Matthews 1954: 30.

tary (cf. Hancock 1973) leadership of East Germany diverges from the increasingly upper-middle-class dominance in West Germany. It is simply not the case that all political elites are either equally unrepresentative or equally middle-class in either origin or occupation. The degree of representativeness may change over time within a system, and in either direction, and there is an absolute abyss between class origins of elite recruitment in capitalist and socialist systems.[7] It is surprising how few of the radical democratic critics of pluralism, or for that matter even Western Marxists, have taken the time to refute this pluralist argument.

4. In general, people will choose to be led, or represented, by their social "betters," who are regarded as more capable of furthering their interests:

> Finally it seems understandable in a society with an accepted stratification system for the electorate to choose men with high social status to represent them in the decision-making process. A man with a fairly high social position has met the society's definition of success. Rightly or wrongly the lawyer is thought to be a better man than the factory worker. Thus when the fac-

7. Only if one tautologically defines all officeholders per se as middle-class and totally ignores social origins (à la Djilas 1961; also Matthews 1954: 55; Rasmussen 1969: 166) can this pluralist argument be held together.

> tory worker votes for the lawyer he is voting for a man who is
> what he would like to be. (Matthews 1954: 32)

> Electors may believe that a politician with a good education and
> with professional experience—a lawyer for example—will make
> more headway in pressing for their interests than a politician
> more like themselves in ability. (Parry 1969: 103)

It must not be forgotten that, in the United States at least, the working class has no choice but to vote for a lawyer or a business owner and has no role whatever in the selection of candidates from the two bourgeois parties. And it must be noted that this is a parochial argument, since Matthews later notes that the British or German voter more often "prefers to be literally represented by an actual member of his class than is true in the more open society of the United States" (1954: 57). Parry too (1969: 97) notes that the tendency for parties to nominate candidates who are representative of their district in their background varies from nation to nation. Finally, Kornberg, Clarke and Watson (1973) have shown that in Canada there is a general tendency among nonradical parties to compete by nominating candidates of high status and for the (nonalienated) electorate to prefer the candidate of highest social status. On the other hand, antisystem or social-protest parties tend to nominate candidates from lower strata, and this is also a viable strategy for garnering antisystem or social-protest votes. In fact, one might posit that this is one test of system-supportive versus antisystem parties.

More conservative pluralists (Schumpeter 1942: 290; Kornhauser 1959; Rasmussen 1969: 172–173; Sartori 1962: 115 ff.) admit that this rationale is their hope, that is, that the social hierarchy will be generally recognized as valid by the working class as well. As Hughes and Dowse note, the success of the Tory party hinges on a considerable percentage of the working class accepting high social status as a "fitness to rule" criterion (1972: 143). But, at the same time, this condition is also variant and cannot be considered as a permanent fixture of the general electorate through thick and thin. Bachrach (1967: chap. 3) and Parry (1969: 143 ff.) have amply summarized the deep-seated distrust among pluralist theorists of the rationality and liberality of the masses, and it is clear that any such rationale as the one presently under discussion is too utopian for the more hard-nosed "realists" of elitist democracy.

5. No matter what elite composition looks like, accountability is retained through elite competition in periodic elections.

This is of course the most universally advertised rationale. It is briefly stated by Lasswell, Lerner, and Rothwell:

> Because of the stress so often put upon the social origins of an elite, and upon the path by which active members of an elite rise to the top, it is sometimes lost sight of that origins are no infallible guide to eliteship. The essential condition to be fulfilled is accountability. To be accountable is to be influenced. We are acquainted with the wide range of devices evolved by representative government in their long struggle to control the executive and to keep all members of the active elite accountable to the passive elements *of the ruling class*. (1952: 21–22) [emphasis mine]

As long as two or mores names of genuinely competing office seekers appear on the ballot once every X years, so the pluralist thesis goes, elites, no matter what the social base of recruitment is, are accountable and by inference *must* take the interests of the lower strata into account.

There are several responses to this rationale. First, every elite must take the interests of the lower strata into some account, unless the elite is willing to risk constant revolt and rebellion. This by no means insures that these interests are equitably or satisfactorily represented, only that for the benefit of stability and order there are certain limits beyond which even the most exploitive elite does not rationally tread.

Second, this rationale does not consider all those terribly important political elites in the government bureaucracy, military/police, economy, and judiciary who are not elected at all but who, in Western democracies, are drawn overwhelmingly from the upper strata, even more heavily than elected elites—the more so the higher one rises in any particular hierarchy (cf. esp. Miliband 1969: chap. 3; Bottomore 1966: chaps. 4, 6; Leggett 1973: 244–286; Hancock 1973).

Third, numerous studies have indicated the cumulative and transferable nature of the participation advantages of the well-born and well-heeled (cf. Connolly 1969; Bottomore 1966: chap. 6; Miliband 1969: chap. 6, among many others), making it difficult for lower-class or disorganized groups to exert influence through the electoral system or to form antisystem parties as viable alternative organizations. Since Berelson et al. (1954), the desirability of nonparticipation by the common people has been widely promoted by the pluralists themselves. The result is an elite consensus (Bachrach 1967: chap. 4; Miliband 1969: chap. 4) which limits the universe of conceivable reform or change to those compatible with the present capitalist order. As Miliband notes, while there are important divisions of opinion among elites in Western democracies (as there are among Soviet elites), these divisions are ideologically confined (with the exception of a few major Communist parties) to questions of "efficiency" and "rationality" *within* the capitalist system. Interestingly, as Taubman (1974: 386–390 esp.) has pointed out in his excellent piece in an otherwise sodden reader on Soviet society, it is on just such grounds that anti-Marxist Sovietologists reject divisions and open competition among Soviet group elites as "spurious" or not "genuine" pluralism (McFarland 1969: 88–89; Skilling 1971: 17).

This ideological elite consensus is the necessary basis for pluralist democracy, which Schumpeter, Aron, and Sartori posited quite early on. In the face of an existing socialist alternative, this makes the American elite competition an ideologically bounded exercise, not neutral in terms of the entire range of social possibility, no matter how this elite consensus is maintained.

Participatory Democrats on Elite Composition

The reaction to the pluralist model's views on the issue of elite representativeness has been slow in developing and has lagged behind the general attack on the pluralist model as a whole. There are a couple of explanations for this lag.

The first major critiques to gain a foothold *within* the academic community came from advocates of participatory democracy whose alternative to the pluralist model involved neither a class-conflict nor a materialist concept of social change, because it did not pose a revolutionary challenge to the economic order.[8] In most cases, advocates of greater decentralization of power and participation took pains to differentiate their positions from Marxist or socialist views.

8. I fully recognize that many individuals in all three camps—pluralist, radical, socialist—have modified their views over the years, some having made the transition from one basic position to another. This is one reason for not making use of Dahl's obviously widely read works of the 1960s, since he waffles on the original pluralist premises. Likewise, quite a few radical democrats have long since come over to a basically Marxist position. Therefore, the following citations must be interpreted only as representative of ideas by individuals at a given point in time and do not necessarily reflect the present thinking of those cited.

Thus Goodman (1963: 116 ff.), after rather crudely misreading Marx's position on the withering away of the state and division of labor, points to the decentralization measures possible within capitalism and notes: "Needless to say, our industrial psychologists cannot pursue their instincts to the logical conclusion, workers' management. Yet questions of degree are not trivial" (p. 134). The basic benefits are seen in terms of greater psychic benefits within the present system:

> The capitalist provides the machinery and materials, but every-thing else—work rules, schedule, hiring—is left to group deci-sion. The group may be half a dozen or a couple of thousand. Humanly, such an arrangement has extraordinary advantages. Men exchange jobs and acquire new skills; they adjust the schedule to their convenience or pleasures. (p. 135)

Goodman must admit that decentralization as he understands it does not lead to an alternative system but to a decentralized capitalist one, one which is from his view more efficient and ra-tional:

> But I am not proposing a system. . . . Rather it seems to me as follows. We are in a period of excessive centralization. In this book I shall try to demonstrate that in many functions this style is economically inefficient, technologically unnecessary, and humanly damaging. Therefore we might adopt a political maxim: to decentralize, where, how, and how much is expe-dient. (p. 27)

Such views maintain the basic social hierarchy in not calling it di-rectly into question. Similarly, Gans, in his book *More Equality*, rather explicitly assumes the continuation of the capitalist market system (1968: 92–95 esp.). In his consideration of more proportional recruitment of elites from all social strata, he makes the pluralist argument that this would not basically alter political outputs (pp. 210–211) and then voices some doubts as to the efficacy of greater equality in political recruitment:

> As more people became part of the political process, they would support politicians more like themselves, and the demographic make-up of Congress would be more similar to that of the total population than at present. Politicians would have to be more astute—and perhaps more manipulative—in order to cope with the greater amount of feedback and access, and they would not

have time to be technical experts on any of the issues with which they have to deal. (p. 212)

Bachrach, perhaps the most widely read critic of pluralist theory from the participatory democracy camp, makes clear that the main issue of democracy is a humanist devolution of sharing of power, a breaking of the elite/mass barriers, and that to this end class composition of the political elite is at best secondary. He indicates that a more representative elite would indeed be more responsive to the interests of the working classes but then concludes:

> But again the argument rests—to reparaphrase Marcuse—on a one-dimensional view of man's interest. The elite-mass nature of society would still remain intact: the few would still count for much, exercising inordinate amounts of power, and the many, faced with a modicum of responsibility and challenge, would still count for little.
>
> The crucial issue of democracy is not the composition of the elite—for the man on the bottom it makes little difference whether the command emanates from an elite of the rich and the wellborn or from an elite of workers and farmers. (1967: 92–93)

In presenting his alternative, Bachrach recognizes the need for industrial democracy and at the same time separates himself on this crucial issue from the socialist position:

> What is called for, at minimum, is discussion and debate on various aspects of the question with the view of possible experimentation with nationalization of one or a few corporate giants. Serious consideration of such a proposal can no longer be left to socialists, nor should controversy centering on such a proposal be fought along traditional socialist-capitalist lines of argument. Today, argument along these lines would border on the irrelevant. For the fundamental issue no longer relates to the problem of production but to the problem of power. (pp. 104–105)

Although it is difficult to imagine an effective industrial democracy without a socialist restructuring of ownership and property rights, it is more difficult to imagine any such restructuring without a political struggle along *other than* capitalist/socialist lines (being careful not to confuse the policies and politics of social democratic parties with socialism). This question aside, however, a general consideration of the radical democratic literature as an alternative to the pluralist position reveals the uncertain or indirect nature of its challenge to industrial capitalism. Of course, this is clear to Marxists from its avowed renunciation of socialist or Marxist theory. Related to this is the uncertain position, often in fact the usual pluralist position, taken on the importance of elite social composition as an indicator of interest representation and equitability.

From their political position, critical of pluralism yet resistant to a materialist class-conflict (Marxist) view of social change, participatory democrats could not and I would argue cannot (as a group) posit a systematic relationship between the social basis of elite recruitment and interest representation, all the more since the goals of widened participation are primarily psychic and humanist, related to self-worth and autonomy and only secondarily concerned with the material bases of these values.

Marxists and Elite Composition: Assimilation of Findings

The Marxist position on the state in capitalist society is both relatively clear in terms of basic functions and, as Miliband says (1969: 5–7), relatively unrefined or underdeveloped and taken to be "self-evident."[9] The position of Marxists on the relationship between class composition of political (state) elites and class representation of interests generally fits this description as well. Indeed, without going further, there is much to be said for the quite straightforward thesis which no pluralist can afford to admit to. For Marxists the relationship, given the perceived linkage between state elite and economic elite, is of basic substantive importance and is even crucial as a defining characteristic of a political system (cf. Bottomore 1966: 121–128; Miliband 1969: chaps. 2, 3, 5). Yet, until the relatively recent comparative elite studies of such Marxist or Marxist-oriented scholars as Bottomore, Miliband, and Jaeggi, little had been done to explore the types or evolution of elite composition compatible with capitalism (or socialism!). The main emphasis of Bottomore's work

9. Recent work on the part of Gold, Lo, and Wright (1975) has added considerably to a Marxist theory of the state, with some implications for elite recruitment which differ from Miliband's basically instrumentalist approach to state elite recruitment.

has been to confirm the upper-middle-class basis for elite consensus in the West, which is of course implicit in the writings of several pluralists. Miliband, using a variety of data, significantly modifies Karl Kautsky's observation that the "capitalist class rules but does not govern" (cited in Miliband 1969: 55) with the finding that capitalist officeholding has been very heavy in the political executive, compared with elected legislatures, but that, with variations, legislative, military, administrative, and judicial elites have been drawn from a narrow upper social stratum (pp. 65–67). Before launching an essay on the political role and purpose of the state in capitalism, Miliband briefly states the Marxist position:

> The reason for attaching considerable importance to the social composition of the state elite in advanced capitalist countries lies in the strong presumption which this creates as to its general outlook, ideological dispositions and political bias. In the case of the governments of these countries, however, we can do much more than merely presume: after all, hardly a day goes by in which political leaders in charge of the affairs of their country do not press upon the public their ideas and beliefs. Much of this may conceal as much as it reveals. But a great deal remains which, together with much other evidence, notably what governments actually do, affords a clear view of what, in large terms, they are about. (p. 68)

The studies presented here indicate several refinements within the basic Marxist orientation:

1. There is considerable variability in the occupational profile of political elites compatible with capitalist economic systems. Transformation of the social basis of recruitment *within* the upper social strata is possible to preserve "representativeness" of recruitment among the dominant social classes. The study (see chaps. 6 and 7) of the German political elite under the Kaiserreich, Weimar, the Third Reich, and the Bonn republic shows a variation of elite recruitment from upper social strata compatible with German capitalism, ranging from heavy representation of the preindustrial aristocracy through the business class in the middle monarchy period to the heavy influx of intellectuals in the latter monarchy years and stable Weimar period. The postwar evolution of German elite recruitment to a system dominated by managerial-professional occupations and the final stage in the *embourgeoisement* of the SPD correspond to the end of ideology assessment of pluralist literature.

2. The most stable bourgeois system (the United States) recruits

its officeholders almost exclusively from the liberal professions and from property owners. The occupational profile of the U.S. political elite over the last century shows great stability and almost total exclusion of lower occupational strata, fulfilling Marx's assessment of the United States as the capitalist social order par excellence. In this respect, contrary to pluralist literature, the U.S., as leader of the capitalist world, has the most rigidly ideological of systems. Of course, given the military as well as the economic predominance of the U.S. and its role in organizing the anticommunist alliance, the pluralist claim that the American government is less ideological than several other "class-bound" capitalist states (cf. Matthews 1954: 57) falls flat for other reasons. For Marxists, it is evident that American foreign policy in practice defines freedom as freedom for private enterprise (the recent cases of Chile and Portugal being only two more blatant examples) and operates to maximize this "freedom."

3. Stabilization of capitalist systems (Mexico and Germany) is associated with consolidation (monopolization) of the social basis of elite recruitment by upper social strata under "normal" circumstances, with a broader middle-class coalition of counterrevolutionary elites (the Third Reich era) under "emergency" circumstances.

Especially salient here is the case of the Mexican Revolution, where analysis of elite composition shows the failure of those from lower social strata to significantly push their way into the elite recruitment process. The reconsolidation of middle-class elements in elite officeholding (chap. 8) in the post-Cárdenas years indicates the impossibility of a socialist development led by the PRI and helps account for the pronounced capitalist development policies taken after Cárdenas.

4. Successful social revolution produces decisive social displacement in the social basis of elite recruitment, not found in strictly political or failed social revolutions (chap. 2). Our studies suggest that, within the Soviet system, generational cleavages rather than social-class cleavages may characterize the elite recruitment process.

Finally, it is obvious from an over-time analysis of the Soviet, Chinese, and East German political elites (cf. esp. Ludz 1972; Clark and Klein 1971), as well as of the leadership of the French (Dogan 1961) and Italian (Putnam 1973) Communist parties, that the most fundamental hierarchical cleavage in the social bases of leadership recruitment is between Communist parties, in or out of power, and everyone else. To be sure, there are some marked differences in composition in the Soviet Communist party leadership over time (cf. chaps. 2–4), as well as between the Soviet and East German industrial communist leaderships and the Chinese agrarian communist leadership, but these differences are secondary compared to the abyss which separates them from all other noncommunist elites, ranging from social democrats through bourgeois parties to fascist groupings (cf. Hancock 1973; Miliband 1969: chaps. 3, 6).

The empirical works which Marxist scholars have been able to put together reinforce the original warnings of Marx (1879) against the growing recruitment of bourgeois managers and professionals into the SPD leadership; they reinforce Marx's belief that the emancipation of the working class must be *primarily* its own doing, including the leadership of its own organizations. In both historical and contemporary contexts, the only parties which recruit leadership *mainly* from the toiling classes are communist.[10] The transcending of bourgeois definitions of rationality, efficiency, and freedom, or even the political consideration of alternatives, is thus internally related to the class basis of elite recruitment, both in the West and in those countries which have started along the road of socialist development (see Ollman 1971 on the use of internal relation analysis rather than cause-effect analysis of whole political systems).

The Political Resolution of Academic Conflict

The prospects for bridging the gap among pluralists, radicals, and Marxists on the relevance of elite representativeness are slim indeed. More studies are now punching holes in the pluralist model, however, and an uneasy coexistence of positions has emerged. The strength of each position will, other things being equal, continue to change with scholarly reaction to real world events. As Hacker (1961: 298) has recognized, the solution to or maintenance of such cleavages depends on the "viability" of the competing ideologies, not on the illusory and/or deceptive façade of a value-free political science. Connolly (1969: 152–153) has called for open and frank admission of the ideological basis on which research is built, and it

10. A few socialist parties, such as the Chilean, which was if anything to the left of the Communist party, have recruited heavily from the working class, but no social democratic parties have any significant representation of workers in their leadership.

seems likely that the present more competitive situation in the discipline may facilitate a dropping (or at least a withering away) of the fig leaf of value freeness from pluralist orthodoxy (cf. also Taubman 1974: 383–391).

But "other things" are not likely to be equal, at least in the U.S. in the short or middle run: the academic market for ideas is not (either in the West or in socialist countries) one of "free" competition, unrelated to the social order in which ideas contend. While it might, as Connolly (1974: 40–41) suggests, be fruitful to realize why there are "essentially contested concepts" in political science, and while such a realization might introduce a "measure of tolerance and receptivity to reconsideration of received views," I perceive perhaps narrower limits to the autonomy of the academic community within the larger political struggle. Intervention by government forces, restrictions by and on publishing outlets, and discrimination by educational financiers and managers *helped* create the pluralist orthodoxy, and, as skeptics of Soviet destalinization are fond of saying, there is no assurance that this could not happen again, especially if the economic situation of the West continues to deteriorate, if détente comes unglued, or if there are further defeats for U.S. foreign policy. Resistance to a stepped-up campaign to restore orthodoxy could be expected to be greater, insofar as the social composition of faculty and students has broadened somewhat and the credibility of anticommunist dogma has been weakened by Vietnam and by destalinization within much of the socialist camp. Still, the struggle for reproduction of capitalist ideology through the institutions of learning (including higher learning) must be hotly pursued by the present system, for to lose this struggle would undermine one more underpinning of acceptance of or resignation to the capitalist order.

Bibliography

1965. Alisky, Marvin. "The Governors of Mexico." Southwestern Studies Monograph 12. El Paso: University of Texas at El Paso.

1969. Anderson, Bo, and James D. Cockcroft. "Control and Cooptation in Mexican Politics." In Irving L. Horowitz, ed., *Latin American Radicalism*. New York: Vintage.

1951. Arendt, Hannah. *Origins of Totalitarianism*. New York: Harcourt Brace.

1966. Armstrong, John. "Party Bifurcation and Elite Interests." *Soviet Studies* 17, no. 3 (April): 417–430.

1950. Aron, Raymond. "Social Structure and the Ruling Class." *British Journal of Sociology* 1, nos. 1–2: 1–16, 126–143.

1967. Bachrach, Peter. *The Theory of Democratic Elitism: A Critique*. Boston: Little, Brown.

1971. ———. *Political Elites in a Democracy*. New York: Atherton.

1970. Bailey, Stephen K. *Congress in the Seventies*. New York: St. Martin's.

1963. Banks, Arthur S., and Robert B. Textor, eds. *A Cross-Polity Survey*. Cambridge, Mass.: MIT Press.

1966. Baran, Paul A., and Paul M. Sweezy. *Monopoly Capital: An Essay on the American Economic and Social Order*. New York: Monthly Review.

1973. Barghoorn, Frederick C. "Trends in Top Leadership in the USSR." In R. Barry Farrell, ed., *Political Leadership in Eastern Europe and the Soviet Union*. Chicago: Aldine.

1973. Baylis, Thomas. "Elites and the Idea of Post-Industrial Society in the Two Germanies." Paper delivered at the annual American Political Science Association meeting in New Orleans, September 4–8.

1973. Beck, Carl, et al. *Comparative Communist Political Leadership*. New York: McKay.

1960. Bell, Daniel. *The End of Ideology: On the Exhaustion of Political Ideas in the Fifties*. New York: Free Press.

1964. ———. *The Radical Right*. Garden City: Doubleday.

1973. ———. *The Coming of Post-Industrial Society: A Venture in Social Forecasting*. New York: Basic Books.

1954. Berelson, Bernard, et al. *Voting: A Study of Opinion Formation in a Political Campaign*. Chicago: University of Chicago Press.

1971. von Beyme, Klaus. *Die politische Elite in der Bundesrepublik Deutschland*. Munich: Piper.

1973. ———. *Die parlamentarische Regierungssysteme in Europa*. Munich: Piper.

1967. Bilinsky, Yaroslav. "Changes in the Central Committee." Monograph Series in World Affairs 4, no. 4. Denver: University of Denver.

1973. Bill, James A., and Robert L. Hardgrave. *Comparative Politics: The Quest for Theory*. Columbus: Merrill.

1961. *Biographical Directory of the American Congress, 1774–1961*. Washington, D.C.: G.P.O.

1972. Blalock, Hubert M. *Social Statistics*. 2d ed. New York: McGraw-Hill.

1966. Bottomore, T. B. *Elites and Society*. London: Penguin.

1973. Boynton, G. R., and Gerhard Loewenberg. "The Development of Political Support for Parliament in Germany." *British Journal of Political Science* 3 (April): 168–189.

1964. Bracher, Karl Dietrich. *Die Auflösung der Weimarer Republik*. Villingen/Schwarzwald: Ring Verlag.

1970. ———. *The German Dictatorship: The Origins, Structure, and Effect of National Socialism*. New York: Praeger.

1964. Brandenberg, Frank. *The Making of Modern Mexico*. Englewood Cliffs, N.J.: Prentice-Hall.

1965. Braunthal, Gerald. *The Federation of German Industry in Politics*. Ithaca: Cornell University Press.

1972. Brezhnev, Leonid I. "Report of the CPSU Central Committee to the 23d Congress of the CPSU." In Joseph L. Nogee, ed., *Man, State, and Society in the Soviet Union*. New York: Praeger.

1963. Brzezinski, Zbigniew K., and Samuel P. Huntington. *Political Power: USA/USSR*. New York: Viking.

1965. Burnham, Walter Dean. "Has Congress a Future?" In Joseph S. Clark, ed., *Congressional Reform: Problems and Prospects*. New York: Crowell.

1971. Camp, Roderic A. "The Cabinet and the *Técnico* in Mexico and the United States." *Journal of Comparative Administration* 3 (August): 188–213.

1972. ———. "The Middle Level Technocrat in Mexico." *Journal of Developing Areas* 6, no. 4 (July): 571–582.

1973. ———. "The National University and Elite Recruitment in Mexico: The 1925 Generation." *Comparative Education Review* 17, no. 1 (February).

1974. ———. "Mexican Governors since Cárdenas." *Journal of InterAmerican Studies and World Affairs* 16, no. 4 (November): 454–481.

1970. Chaffey, Douglas. "The Institutionalization of State Legislatures." *Western Political Quarterly* 23, no. 1 (March): 180–196.

1928. Chang, Wei-Chiu. *The Speaker of the House of Representatives since 1896*. New York: Columbia University Press.

1968. Churchward, L. G. *Contemporary Soviet Government*. New York: American Elsevier.

1965. Claessens, Dieter, Arno Klönne, and Armin Tschoepe. *Sozialkunde der Bundesrepublik Deutschland*. Dusseldorf: Diederichs.

1963. Clapp, Charles L. *The Congressman: His Role As He Sees It*. Garden City: Doubleday.

1971. Clark, Anne B., and Donald Klein. *Biographical Dictionary of Chinese Communism: 1921–1965*. 2 vols. Cambridge, Mass.: Harvard University Press.

1963. Cline, Howard F. *The U.S. and Mexico*. 2d ed. Cambridge, Mass.: Harvard University Press.

1968. Cochrane, J. D. "Mexico's New *Científicos*: The Díaz Ordaz Cabinet." *InterAmerican Economic Affairs* 21, no. 1 (Spring): 61–72.

1968. Cockcroft, James D. *Intellectual Precursors of the Mexican Revolution, 1900–1913*. Austin: University of Texas Press.

1972. ———. "Coercion and Ideology in Mexico." In Cockcroft et al., eds., *Dependence and Underdevelopment: Latin America's Political Economy*. Garden City: Doubleday.

1965, 1969, 1973. *Congressional Directory*. Washington, D.C.: G.P.O.

1967. Connolly, William E. *Political Science and Ideology*. New York: Atherton.

1969. ———. *The Bias of Pluralism*. New York: Atherton.

1974. ———. *The Terms of Political Discourse*. Lexington, Mass.: D. C. Heath.

1968. Conquest, Robert. *The Great Terror: Stalin's Purges of the Thirties*. New York: Macmillan.

1974. Conradt, David P. "West Germany: A Remade Political Culture." *Comparative Political Studies* 7, no. 2 (April): 222–238.

1973. ———, and Dwight Lambert. "The Legitimation of Competitive Politics in West Germany." Paper delivered at the Conference Group on German Politics meeting in Athens, Georgia, September 3–4.

1973. Cornelius, Wayne A. "Nation Building, Participation, and Distribution: The Politics of Social Reform under Cárdenas." In Gabriel A. Almond et al., eds., *Crisis, Choice, and Change: Historical Studies of Political Development*. Boston: Little, Brown.

1974. ———. "Urbanization and Demand Making." *American Political Science Review* 68, no. 3 (September): 1125–1146.

1970. Cutler, Neal. "Generational Succession As a Source of Foreign Policy Attitudes: A Cohort Analysis of American Opinion, 1946–1966." *Journal of Peace Research* 7, no. 1: 33–48.

1971. ———. "Generational Analysis in Political Science." Paper delivered at the annual American Political Science Association meeting in Chicago, September 7–11.

1961. Dahl, Robert A. *Who Governs: Democracy and Power in an American City*. New Haven: Yale University Press.

1959. Dahrendorf, Ralf. *Class and Class Conflict in Industrial Society*. Stanford: Stanford University Press.

1967. ———. *Society and Democracy in Germany*. London: Weidenfeld & Nicolson.

1960. Daniels, Robert V. *The Conscience of the Revolution: Communist Opposition in Soviet Russia*. New York: Clarion.

1969. Davidson, Roger H. *The Role of the Congressman*. New York: Pegasus.

1966. ———, Michael K. O'Leary, and Daniel M. Kovenock. *Congress in Crisis: Politics and Congressional Reform*. Belmont, Calif.: Wadsworth.

1968. Deutscher, Isaac. *Russia after Stalin*. Indianapolis: Bobbs-Merrill.

1871, 1878, 1881, 1884. *Deutscher Parlaments-Almanach*. Leipzig: Georg Hirth.

1961. Djilas, Milovan. "The New Class." In A. Mendel, ed., *Essential Works of Marxism*. New York: Bantam Books.

1961. Dogan, Mattei. "Political Ascent in a Class Society." In Dwaine Marvick, ed., *Political Decision-Makers: Recruitment and Performance*. New York: Free Press.

1967. Domhoff, G. William. *Who Rules America?* Englewood Cliffs, N.J.: Prentice-Hall.

1972. Donaldson, Robert H. "The 1971 Soviet Central Committee: An Assessment of the New Elite." *World Politics* 24, no. 3 (April): 382–409.

1970. ———, and Derek Waller. "The 1956 Central Committees of the Chinese and Soviet Communist Parties: A Comparative Analysis of Elite Composition and Change." Paper delivered at the annual American Political Science Association meeting in Los Angeles, September 7–11.

1962. Dreitzel, H. P. *Elitebegriff und Sozialstruktur*. Stuttgart: F. Enke.

1965. Durden, Robert F. *The Climax of Populism: The Election of 1896*. Lexington: University of Kentucky Press.

1934. Dutt, R. Palme. *Fascism and Social Revolution*. New Delhi: India Publishing House.

1968. Edinger, Lewis J. *Politics in Germany*. Boston: Little, Brown.

1975. ———, et al. *Political Elites and Social Structure in Parliamentary Democracies*. Cambridge, Mass.: MIT Press.

1960. Ehrlich, Alexander. *The Soviet Industrialization Debate, 1924–1928*. Cambridge, Mass.: Harvard University Press.

1966. Eisenstadt, S. N. "Breakdowns of Modernizations." In Jason L. Finkle and Richard W. Gable, eds., *Political Development and Social Change*. New York: Wiley.

1884. Engels, Friedrich. *On the Origin of the State*. In Robert C. Tucker, ed., *The Marx-Engels Reader*. New York: Norton, 1972.

1959. Etzioni, Amitai. "The Functional Differentiation of Elites in the Kibbutz." *American Journal of Sociology* 64, no. 1: 476–486.

1972. Fagen, Richard R., and William S. Tuohy. *Politics and Privilege in a Mexican City*. Stanford: Stanford University Press.

1963. Fainsod, Merle. *How Russia Is Ruled*. Rev. ed. Cambridge, Mass.: Harvard University Press.

1973. Farrell, R. Barry, ed. *Political Leadership in Eastern Europe and the Soviet Union*. Chicago: Aldine.

n.d. Fiorina, Morris, et al. "Congressional Replacement: An Historical Examination." Unpublished paper.

1968. Fischer, George. *The Soviet System and Modern Society*. New York: Atherton.

1968. Fleron, Frederic J., Jr. "Soviet Area Studies and the Social Sciences." *Soviet Studies* 19, no. 3 (January): 313–339.

1969. ———. "Cooptation As a Mechanism of Adaptation to Change: The Soviet Political Leadership System." *Polity* 2, no. 2 (Winter): 176–190.

1969a. ———. "Research Strategies for the Study of Communist Systems." *Canadian Slavic Studies* 3, no. 3 (Autumn): 544–552.

1966. Friedrich, Carl J., and Zbigniew K. Brzezinski. *Totalitarian Dictatorship and Autocracy*. Rev. ed. New York: Praeger.

1968. Gans, Herbert J. *More Equality*. New York: Pantheon.

1971. Garson, G. David. *Introductory Handbook of Political Science Methods*. Boston: Holbrook.

1966. Gehlen, Michael P. "The Educational Backgrounds and Career Orientations of the Members of the Central Committee of the CPSU." *American Behavioral Scientist* 9, no. 8 (April): 11–14.

1968. ———, and Michael McBridge. "The Soviet Central Committee: An Elite Analysis." *American Political Science Review* 62, no. 4 (December): 1232–1241.

1962. Gershenkron, Alexander. *Economic Backwardness in Historical Perspective*. Cambridge, Mass.: Harvard University Press.

1952. Gerth, Hans. "The Nazi Party: Its Leadership and Composition." In Robert K. Merton et al., eds., *Reader in Bureaucracy*. New York: Free Press.

1975. Gold, David, Clarence Lo, and Erik Wright. "Recent Developments in Marxist Theories of the Capitalist State." *Monthly Review* 27, nos. 5–6 (October–November): 29–43, 36–51.

1970. González Casanova, Pablo. *Democracy in Mexico*. Translated by Danielle Salti. New York: Oxford University Press.

1963. Goodman, Paul. *People or Personnel: Decentralizing and the Mixed System*. New York: Random House.

1973. Gorz, André. *Socialism and Revolution*. Translated by Norman Denny. Garden City: Doubleday.

1973. Gregor, A. J. "Fascism: Its Contemporary Interpretations." Morristown, N.J.: General Learning Press.

1968. Grew, Raymond, and Sylvia L. Thrupp. "Horizontal History in Search of Vertical Dimensions." In Charles L. Taylor, ed., *Aggregate Data Analysis: Political and Social Indicators in Cross-National Research*. Paris: Mouton.

1971. Gruber, Winfried. "Career Patterns of Mexico's Political Elite." *Western Political Quarterly* 24, no. 3 (September): 467–482.

1957. Gusfield, Joseph R. "The Problem of Generations in an Organizational Structure." *Social Forces* 35, no. 2 (May): 323–330.

1973. Habermas, Jurgen. *Legitimationsprobleme im Spätkapitalismus.* Frankfurt: Suhrkamp.

1961. Hacker, Andrew. "Sociology and Ideology." In Max Black, ed., *Social Theories of Talcott Parsons.* Englewood Cliffs, N.J.: Prentice-Hall.

1974. Hagopian, Mark. *The Phenomenon of Revolution.* New York: Dodd, Mead.

1973. Hancock, M. Donald. "The Bundeswehr and the National People's Army." Monograph Series in World Affairs 10, no. 2. Denver: University of Denver.

1971. Hansen, Roger D. *The Politics of Mexican Development.* Baltimore: Johns Hopkins.

1959. Harcave, Sidney. *Russia: A History.* Philadelphia: Lippincott.

1968. Hardt, John P., and Carl Modig. "Stalinist Industrial Development in Soviet Russia." In Kurt London, ed., *The Soviet Union: A Half Century of Communism.* Baltimore: Johns Hopkins.

1963. Heberle, Rudolf. *Landbevölkerung und Nationalsozialismus.* Stuttgart: Deutsche Verlagsanstalt.

1971. Heidenheimer, Arnold J. *The Governments of Germany.* 3d ed. New York: Crowell.

1971. Hinckley, Barbara. *The Seniority System in Congress.* Bloomington: Indiana University Press.

1960. *Historical Statistics of the United States: Colonial Times to 1957.* Washington, D.C.: G.P.O.

1967. Hitchener, Dell, and Carol Levine. *Comparative Government and Politics.* New York: Dodd, Mead.

1973. Hobsbawm, E. J. *Revolutionaries.* New York: Meridian.

1966. Hodge, Robert, Paul Siegel, and Peter Rossi. "Occupational Prestige in the United States, 1925–1963." In Reinhard Bendix and Seymour M. Lipset, eds., *Class, Status, and Power: A Reader in Social Stratification.* New York: Free Press.

1966. ———, J. Treiman, and Peter Rossi. "A Comparative Study of Occupational Prestige." In Bendix and Lipset, eds., *Class, Status, and Power: A Reader in Social Stratification.* New York: Free Press.

1967. Hough, Jerry F. "The Soviet Elite." *Problems of Communism* 16, nos. 1 and 2 (January–February, March–April): 28–35, 18–25.

1972. ———. "The Soviet System: Petrification or Pluralism?" *Problems of Communism* 21, no. 2 (March–April): 25–45.

1972. Hughes, John, and Robert Dowse. *Political Sociology.* New York: Wiley.

1964. Hunt, Richard N. *German Social Democracy.* New Haven: Yale University Press.

1963. Hunter, Floyd. *Community Power Structure*. Garden City: Double-day.

1965. Huntington, Samuel P. "Congressional Responses to the Twentieth Century." In D. Truman, ed., *The Congress and America's Future*. Englewood Cliffs, N.J.: Prentice-Hall.

1968. ———. *Political Order in Changing Societies*. New Haven: Yale University Press.

1971. Inglehart, Ronald. "The Silent Revolution in Europe: Intergenerational Change in Post-Industrial Society." *American Political Science Review* 65, no. 4 (December): 991–1017.

1956. Inkeles, Alex, and Peter Rossi. "National Comparisons of Occupational Prestige." *American Journal of Sociology* 61, no. 1 (January): 329–339.

1969. Jaeggi, Urs. *Macht und Herrschaft in der Bundesrepublik*. Frankfurt am Main: Fischer.

1974. Jancar, Barbara. "Women and Soviet Politics." In Henry W. Morton and Rudolf L. Tokes, eds., *Soviet Politics and Society in the Seventies*. New York: Free Press.

1958. Janowitz, Morris. "Social Stratification and Mobility in West Germany." *American Journal of Sociology* 64, no. 1.

1955. ———, and Dwaine Marvick. "Competitive Pressure and Democratic Consent." *Public Opinion Quarterly* 19, no. 4 (Winter): 381–400.

1973. Jewell, Malcolm E. "Linkages between Legislative Parties and External Parties." In Allan Kornberg, ed., *Legislatures in Comparative Perspective*. New York: McKay.

1971. Johnson, Kenneth F. *Mexican Democracy: A Critical View*. Boston: Allyn & Bacon.

1964. Jones, Charles. "Inter-Party Competition for Congressional Seats." *Western Political Quarterly* 17, no. 3 (September): 461–476.

1974. Kaack, Heino. *Geschichte und Struktur des deutschen Parteiensystems*. Opladen: Westdeutscher Verlag.

1961. Kaufmann, Karlheinz, Helmut Kohl, and Peter Molt. *Kandidaturen zum Bundestag*. Köln/Berlin: Kiepenheuer & Witsch.

1968. Kautsky, John H. *Communism and the Politics of Development: Persistent Myth and Changing Behavior*. New York: Wiley.

1903. Kautsky, Karl. *The Social Revolution*. Chicago: C. H. Kerr.

1970. Keniston, Kenneth. "Youth: A New Stage of Life." *American Scholar* 39, no. 3 (Autumn): 631–654.

1956. Khrushchev, Nikita S. "Special Report by N. S. Khrushchev to Closed Session of the Twentieth Congress of the CPSU." In David Lane, *Politics and Society in the USSR*. New York: Random House, 1971.

1966. Kirchheimer, Otto. "The Transformation of the Western European Party Systems." In Joseph LaPalombara and M. Weiner, eds., *Political Parties and Political Development*. Princeton: Princeton University Press.

1960. Kitzinger, Uwe W. *German Electoral Politics: A Study of the 1957 Campaign*. Oxford: Clarendon.

1971. Klecka, William. "Some Strategies for Seeking Age Relationships in Political Science." Paper delivered at the annual American Political Science Association meeting in Chicago, September 7–11.

1972. Knauerhase, Ramon. *An Introduction to National Socialism, 1920–1939*. Columbus: Merrill.

1952. Knight, Maxwell E. *The German Executive, 1890–1933*. Stanford: Stanford University Press.

1969. Knights, Peter. "Population Turnover, Persistence, and Residential Mobility in Boston, 1830–1860." In Stephan Thernstrom and Richard Sennett, eds., *Nineteenth-Century Cities: Essays in the New Urban History*. New Haven: Yale University Press.

1973. Kornberg, Allan, Harold D. Clarke, and George L. Watson. "Toward a Model of Parliamentary Recruitment in Canada." In Kornberg, ed., *Legislatures in Comparative Perspective*. New York: McKay.

1959. Kornhauser, William. *Politics of Mass Society*. New York: Free Press.

1971. Kuehnl, Richard. *Formen bürgerlicher Herrschaft: Liberalismus-Faschismus*. Reinbek bei Hamburg: Rowohlt.

1954–1973. *Kürschners Volkshandbuch deutscher Bundestag*. Darmstadt: Neuer Darmstädter Verlagsanstalt.

1971. Lambert, T. Allen. "Generational Factors in Political-Cultural Consciousness." Paper delivered at the annual American Political Science Association meeting in Chicago, September 7–11.

1971. Lane, David. *Politics and Society in the USSR*. New York: Random House.

1952. Lasswell, Harold D., Daniel Lerner, and C. Easton Rothwell. *The Comparative Study of Political Elites*. Stanford: Stanford University Press.

1965. ———, and Daniel Lerner. *World Revolutionary Elites: Studies in Coercive Ideological Movements*. Cambridge, Mass.: MIT Press.

1973. Leggett, John C. *Taking State Power: The Sources and Consequences of Political Challenge*. New York: Harper & Row.

1966. Lenski, Gerhard. *Power and Privilege: A Theory of Social Stratification*. New York: McGraw-Hill.

1973. Levin, Alfred. *The Third Duma, Election and Profile*. Hamden, Conn.: Shoe String.

1967. Lewytzkyj, Borys. "Generations in Conflict." *Problems of Communism* 16, no. 1 (January–February): 36–40.

1970. ———. *The Soviet Political Elite*. Stanford: Hoover Institution.

1970a. ———. "The Third Generation of Soviet Leaders." *Bulletin* 17, no. 11 (November): 5–17.

1968. Lieuwen, Edwin. *Mexican Militarism: The Political Rise and Fall of the Revolutionary Army, 1910–1940*. Albuquerque: University of New Mexico Press.

1966. Linden, Carl A. *Khrushchev and the Soviet Leadership, 1957–1964.* Baltimore: Johns Hopkins.

1963. Lipset, Seymour M. *Political Man: The Social Bases of Politics.* Garden City: Doubleday.

1970. ———. *Revolution and Counter-Revolution: Change and Persistence in Social Structure.* Garden City: Doubleday.

1971. ———, and E. C. Ladd. "The Politics of American Political Scientists." *PS* 4, no. 2 (Spring): 135–144.

1967. ———, and Aldo Solari, eds. *Elites in Latin America.* New York: Oxford University Press.

1968. Lodge, Milton. "Groupism in the Post-Stalin Period." *Midwest Journal of Political Science* 12, no. 3 (August): 330–351.

1967. Loewenberg, Gerhard. *Parliament in the German Political System.* Ithaca: Cornell University Press.

1971. ———. "Participants in Debates of the Third German Bundestag." Codebook. Iowa City: Regional Social Science Data Archive in Iowa.

1968. Lowenthal, Richard. "The Soviet Union in the Post-Revolutionary Era." In Alexander Dallin and Thomas B. Larson, eds., *Soviet Politics since Khrushchev.* Englewood Cliffs, N.J.: Prentice-Hall.

1972. Ludz, Peter Christian. *The Changing Party Elite in East Germany.* Cambridge, Mass.: MIT Press.

1974. Mabry, Donald J. "Mexico's Party Deputy System." *Journal of InterAmerican Studies and World Affairs* 16, no. 2 (May): 221–233.

1969. McFarland, Andrew S. *Power and Leadership in Pluralist Systems.* Stanford: Stanford University Press.

1971. McHale, Vincent, and Dennis Paranzino. "Correlates of Political Longevity among the Soviet Leadership, 1952–1966." Anspach Institute Series on International and Comparative Politics 1.

1973. MacPherson, C. B. *Democratic Theory: Essays in Retrieval.* Oxford: Clarendon.

1972. Mandel, Ernest. "The Soviet Economy Today." *International Socialist Review* 33, no. 6 (June): 6–19.

1952. Mannheim, Karl. "The Problem of Generations." In Paul Kecskemeti, ed., *Essays on the Sociology of Knowledge.* New York: Oxford University Press.

1961. Marvick, Dwaine, ed. *Political Decision-Makers: Recruitment and Performance.* New York: Free Press.

1845–46. Marx, Karl. *The German Ideology.* In Robert C. Tucker, ed., *The Marx-Engels Reader.* New York: Norton, 1972.

1848. ———. *Manifesto of the Communist Party.* In Tucker, ed., *The Marx-Engels Reader.*

1852. ———. *Eighteenth Brumaire of Louis Bonaparte.* In Tucker, ed., *The Marx-Engels Reader.*

1879. ———. "Circular Letter to Bebel, Liebknecht, Bracke, and Others." In Tucker, ed., *The Marx-Engels Reader.*

1954. Matthews, Donald R. *The Social Background of Political Decision-Makers*. New York: Random House.

1965. Merkl, Peter H. *Germany: Yesterday and Tomorrow*. New York: Oxford University Press.

1967. ———. *Political Continuity and Change*. New York: Harper & Row.

1970. ———. *Modern Comparative Politics*. New York: Holt, Rinehart & Winston.

1970. Merritt, Richard. *Systematic Approaches to Comparative Politics*. Chicago: Rand-McNally.

1973. Mickiewicz, Ellen P., ed. *Handbook of Soviet Social Science Data*. New York: Free Press.

1969. Miliband, Ralph. *The State in Capitalist Society: An Analysis of the Western System of Power*. New York: Basic Books.

1973. ———. "Marx and the State." In T. B. Bottomore, ed., *Karl Marx*. Englewood Cliffs, N.J.: Prentice-Hall.

1888. Mill, John Stuart. *A System of Logic*. New York: Harper & Row.

1956. Mills, C. Wright. *The Power Elite*. New York: Oxford University Press.

1962. ———. *The Marxists*. New York: Dell.

1963. Molt, Peter. *Der Reichstag vor der improvisierten Revolution*. Opladen: Westdeutscher Verlag.

1960. Moore, H., and G. Kleining. "Das soziale Selbstbild der Gesellschaftsschichten in Deutschland." *Kölner Zeitschrift für Soziologie und Sozialpsychologie* 12, no. 1 (Spring): 86–119.

1970. Nagle, John D. *The National Democratic Party: Right Radicalism in the Federal Republic of Germany*. Berkeley & Los Angeles: University of California Press.

1973. ———. "System and Succession: A Generational Analysis of Elite Turnover in Four Nations." Paper delivered at the annual Southern Political Science Association meeting in Atlanta, November 2.

1975. ———. "A New Look at the Soviet Elite: A Generational Model of the Soviet System." *Journal of Political and Military Sociology* 3 (Spring): 1–13.

1961. Needler, Martin. "The Political Development of Mexico." *American Political Science Review* 55, no. 2 (June): 308–312.

1942. Neumann, Franz L. *Behemoth: The Structure and Practice of National Socialism, 1933–1944*. New York: Oxford University Press.

1972. Offe, Claus. *Strukturprobleme des kapitalistischen Staates*. Frankfurt: Suhrkamp.

1973. ———. "The Abolition of Market Control and the Problem of Legitimacy." *Kapitalistate*, nos. 1 and 2.

1971. Ollman, Bertell. *Alienation: Marx's Conception of Man in Capitalist Society*. New York: Cambridge University Press.

1970. Osborn, Robert J. *Soviet Social Policies: Welfare, Equality, and Community*. Homewood, Ill.: Dorsey.

1974. ———. *The Evolution of Soviet Politics*. Homewood, Ill.: Dorsey.

1965. Padgett, L. Vincent. *The Mexican Political System*. Boston: Houghton Mifflin.

1969. Parry, Geraint. *Political Elites*. New York: Praeger.

1968. Polsby, Nelson W. "The Institutionalization of the U.S. House of Representatives." *American Political Science Review* 62, no. 1 (March): 144–168.

1969. ———, Miriam Gallaher, and Barry Rundquist. "The Growth of the Seniority System in the U.S. House of Representatives." *American Political Science Review* 63, no. 3 (September): 787–807.

1965. Price, H. Douglas. "The Electoral Arena." In D. Truman, ed., *The Congress and America's Future*. Englewood Cliffs, N.J.: Prentice-Hall.

1973. Putnam, Robert D. *The Beliefs of Politicians: Ideology, Conflict, and Democracy in Britain and Italy*. New Haven: Yale University Press.

1970. Quandt, William B. "The Comparative Study of Political Elites." Beverly Hills: Sage Publications.

1967. Rae, Douglas W. *Political Consequences of Electoral Laws*. New Haven: Yale University Press.

1969. Rasmussen, Jorgen S. *The Process of Politics*. Chicago: Aldine.

1881–1912. *Reichstag-Handbuch, Amtliches*. Berlin: Office of the Reichstag.

1968. Rejai, Mostafa, W. L. Mason, and D. C. Beller. "Political Ideology: Empirical Relevance of the Hypothesis of Decline." *Ethics* 78, no. 4 (July): 303–312.

1924. Rice, Stuart A. *Farmers and Workers in American Politics*. New York: Columbia University Press.

1950. Riesman, David, Nathan Glazer, and Reuel Denney. *The Lonely Crowd: A Study of the Changing American Character*. Garden City: Doubleday.

1958. Rintala, Marvin. "The Problem of Generations in Finnish Communism." *American Slavic and East European Review* 17, no. 2 (April): 190–202.

1962. ———. *Three Generations: The Extreme Right Wing in Finnish Politics*. Bloomington: Indiana University Press.

1967. Rogin, Michael P. *The Intellectuals and McCarthy: The Radical Specter*. Cambridge, Mass.: MIT Press.

1965. Rush, Myron. *Political Succession in the USSR*. New York: Columbia University Press.

1964. Russett, Bruce M. *World Handbook of Political and Social Indicators*. New Haven: Yale University Press.

1966. Rustow, Dankwart A. "The Study of Elites." *World Politics* 18, no. 4 (July): 690–717.

1965. Ryder, Norman. "The Age Cohort as a Concept in the Study of Social Change." *American Sociological Review* 30, no. 4 (November): 843–861.

1962. Sartori, Giovanni. *Democratic Theory*. New York: Praeger.

1956. Schattschneider, Elmer E. "United States: The Functional Approach to Party Government." In Sigmund Neumann, ed., *Modern Political Parties: Approaches to Comparative Politics*. Chicago: University of Chicago Press.

1960. ———. *The Semisovereign People: A Realist's View of Democracy in America*. New York: Holt, Rinehart & Winston.

1969. Schellenger, Kurt. *The SPD in the Bonn Republic*. The Hague: Martinus Nijhoff.

1966. Schlesinger, Joseph A. *Ambition and Politics: Political Careers in the United States*. Chicago: Rand-McNally.

1951. Schueller, George K. *The Politburo*. Stanford: Stanford University Press.

1942. Schumpeter, Joseph A. *Capitalism, Socialism, and Democracy*. New York: Harper & Row.

1964. Scott, Robert E. *Mexican Government in Transition*. Rev. ed. Urbana: University of Illinois Press.

1969. Searing, Donald D. "The Comparative Study of Elite Socialization." *Comparative Political Studies* 1, no. 4 (January): 471–500.

1967. ———, and Lewis J. Edinger. "Social Background in Elite Analysis: A Methodological Inquiry." *American Political Science Review* 61, no. 2 (June): 428–445.

1971. Skilling, H. Gordon. "Interest Groups and Communist Politics." In Skilling and Franklyn Griffiths, eds., *Interest Groups in Soviet Politics*. Princeton: Princeton University Press.

1974. Smith, Michael. "A Shift to Grass Roots Politics in the Soviet Union, 1917–1971." Unpublished Ph.D. dissertation, Syracuse University.

1974. Smith, Peter. "Political Mobility in Contemporary Mexico." Paper delivered at the annual American Political Science Association meeting in Chicago, August 28–September 2.

1966. Snowiss, Leo. "Congressional Recruitment and Representation." *American Political Science Review* 60, no. 3 (September): 627–639.

1968. *Statistical Abstract of the United States*. Washington, D.C.: G.P.O.

1972. Stewart, Philip, et al. "Political Mobility and the Soviet Political Process." *American Political Science Review* 66, no. 4 (December): 1269–1290.

1973. Stojanovic, Svetozar. *Between Ideals and Reality: A Critique of Socialism and Its Future*. Translated by Gerson S. Sher. New York: Oxford University Press.

1971. Stokes, Donald, and Warren Miller. "Party Government and the Saliency of Congress." In Raymond E. Wolfinger, ed., *Readings on Congress*. Englewood Cliffs, N.J.: Prentice-Hall.

1942. Sweezy, Paul M. *The Theory of Capitalist Development*. New York: Monthly Review.

1971. ———, and Charles Bettelheim. *On the Transition to Socialism*. New York: Monthly Review.

1970. Tatu, Michel. *Power in the Kremlin: From Khrushchev to Kosygin.* New York: Viking.

1974. Taubman, William. "The Change to Change in Communist Systems." In H. Morton and R. Tokes, eds., *Soviet Politics and Society in the Seventies.* New York: Free Press.

1969. Thernstrom, Stephan. "Immigrants and WASPS: Ethnic Differences in Occupational Mobility in Boston, 1890–1940." In Thernstrom and Richard Sennett, eds., *Nineteenth-Century Cities: Essays in the New Urban History.* New Haven: Yale University Press.

1970. ———, and Peter Knights. "Men in Motion." *Journal of Inter-Disciplinary History* 1, no. 1 (Autumn): 7–36.

1940. Trotsky, Leon. *In Defense of Marxism.* New York: Pathfinder Press.

1957. ———. *The Revolution Betrayed.* London: Plough Press.

1972. Tucker, Robert C., ed. *The Marx-Engels Reader.* New York: Norton.

1969. Unger, A. L. "Stalin's Renewal of the Leading Stratum: A Note on the Great Purge." *Soviet Studies* 20, no. 1 (January): 321–330.

1965. Verba, Sidney. "Germany: The Remaking of Political Culture." In Lucien W. Pye and Sidney Verba, eds., *Political Culture and Political Development.* Princeton: Princeton University Press.

n.d. Welsh, William A. "Methodological Problems in the Study of Political Leadership in Latin America." Iowa City: University of Iowa Laboratory for Political Research.

1969. ———. "Towards a Multiple-Strategy Approach to Research on Comparative Communist Political Elites." In Frederic J. Fleron, Jr., ed., *Communist Studies and the Social Sciences: Essays on Methodology and Empirical Theory.* Lexington: University of Kentucky Press.

1972. Wesson, Robert G. *The Soviet State: An Aging Revolution.* New York: Wiley.

1972a. ———. "The USSR: Oligarchy or Dictatorship." *Slavic Review* 31, no. 2 (June): 314–322.

1973. Wiarda, Howard J. "Towards a Framework for the Study of Political Change in the Iberic-Latin Tradition: The Corporative Model." *World Politics* 25, no. 1 (January): 206–235.

1964. Witmer, T. Richard. "The Aging of the House." *Political Science Quarterly* 79, no. 4 (December): 526–541.

1969. Womack, John, Jr. *Zapata and the Mexican Revolution.* New York: Vintage.

1965. Zapf, Wolfgang. *Wandlungen der deutschen Elite.* Munich: Piper.

Index

Date Due
